STAGE LEFT

Books by Jay Williams

FICTION
The Good Yeomen
The Rogue from Padua
The Siege
The Witches
Solomon and Sheba
The Forger
Tomorrow's Fire
Uniad

NON-FICTION
Fall of the Sparrow
A Change of Climate

MYSTERY NOVELS (as Michael Delving)
Smiling the Boy Fell Dead
The Devil Finds Work
Die Like a Man
A Shadow of Himself

JAY WILLIAMS

STAGE LEFT

Charles Scribner's Sons
New York

Library of Congress Cataloging in Publication Data

Williams, Jay, 1914–
    Stage left.

    Includes bibliographical references.
    1. Theater—United States—History. I. Title.
PN2266.W5   792'.0973   73–1118
ISBN 0–684–13660–0

1 3 5 7 9 11 13 15 17 19 H/C 20 18 16 14 12 10 8 6 4 2

Printed in the United States of America

Good my lord, will you see the players well bestowed? Do you hear, let them be well used; for they are the abstracts and brief chronicles of the time: after your death you were better have a bad epitaph than their ill report while you live.

Hamlet, II, ii, 555

STAGE LEFT

In 1969, I was living in London, trying to finish a crime novel about an American in England. Between three and six in the afternoon, when the pubs were closed, I was able to avoid overwork by visiting friends. One of them was Michael Dean, whose shop, Nihon To Ken, full of Japanese works of art, was a rendezvous for a number of active theatre people. Early in April, Michael told me that he had organized a festival of underground or experimental theatrical groups. It would run for five Sundays in an upper room of Ronnie Scott's night club in Soho, and from about three in the afternoon until past midnight different groups and solo performers would present samples of their work. Among them were The People Show, The Portable Theatre, Will Spoor's Mime Company from Amsterdam, Pip Simmons' Theatre Group, and the Freehold Theatre Company, as well as an assortment of folk singers, pantomimists, comedians, and poets.

I went to three of these marathons and talked to many of the performers. They were young, mostly under thirty, furiously opposed to whatever Establishment was around, and full of a pioneering zeal. They spoke about abolishing the proscenium, about taking theatre to the people, about performing in the streets, and they used words like "agit-prop" and "improvisation." Their plays were heavy-handed and their acting often amateurish, but they were bursting with energy; they were irrational and sometimes incoherent, but along the way they fired off salvos in the most high-spirited way at Church and State and any other institution that offered itself.

It must have seemed new and fresh to them and to most of their audience. To me, however, it had all the nostalgia of a Currier and Ives print. It was like a trip back to Grandma's house for Christmas, or watching kids play one o' cat in a school playground. Thirty-five years before, but in another country, I had taken part in similar festivals; I had been a member of a group something like these, and we had used much the same language in describing what we were doing.

There was a profound difference. We had been at the hub of change. In America, we had been part of a metamorphosis; after us, the American theatre was never the same again. It had all happened in a couple of decades, at the beginning of which the theatre was a chaste and elegant home for two nice old ladies, Beauty and Entertainment, and at the end of which its windows had been thrown open to all sorts of weather. Audiences were to find themselves involved in argument, shot at, or impelled to take part in the performances. The political and economic realities of life were dragged up on stage and dissected in plain sight with much kicking and screaming. The actors' approach to acting underwent the most striking change since the abandonment of the Delsarte method of Applied Aesthetics. The word "propaganda" lost its energy as a critical thunderbolt. It is at least arguable that whatever in the past thirty years has been interesting, or stimulating, or important in the American theatre grew in one way or another out of that period.

The funny thing is that it all seems to be forgotten. Few college drama courses give more than a passing nod in the direction of the Group Theatre or the New Playwrights Theatre, although the former was responsible for a change in acting technique that affected the entire theatrical scene and the latter was the first organized attempt at expressionist theatre in this country. Most histories of the drama acknowledge the importance of Tennessee Williams and Arthur Miller but ignore the fact that the groundwork for the acceptance and recognition of their plays, as well as the directing and acting methods that would give them their due, was developed somewhat earlier. The extensive and exciting workers' theatre movement which, if it did nothing else, changed the atmosphere around strictly hortatory plays, has been treated in only one book, which attempts to prove, firstly, that it didn't exist, and secondly that if it did it was a Communist plot to seize control of Broadway and start the tumbrils rolling along Shubert Alley.

The pivot on which everything turned was what, for want of a better word, may be called socially-conscious drama, that is, plays which took account of the fact that grim and disagreeable things went on outside playhouses and might, with some profit, be dealt with inside them. It is hard to remember that there was a time when poverty, war, or political chicanery were considered unfit subjects for the drama, and almost the only notice that was taken of the frightful condition of black Americans was to present it as quaint or comic. The theatre was firmly in the hands of businessmen who ran it as a business resting on the lucrative star system and who were frightened out of their wits at the thought of presenting their public with anything so unpleasant that it might make them walk out. The critic, William Winter, said in 1913 of one pernicious radical:

> Granting to Ibsen and his followers the highest and best motives, they have altogether mistaken the province of the theatre in choosing it as the medium for the expression of social views . . . which once adopted, would disrupt society. . . . Since when did the theatre become a proper place for a clinic of horrors and the vivisection of moral ailments?[1]

Nevertheless, in the mid-1920s a few ripples were made in that generally placid surface which began to spread in all directions. This book is concerned with the people who threw the stones.

They were people of a wide variety of backgrounds and persuasions. They included established professionals, some of whom had their own permanent theatres, and amateurs whose stage was a picket line or the back of a truck. Many of them banded together and issued manifestos—it is almost the first requisite for innovators in the arts—and they ranged from relatively conservative organizations like the Theatre Guild to left-wing groups like the Workers Laboratory Theatre. Some of them had grown up out of the reaction against American philistinism after the First World War, others from the economic struggles of the Great Depression. Almost all were influenced in one way or another by European experimenters, and all tried to find ways of translating that European influence into purely American terms.

This book is an attempt to describe what it was like to be part of those changeful times. It is neither a scholarly work nor a text book, nor even, in the pedagogic sense, a history complete with cross-references, statistics, and lists of the names of first-nighters. My credentials for writing it are the slenderest and most basic. I saw, or took an active part in, much of what I write about, and knew and worked with many of the people I mention. I have tried to supplement the wide gaps in my knowledge by careful research and personal interviews, but I cannot promise the reader scientific accuracy. I am far from being a scientist or a savant. Like everyone who ever worked in show business, I am romantic, sentimental, and unreliable.

I am profoundly grateful to the many people who generously gave me so much of their time in talks and interviews, and loaned me reference material or allowed me to make use of their records. I wish particularly to express my thanks to the staff of the Theatre Collection of the New York Public Library at Lincoln Center; to my wife, Barbara, for her assistance in the laborious task of research; to Ruth Eliot and Michael Gordon for special courtesies; to Ben Berenberg, Will Lee, and Perry Bruskin for exhaustive reading and correction of the manuscript; and to Nicholas Ray, whose idea it was in the first place that this book should be written.

1915-1929

Only someone whose ideal is *Peter Pan* can seriously believe that the theatre's sole purpose is entertainment. Since its primeval opening night the theatre has been a vehicle for the wielding of magical powers, as all art is for its practitioners. At its best, that power is used to express profound and moving statements about the realities of life. It is only at its crudest that it juggles balls and dishes for amusement alone. In the beginning, the theatre told of the gods and of men's dealings with them. During the middle ages it continued that ritual and mythic tradition. When it became secular, it flowered with the plays of Shakespeare, which are crammed with political propaganda and the exposure of social evils, most of which is so topical that it became impenetrable to later audiences, thus winning the Bard an ill-deserved reputation for pure high-minded respectability. Eighteenth-century dramatists took no chances on being misunderstood and gave their characters names like Surface and Malaprop instead of Smith or Jones; the Victorians recognized that the theatre could serve a high moral purpose; and even the early twentieth century's Pulitzer Prize was to be awarded to a play "which shall best represent the educational value and power of the stage," even though that was to be expressed in nothing rowdier than "good morals, good taste and good manners."

So why all the hullabaloo about "social-conscious" drama? Simply because it meant drama that was conscious of *unpopular* social ills. Its proponents were young Doctor Kildares trying to treat venereal diseases in patients too well brought-up to admit that sex existed.

The place of the theatre in America, like that of all the arts, was uneasy almost from the outset. To the Puritan mind, art ran perilously close to sin, and the very word "playhouse" had bawdy connotations. Thrifty Dutch farmers were no readier than New Englanders to spend their money on frippery. As a result, playwrights and producers, if they wanted to make enough money to survive, had to present unimpeachable classics or plays which were, in the words of one historian, "clean, moral, inoffensive, amusing, and innocuous."[2] A handsome and energetic actor who could roar around and tear up the scenery was a safe financial bet, and as early as 1847 Walt Whitman was complaining that there was no really good theatre in New York and that the star system was a curse which kept what there was from developing. By the end of the century, the box office had become the most important location in a playhouse, and drama shamelessly changed its name to show business. A kind of octopus booking-office, the Theatrical Syndicate, headed by Charles Frohman, controlled the road—the profitable cross-country circuit, which was generally fed by long-running plays cast in New York. Although several actors and managers, among them David Belasco and Minnie Maddern Fiske, tried fighting it, the Syndicate's major rivals were the Shubert brothers, equally sharp traders less concerned with art than profit. The theatre was beginning to suffer from economic pressures, unemployment, and the decline of the road resulting from the grip of monopoly. Everyone wanted a sure thing. Nothing was encouraged that would rock the boat. By the early 1900s, Clyde Fitch was America's most serious playwright with works like *Barbara Frietchie* or *The Climbers*. And when, in 1905, George Bernard Shaw's *Mrs. Warren's Profession* opened in New York in competition with *The Squaw Man* and *Peter Pan*, the papers joined in condemning it. "An insult to decency," said the *Herald*; "Has absolutely no place in a theatre before a mixed assembly," boomed the *Times*; "Vile!" whimpered the *Sun*; while the *Post* huffed, "Contemptible and abominable."

America in those days wasn't quite ready for so public an announcement of what might lurk under a comfortable exterior. It had come a long way from its brash youth. Its new tycoons were building palaces and collecting art. Giant trusts controlling steel, coal, railroads and oil disposed of more wealth than most European kingdoms could conceive of. A well-to-do middle class was rising, and such things as poverty, corruption in government, or the bloody repression of workingmen were successfully hidden. The theatre, which depended on the carriage trade to fill its expensive seats, was naturally not going to offend its patrons.

There were, however, a good many people who still thought of the drama as one of the arts and so privileged to regard all aspects of life. Out of their ranks came the Little Theatre movement.

It began about the time of the First World War, as if the military thunder was somehow clearing the air. Around 1910, the Wisconsin Players were formed; in 1911 Chicago had its Little Theatre, the Goodman. These were perhaps the trailblazers. In 1912, Professor George Pierce Baker, who for some years had been giving courses in the history and techniques of playwriting at Harvard, formed the 47 Workshop which was to have incalculable effects on the theatre's history. Three years later, the Neighborhood Playhouse opened its doors on New York's East Side under the wings of the indefatigable Lewisohn sisters, Alice and Irene; in twelve years of performing it would set a high standard of elegance, not only for Little Theatres but for Broadway as well. Within a couple of decades there were hundreds of groups, from tiny college-based companies with a budget of a couple of hundred dollars, to the Cleveland Playhouse with its $325,000 theatre, a budget of $100,000, and some quarter of a million annual admissions.

These Little Theatres and Community Theatres filled the gap left by the decline of the road, and weren't afraid to try out unusual plays or novel techniques of production. The two most important, in terms of future influences, were a company in a corner of Cape Cod, and another in a minute playhouse some distance from Broadway, both organized in the same year, 1915.

Up in Provincetown, Massachusetts, a group of summer residents got together to do plays for fun. There were some professional theatre people among them. The others were artists, teachers, novelists, journalists, and the like, but they were all bitten by the same bug. They were in and out of each other's houses a good deal: John Reed, who later wrote *Ten Days That Shook The World*, Susan Glaspell and her husband George Cram Cook, Wilbur Steele, the designer Robert Edmond Jones, the painter William Zorach, altogether some twenty-five to thirty people. They did their first program in Hutchins Hapgood's living room and had such a good time that they agreed to branch out. Mary Heaton Vorse owned a shack on the wharf. They put in some benches, decorated it in nautical style, and christened it the Wharf Theatre. There, they unveiled their living room dramas, *Freedom*, a prison play by Reed, *Suppressed Desires*, by Glaspell and Cook, and *Winter's Night*, by Neith Boyce. At fifty cents a ticket, the bill was a sell-out.

It sharpened their taste for more. Cook wrote letters asking for subscribers at a dollar a head for the next three bills, and set a tone from which the group never departed when he said that their purpose was "to give American playwrights a chance to work out their ideas in freedom."[3] He got enough responses to carry them over to the next summer.

That year, somebody brought to one of the early meetings a painfully thin young man with burning eyes. His name was Eugene O'Neill. He had written a number of short plays. One, *Bound East for Cardiff*, was put into rehearsal for the second program. O'Neill himself, "sick with stage-fright,"[4] had a part that called for him to speak one line. The play was received so well that later in the season another of his scripts, *Thirst*, was done. O'Neill played a black sailor in this one and showed considerably more stage presence. Fortunately, however, he refused to let his success as an actor turn him from writing.

Towards the end of that summer, John Reed proposed that they think about transferring their activities to the city. It was an exciting idea. Eight of the members put up thirty dollars each, and they had a treasury. A brownstone house was rented at 139 Macdougal Street, in Greenwich Village, where the living room, as if to echo their original stand, was fitted up with precarious bleachers to make an auditorium that would just hold 150 people. The dining room, with the connecting doors opened, provided a stage. At a meeting of all hands they named themselves the Provincetown Players, and called the Macdougal Street house The Playwrights Theatre. A constitution was drawn up, George Cram Cook was elected president, and Margaret Nordfeldt secretary. Reed wheedled the New York Stage Society into taking 400 subscriptions, and they found themselves properly launched.

After a couple of years, they were doing well enough to need more space. In 1919, they moved a few doors along the street to Number 133, which was variously described in their publicity as a made-over stable and a made-over barn. They established a system of admissions which they felt would give them greater freedom: tickets for performances were available only to subscribers. This, they said, kept them from being a "public theatre," and hence free to experiment as they pleased. Their subscribers sat on hard backless benches, cold without but warmed within by daring words written by newcomers like O'Neill, Glaspell, Edna St. Vincent Millay, Alfred Kreymbourg, Edna Ferber, Djuna Barnes, and Wallace Stevens.

Their second year there was marked by an unexpected windfall. They had done a number of O'Neill's short plays, and now they did a long one, *Beyond the Horizon*. The bedazzled critics acclaimed it and it won that year's Pulitzer Prize. O'Neill's eminence was established, and the Provincetown was at least temporarily solvent.

Early in 1922, George Cram Cooke went to live in Greece where, two years later, he died. In 1923, the Provincetown was reorganized with O'Neill, Robert Edmond Jones, and Kenneth MacGowan at the head of the company. MacGowan had been a drama critic for various major newspapers for twelve years and was by now not only *Vogue*'s reviewer but an associate editor of *Theatre Arts Monthly*. Jones's reputation as a scene designer had been established since 1911, and in addition he had staged some plays. The following year, the Greenwich Village Theatre was taken over and these three supervised its operation while James Light acted as director of the old theatre. They had mixed success, managing in most cases just to break even, but their boast was that their work testified to "our mission of discovering and giving to the theatre new playwrights and new and fruitful impulses."[5]

The Provincetown's rival was a band of amateurs who at first called themselves the Washington Square Players. They started off with a program of three and a half plays, presented Friday and Saturday evenings at the Band Box Theatre on East 57th Street in

New York. The three plays were *Licensed,* by one of the founders, an attorney named Lawrence Langner writing under a pen name, *Eugenically Speaking,* by Edward Goodman, and *Interior,* by Maurice Maeterlinck. The half was *Another Interior,* a pantomime which took place inside a human stomach, with still another founder, Philip Moeller, as a villainous liqueur. The critics, when they drifted over to see the show, liked it, and the group were so much in business that they added a third performance each week.

They managed to continue performing all during the war years, moving to a larger theatre, paying their actors and stagehands as much as $25 a week, and even doing more ambitious productions, such as Ibsen's *Ghosts.* In May, 1918, when it became clear they couldn't meet their bills, they closed down. Only temporarily, however. Langner, with ideas for a new organization in his head, began calling meetings of some of the original members and some new people. Those who could afford it put up some money—their stake was larger than the Provincetown's and came to something over a thousand dollars. A board of managers was set up which included Langner, Moeller, Helen Westley, Justus Sheffield, Maurice Wertheim, Helen Freeman, Lee Simonson, and Rollo Peters. A name vaguely hinting at some medieval notion of cooperative craftsmanship was chosen: the Theatre Guild.

With some help from the financier Otto Kahn, they leased the Garrick Theatre—that very house in which *Mrs. Warren's Profession* had opened to such hostile reviews and had been closed almost at once by the police. Their first play couldn't have been further from Shaw; it was a harlequinade by Benevente, with Edna St. Vincent Millay as Columbine and Dudley Digges as Polichinelle. Since their budget was very small they had to scrimp on sets and costumes. A particularly dazzling gown was made for one of the actresses, Amelia Somerville, out of oilcloth and gold radiator paint, and when, in her first scene, she sat down, she stuck to the chair. She was pulled free, but had to be careful not to turn her back to the audience for the rest of the play.

The Guild's second production was a somber Irish drama of rape and murder, *John Ferguson,* by St. John Ervine. When it opened, the group had less than twenty dollars left in the bank. By the time it closed, some 177 performances later, they were in the black once more.

This was in 1919. The next six years saw them slowly gaining ground, forging themselves into a tighter working organization, approaching their ideal of a theatre which "will not be employed for either personal or commercial exploitation, but for the creation . . . of the best drama of one's time, drama honestly reflecting the author's vision of life or sense of style and beauty."[6] There were upheavals in the managerial board over an issue that was often to divide other bands like theirs, whether the theatre could be run by a group with equal voices, or had to be firmly controlled by a dictator. Several members resigned although not necessarily over that issue—Rollo Peters, Helen Freeman, and Justus Sheffield —and a new one was added, their play reader, Theresa Helburn, bringing the board to the six members it was to continue with almost to the end. Meeting in the dingy partitioned attic at the Garrick which was their office, or at one another's houses for dinner, they argued hotly over productions and hammered out policies. They read plays endlessly. They supervised rehearsals, criticizing the work of director and cast as ruthlessly but as constructively as they could. And by degrees they made themselves into a cohesive, well-functioning group. "It has often been said that a theatre can be run successfully only by an autocrat," said Miss Helburn, later, "and there may be some truth in the theory provided that the autocrat is a genius. Failing the genius, give me six good theatrical minds working together for a common end."[7]

From the beginning, they recognized that they would have to rely on like-minded people for their support, and this meant a subscription list which would guarantee audiences and money in advance of every season, although, unlike the Provincetown, they would then sell tickets publicly at the box office. This had its limitations; they had to provide five or six plays a year to the subscribers, and they couldn't risk alienating their friends by giving them unduly strong meat. They wanted to present plays by Americans about America, but the right ones were hard to find if they were to compete with Broadway. So, while they were far from abandoning their ideals, they found themselves relying more often on works by established European authors. These included Masefield, St. John Ervine (a second play by him helped them recover the losses of three flops in a row), Shaw, and A. A. Milne, whose *Mr. Pim Passes By,* a mild, domestic, Winnie-the-Poohish comedy done early in 1921, set them solidly in their bank's good books. *Liliom,* by Molnar, which followed it, was an even greater hit. But they were always ready to risk financial failure if a play seemed to them to say something important and to say it in the highest theatrical terms. Shaw's *Back to Methuselah,* which followed, appeared to them just such a risk. It took three nights to perform and was expensive to do, nor was it altogether comprehensible even to the Guild's most loyal supporters. When, during its run, Wertheim asked the doorman how things were going, he was told, "Better and better every evening. Less people are leaving before it's over." They had prepared themselves to lose as much as $30,000 on the play, and when the final loss turned out to be $20,000 Shaw said that the Guild had made ten thousand dollars out of his name alone.

The group continued to search for American plays, and significantly, not for those which would imitate Broadway successes. The profits from Shaw's *Heartbreak House,* which had been done in 1920, allowed them to give six matinées of a tough, serious play about southern hillbillies, called *John Hawthorne,* by David Liebovitz. That was only an appetizer. In 1923, they presented to the regular subscription list *The Adding Machine* by Elmer Rice. Broadway's table, that season, was spread with such goodies as *Shore Leave, Rain, Merton of the Movies, The Old Soak, The Gingham Girl,* two "colored vaudevilles", and, for heavier fare, Jane Cowl as Juliet, and John Barrymore as Hamlet. *The Adding Machine* was a quite different dish.

Rice had had a hit at the age of twenty-two with *On Trial.* Two other plays had done well. He was now thirty-one, an earnest, round-faced, bespectacled young man. *The Adding Machine* was a lively attack on the dreariness and soullessness of modern life. Its characters, chained to computations of profit and loss, had digits instead of names, and when its protagonist, Mr. Zero, went to heaven, he found there only another giant adding machine.

It was not precisely a success, chalking up only 72 performances. However, it was to be remembered as one of the earliest unveilings in America of expressionist theatre—certainly, the first full-length one to be done professionally.

Expressionism lent itself to plays with a social message. It had developed in Germany through the work of Bertolt Brecht, Ernst

Toller, and Erwin Piscator, and in Russia under Vsevolod Meyerhold's direction. As a revolutionary form it addressed itself to that class its authors saw as most revolutionary, the proletariat. In practice, however, the proletariat was hardly the mainstay of the theatre, and when it did buy tickets it wanted to understand what was going on, so that avant-garde plays tended to appeal largely to radical intellectuals and middle-class liberals. Expressionism had at its root the notion that theatrical form was by definition unreal. You did not actually see real people on the stage but performers playing at reality. Why not, then, abandon the constricting drawing room and broaden the theatre into the most interesting and entertaining of lecture halls? The job of the dramatist was to use the devices of the stage—movement, settings, dance, lighting, music, acting—to expose the ills of the human condition in a society based on material rather than spiritual gain, and to educate audiences in their eradication. What was done on the stage was not reality but symbolic of reality. It was not surprising that many American playwrights, trying their best to sum up the rampant confusion of the time, chose to call their main characters He, The Boy, or Adam, and just stopped short of Everyman. Expressionism was, in a sense, a return to the medieval Morality play, and imitating that predecessor tried to root itself in popular taste while maintaining an elevated tone.

This, in a somewhat watered-down form, was what *The Adding Machine* attempted. Rice and his producers failed gallantly. They were not to be the last.

Undaunted, the Guild tried again the following year. They did *Man and the Masses (Massemensch)* by Ernst Toller, in a splendid translation by the poet, Louis Untermeyer. It had been one of the early expressionist plays and had deeply impressed Lee Simonson when he saw it in Germany. It was considerably more somber and revolutionary than *The Adding Machine,* and it closed after less than half as many performances.

The Guild's position was to be voiced by Philip Moeller, some time later. "We made some money last season, so now we felt we could afford to lose some."[8] Accordingly, they didn't give up. In January, 1925, they presented a third expressionist play, *Processional.* Again, it was by an American, John Howard Lawson. It dealt more specifically than *The Adding Machine* with contemporary problems, and spoke more sharply in the accents of protest.

Lawson's passionate attachment to the theatre had begun early. His family had been well off and theatre-going had been a normal part of his life. He had written his first play, a poetic Hindu love drama in blank verse, at the age of fourteen, noting that for some reason it had given him a lot of trouble to write. A second, done in his senior year at Williams College, was seriously considered by Walter Hampden, and this confirmed Lawson in his desire to be a playwright. After graduation, he went to work as a cable editor —his father was the American representative of Reuter's—but kept on writing, and within the next year or so had had two plays produced outside New York.

When the United States entered the First World War, Lawson, like many other American artists, made his protest against it by going to Europe as a Red Cross ambulance driver. He had already been something of a radical in college, and what he saw during the war made him lean even more strongly toward pacifism and socialism. After the war, he sold a script to Paramount for what was then a useful sum, $5,000, and with his new wife took the well-beaten trail to Paris. There, he settled down to work and turned out two plays, *Roger Bloomer* and *Processional.* The first was a kind of fantasy about a youth's struggle against a hard-hearted commercial world; the second dealt rather loosely with a miners' strike in West Virginia.

He had been much struck by the work of the expressionists, and their influence was strong in both pieces. But "I looked," he said, "for a more American expression in words, music, pantomime, that would carry a sense of a modern kind of projection, that would be *artificial* like musical comedy, like vaudeville, like burlesque." He referred to *Processional* as a "jazz symphony," and in his notes in the typescript of the play, wrote, "An attempt has been made to build something of a definitely American character and rhythm. A conception of the stream of American life carried along on a current of vaudeville patter and jazz noises." To reinforce this quality, he used snatches of jazz as musical emphasis, and constructed the play out of brief scenes which were sometimes reminiscent of vaudeville sketches. *Roger Bloomer*, too, was composed of short scenes which melted into one another, and at the end of the play there was what he called a "Freudian dream-ballet" which reflected the influence Diaghilev's ballets had had on him in Paris. His stage directions for a section of this sequence read: "This should be performed like a Black Mass in a Christian Science church." Henry Hull, who read the play, said to him, "Look here, there's no such thing." "I know," said Lawson, airily. "That's just what I mean."

When he returned to New York, *Roger Bloomer* was done by the Actors' Theatre, a short-lived venture under the sponsorship of Actors Equity. *Processional* had to wait for a couple of years until the Guild produced it. Neither play made money, although *Processional* ran for twelve weeks. Both, however, attracted a good deal of critical attention, and together with *The Adding Machine* and Eugene O'Neill's short try at expressionism, *The Hairy Ape*, had the distinction of being trailblazers. Rice and Lawson had developed an American form based on the European inspiration which was to have its effect on many other playwrights, and Lawson was to be considered one of the leaders of expressionism long after he himself felt that he had gone beyond it.

While the Guild was thus occupied, the Provincetown had been taking an equally long step in another new direction. Plays about blacks which showed them as something other than beastly primitive types were rare almost to the point of improbability. Yet the Provincetown had done four.

They were by white playwrights, of course, and good as they were they could not escape the limitations of a culture which had made slaves of black men. But then, with only two exceptions, *all* the plays done professionally about blacks up to this time were by whites. The exceptions were *The Clip Woman's Fortune*, done by the Ethiopian Art Players for a single week, and *Appearances*, by Garland Anderson. The latter perhaps merits a closer look.

Not only was it the first full-length drama by a black to reach Broadway (*The Clip Woman's Fortune* was a one-acter), it was also the first to make a point about prejudice unencumbered by any mythology from Darkest Africa. Its story concerns a bellhop in a western hotel who is framed by a crooked lawyer on a charge of raping a white woman. Appearances are against him and he is threatened with lynching, but he makes a vigorous defense in the course of which he attacks racial intolerance, and at the last moment is vindicated. Anderson knew what he was writing about. He had been a bellhop in a hotel in San Francisco for fifteen years. His characters were drawn from life. There were no crap games, no razor fights, no bug-eyed flights from ghosts, no voodoo drums, no childlike darkies who, in their simplicity, seemed almost human. There was, instead, for all the awkwardness of the play's construction, a note by the author: "This play is the outward expression of an inner burning desire to serve humanity."

Anderson had had only four years of schooling. He had used his spare time to teach himself, to such good effect that the *Sun's* interviewer declared no one could tell from his speech that he wasn't a college graduate. His announced philosophy was that "any man can make anything of himself if he wills it." He had willed to write a play and had done so.

Al Jolson was sufficiently impressed by the script of *Appearances* to put up the money to send Anderson to New York, to find a backer. Against all odds, one turned up, L. W. Sagar, a former Shubert associate. Another innovation was a mixed cast, blacks being played by blacks instead of white actors in blackface. After rehearsals started, two of the leading women, discovering that they would have to share the stage with Lionel Monagas, who played the lead, and Doe Doe Green, a very funny black comic, walked out. Replacements were found, and the play opened at the Frolic Theater in October, 1925. Although it got wide publicity and sympathetic reviews, it began to die, and Sagar announced that he was pulling out. Anderson's answer was to turn up three more backers—all three white Texans. After another few weeks the play was wrapped up and taken to San Francisco, where it ran for over three months. It was shown in cities all over the country, and was revived in New York in 1929 to renewed praise. The next year it went to London where Anderson was a PEN Club guest and had his portrait painted by A. Christie. Then—nothing more. Although it was announced that he was working on another play, no more is known of him. Unlike most people, however, he had achieved exactly what he had set out to do.

Three of the four black plays the Provincetown did were by Eugene O'Neill. Their first bill in 1919 had included his one-act, *The Dreamy Kid,* about a hunted criminal. The following year, *The Emperor Jones* had appeared, with the fine black actor Charles Gilpin in the lead. In spite of its doomful Moussorgskian quality, it contained little that was pertinent to American blacks except to reinforce the white notion that they were hardly better than savages, but it did succeed in elevating its central character to a grand, tragic level. In 1924, however, *All God's Chillun Got Wings* was shown, with Paul Robeson as Jim Harris. If O'Neill displayed his grim power to great advantage in this drama of miscegenation, the Provincetown showed great bravery in producing it. A story of the racial tensions which destroy a marriage between a black man and a white woman, it provoked such a hurricane of whispers about its immorality (Paul Robeson actually kissed Mary Blair's hand on stage) that the Provincetown was forced to write to its subscribers complaining that their aims and those of the author had been distorted. "We are not the least interested in either sensationalism or propaganda," they snapped. "To us, *All God's Chillun Got Wings* is neither of these things."[9] Notwithstanding this disclaimer, the play *was* propaganda. There could be little doubt in the minds of those who saw it that something was wickedly wrong in the relations between blacks and whites.

The Provincetown's twelfth season, that of 1926–27, featured *In Abraham's Bosom,* by Paul Green. Its blacks were also patterned after life, and its hero was a man burning to better himself but doomed by the defects in his own character. It contained a plea no less passionate for being couched in a way that wouldn't frighten white audiences: "I don't say the colored ought to be made equal to the white. . . . We are not ready for it yet," cries Abe. "But I do say we have equal rights to education and free thought and living our lives."

Paul Green was then thirty-three, a lanky, long-nosed man with an engaging manner, a teacher of English at the University of North Carolina. He had written a number of plays for Little Theatres, and with his colleague, Professor Frederick Koch, who founded the North Carolina Playmakers, was concerned not only to produce American dramas but regional ones which would deal with the special problems of the South. No one could have been more surprised than he, except possibly his producers, when *In Abraham's Bosom* received the Pulitzer Prize. It not only marked a milestone, it revived the Provincetown and kept its doors open on Macdougal Street for a little while longer.

As the Provincetown's fortunes waned—in another couple of years it was to disband for good—those of the Guild increased. Langner had always insisted that the organization must have its own theatre and a permanent company. Like the Provincetown, the Guild had depended on a subscription list, and by the end of 1923 they held a bond sale to which 2500 of their subscribers responded by buying over half a million dollars' worth. This meant that a permanent house was possible. They inaugurated it on April 5th, 1925, with Shaw's *Caesar and Cleopatra*. Shaw was invited to be present but said he was more accustomed to closing theatres than to opening them. The first season found them nearly broke again, with a four hundred thousand dollar mortgage and a number of subscribers not altogether satisfied with their plays. Not even this could stop them. They achieved their second goal, that of a permanent company which included most of their regulars, among them Helen Westley, Lynn Fontanne, Alfred Lunt, Dudley Digges, Margalo Gilmore, Philip Loeb, Edward G. Robinson, Clare Eames, Earl Larimore, and Henry Travers. And so obvious was the value and importance of their work that in defiance of every obstacle the end of their second year in the new theatre saw their subscription list increased to 23,000. As if in further vindication, they now had one of their biggest hits, and strikingly enough it, like the Provincetown's success, was about American blacks.

Looked at from the perspective of its own times, *Porgy* is clearly an honest attempt to present black life, just as the novel by Dubose Heyward, from which it was taken, had been. The brawling precincts of Catfish Alley seethe with real people; the language is full of truth. And yet the total effect was, in those days, curiously quaint and foreign, rather like watching a pageant of folk customs in Outer Mongolia. It is easy to see why *Porgy* went down so smoothly in 1927; it did nothing to alter white audiences' convictions about blacks. Only from the colder vantage point of today can it be seen how much it had to do with the terrible running sore of black life in America.

Despite the courage shown by the Guild and the Provincetown in experimentation, there was very little being done in the opinion of some playwrights to shake the theatre's complacency. Something new, something more revolutionary, was needed. Provocative samplings from Europe had been seen. Jacques Copeau had appeared in 1917—and at that storm center, the Garrick Theatre. In 1922 and again in 1923 the Moscow Art Theatre, under its brilliant leader Konstantin Stanislavsky, had been the rage of New York, although hardly anyone could understand a word of what they said. Stanislavsky had visited the Guild to see *Peer Gynt*, and to their chagrin had told them that it was only "surface." In 1926, the work of many European directors was shown in an International Theatre Exhibition in New York. As an indirect result, four earnest, rebellious theatre people were brought together: John Howard Lawson, Em Jo Basshe, Michael Gold, and Francis Faragoh.

They were all about the same age, in their early thirties. Basshe had been an early member of the Provincetown, and had had his play, *Adam Solitaire*, produced by them the season before. Faragoh was less well known, having had little produced and that by Little Theatres. Gold had also been one of the original Provincetowners and a good friend of John Reed's; in addition, he had been a journalist, had worked in oil fields and on ranches in Mexico, and had started an anarchist paper which was suppressed by the police after two issues. An avowed Communist, he was at this time working as an editor of the *New Masses*. Unlikely as it may seem, he was also on friendly terms with the banker, Otto Kahn.

Kahn was a great patron of the arts, especially of the theatre. He had been actively involved in bringing Copeau to America, and in the promotion of the Metropolitan Opera Company. He had been a backer of both the Guild and the Provincetown. He was always open to new ideas and wasn't afraid to lose money standing up for them. Now, after some initial discussions, he invited the four to lunch with him in his club, on the top floor of an office building with a grand view over Wall Street.

Lawson remembers him as looking "a bit like the White Rabbit in *Alice in Wonderland*, a brisk, alert, hurrying man." They put their plan to him, the formation of an avant-garde theatre which would be in the hands of playwrights. Both the Guild and the Provincetown, they said, were hopelessly middle-class and commercial. Theirs would be a theatre of youth, a theatre without commercialism, and one which would address itself, as did the European companies they admired, to the progressive working class, the real core of America. If Kahn had any reservations he kept them to himself. It was not his style to dictate policy; a true patron, he believed in letting people have their heads. He put up $30,000 with no strings attached.

Lawson suggested adding two members. One was his friend John Dos Passos, whom he had met on the boat which took them to their ambulance driving during the war. Dos Passos had made his reputation with his novels, *Manhattan Transfer* and *Three Soldiers*, and had made a stab at the stage with a rather diffuse and scrappy piece, *The Moon is a Gong*, which had been done at the Cherry Lane Theatre. The other name was Eugene O'Neill. Lawson was certain Dos Passos, who was then abroad, would join and he was right. O'Neill, however, wrote a cold refusal. It shocked Lawson but was perfectly understandable. O'Neill was by then generally accepted as one of the most successful playwrights around, and was no longer interested in starting new ventures. Furthermore, from 1923 to 1925 he, along with Kenneth MacGowan and Robert Edmond Jones, had worked hard to keep the Provincetown alive and presumably he had had his fill of being an executive.

The group now had a managerial board of five. It had a name —the New Playwrights Theatre. It had its first bill, which was to consist of Lawson's *Loud Speaker*, *Earth*, by Basshe, and Gold's *Fiesta*. What it lacked was a stage director.

They got in touch with Jasper Deeter, who ran a small but highly thought of cooperative theatre, the Hedgerow, near Philadelphia, and who had directed *In Abraham's Bosom* for the Provincetown. Deeter came to New York and said that he was willing to take over the direction of the plays at once, but that he would have to have complete authority over all productions. It seemed to the five playwrights that autocracy would edge out their democracy, and they replied that they must retain control. Deeter bowed out. In the end, since the first play was a farce, they hired a man with considerable experience in Broadway comedy, Harry Wagstaff Gribble. *Loud Speaker* was put into rehearsal and scheduled for March 2nd, 1927, at the 52nd Street Theatre. It had once been Bim's Music Hall, and was a big, echoing barn of a place, but it was only a block away from the Guild's new theatre and it seemed a good vantage point from which to challenge them.

There was trouble from the start. *Loud Speaker* was a difficult play, a satire on politics and journalism, a fantasy, a farce comedy, and what Joseph Wood Krutch called "an American example of the Comedia dell'Arte," all at once. Lawson, pursuing his notion of a new kind of American expressionism, demanded a constructivist set. He wanted characters to make surprise entrances sliding down chutes, and scenes to dissolve into one another as they did in a burlesque show. His vision was a swift-paced ordered confusion which would express the Jazz Age, the chaos and comedy of modern society. It called for a director like Meyerhold. What it got was a good, sound craftsman who played it for laughs, and that wasn't quite enough.

Mordecai Gorelik, a brilliant and imaginative designer who had done the sets for *Processional*, turned out one of the first constructivist settings ever seen in America, a dazzling red and green arrangement of levels, platforms, staircases and chutes. Seth Kendall, the actor who played a millionaire candidate for Governor of New York, was a dignified, heavyset man. When it was explained to him that he had to make his first entrance sliding down one of the Coney Island chutes, he threatened to quit. Many of the other actors felt, too, that the whole operation was too dangerous for them, and in consequence much of the effect of the set was lost.

There was tension between Lawson and Gribble, neither of whom really understood the other. To Gribble, farce was farce and you directed it in a certain way. For Lawson, things were more serious; you could use the skills of the commercial theatre but what you turned out had to go considerably deeper. During one rehearsal, Lawson, never reticent about speaking his mind, interrupted a scene and Gribble, in a fury, told him to shut up. Lawson went to the office feeling that the whole concept of playwrights' control of the theatre was at stake. He sent his secretary to ask Gribble to come upstairs, and then sat biting his nails and wondering whether he had gone too far. However, Gribble dismissed the actors and came. He apologized—after all, the company had hired him to do a job for them—and Lawson in his turn apologized. They got on better after that, but they still weren't any closer to understanding each other.

Inevitably, the play suffered. It was greeted with puzzlement and derision for the most part, some critics wanting to know what all those ladders and slides were for, others, like the *Sun*'s Gilbert

Gabriel, remarking that "most of the comedy has the substance of hiccups in a gale."

The mistakes of the first play were to be repeated in later ones. Partly, it was the result of inexperience on the part of the five managers, but partly it was simply that they were ahead of their times. They were unable to find a director capable of translating what they wanted into what was possible onstage.

Em Jo Basshe's *Earth*, the second production, was a little more successful. Basshe had lived in Alabama, and wrote about the struggle between voodoo and Christianity among blacks. What emerged was the familiar "study of primitive Negro life . . . a portrait of religious fervor among semi-barbaric people," to quote the New Playwrights' handbill. It came somewhere between *In Abraham's Bosom* and *Porgy* and couldn't quite compete with them being less beautifully produced than the latter and more incoherent than the former.

Fiesta, Mike Gold's play about Mexico, was carried to the dress rehearsal stage and then, since everyone was uneasy about it, postponed until the following season. In any case, they had run out of money.

Kahn came through with another $30,000. The playwrights took stock of their situation and decided that to begin with they must stop trying to tilt against Broadway. They moved to the tiny Cherry Lane Theatre, in Commerce Street, and set up a loose sort of workshop in the hope of developing a more unified company. The five managers divided responsibility and planned to work full-time on the business of the theatre. In return, they allotted themselves $25 a week each, and the actors got paid about the same amount. They still thought of themselves as a "working-class" theatre, by which each of them may have meant different things, but in general that they were out to break with tradition, that their productions would be revolutionary both in technique and in their attack on the established order of society.

The season from the fall of 1927 to the spring of 1928 comprised four plays, all interesting, all well written, all certainly in line with the theatre's policy. *The Belt*, by a newspaperman named Paul Sifton, was based on the Ford assemblyline method and dealt realistically with the conditions of factory workers under a speed-up. *The Centuries*, written and staged by Em Joe Basshe, was a muscular portrait of a slum tenement with the action centered firmly on a single house. It was almost balletic in treatment but sharply political in tone, calling upon the poor to organize themselves against their miserable condition. (It is interesting to note, in passing, that a little more than a year later Elmer Rice's *Street Scene* opened on Broadway and soon after took the Pulitzer. It, too, portrayed tenement life and was centered around a single house which in Rice's words was "the real protagonist of the drama." It had been rejected by the Guild among others, and when a backer was found Rice had to do his own directing. This play ended with no sort of revolutionary message, but St. John Ervine fastidiously referred to it as "a garbage can.") The third of the New Playwrights' plays was Lawson's *The International,* an attempt to set an anti-war play to a complex musical rhythm, which included formal choruses and gymnastic dances. The fourth was by Mike Gold and replaced *Fiesta.* It was called *Hoboken Blues* and dealt, in a form as disjointed as a revue, with New York's Harlem. To reinforce its satiric bite it was performed by white actors in blackface, a reverse foreshadowing of Genet's *The Blacks* which was a little too mysterious for the 1920s.

It was, on the whole, an unusual mixed bag, and though there were crudities in the scripts and some clumsiness in the staging, it provided an exhilarating contrast to much of what was being done uptown. Some interesting new actors were seen, among them Franchot Tone and George Tobias. Yet the mistakes and awkwardnesses of the group were charged harshly against it, and few critics were ready to give it credit for pioneering. *Hoboken Blues,* directed by Edward Massey, was described by one viewer in terms that give a sense of its visual interest: "In one scene in a hospital a Negro is being given an anaesthetic: ether is hissing, in the trembling green light a policeman is dancing on the Negro's chest, and every ladder and scaffold becomes peopled with hooded and shrouded figures of hags and goblins. It was decidedly good theatre."[10] But the strangeness of its visions only put most reviewers off; Alexander Woollcott, for instance, complaining that the "backdrop revolved this time like a roller towel. . . ."

There were some serious blunders. The stage of the Cherry Lane Theatre was really not large enough to take such ambitious efforts as setting a whole tenement onstage, as in *The Centuries,* or danced-out battle scenes such as *The International* called for. Nor were matters helped by the fact that Basshe and Lawson chose to direct their own plays. They knew what they wanted but, not being directors, didn't know how to convey the message to the actors. "When I directed *The International*," Lawson recalls, "the actors came to a point almost of revolt because they thought I didn't know what I was doing—and I must say they were largely right." The settings were not always by professionals, for instance, those for *The International* were done by John Dos Passos, whose gifts as a novelist were perhaps no qualification for scene design. And the theatre itself was small and uncomfortable, with hard seats, so that watching a long play there may have taken the edge off the critics' appreciation.

At the end of the season, the New Playwrights had used up every penny of their capital. Lawson, with a family to support, decided to migrate to Hollywood and the films. Faragoh went, too, and was to work on movies as far removed from what he had been writing as *Little Caesar, Frankenstein,* and *My Friend Flicka.* Gold had become convinced that the development of workers' theatre lay elsewhere; as for his unproduced play, *Fiesta,* he took it to the Provincetown the following year.

Basshe, with some help from Dos Passos, tried to keep the company going, although there was no more money to be had from Otto Kahn. He announced the election of Paul Sifton and Edward Massey to the board of directors, and rented the Provincetown Playhouse for the next bill, which was to consist of a dramatization of a longshoremen's strike in California, *Singing Jailbirds,* by Upton Sinclair, and Dos Passos's play, *Airways, Inc.* He tried to develop a sustaining fund of gifts from well-wishers, and set up an organization called En-Ti-Pi Shops, through which he hoped to sell books and works of art, the profits to go into the sustaining fund.

Sinclair had written *Singing Jailbirds* out of first-hand experience. In 1923, he had taken part in a strike of the Marine Transport Workers Union, at San Pedro, the harbor of Los Angeles. It had been a small enough part; he had attempted to read an incendiary document—the Constitution of the United States—on private land and had been arrested. He had spent eighteen hours in jail, incommunicado, along with some six hundred other people who were scooped up for cheering and singing in sympathy with the strikers. The play dealt with the imprisonment and grisly death of the leader of such a strike, and for once the reviewers were impressed. The play, which had been effectively staged by Basshe, ran for seventy-nine performances.

But after this promising beginning, *Airways, Inc.* was a disaster. Dos Passos and Basshe disagreed over the production, and in the end Dos Passos resigned. It was the last straw. The New Playwrights was out of business for good.

Their failure stemmed largely from the causes which were always to plague such groups. One major one was misjudgment of the size of the theatre. An intimate play might be destroyed by too roomy a house or a complex one cramped by too small a stage. A play calling for a large cast and elaborate sets might draw crowds but its costs would be bound to eat up the income. The right combination of play, director, cast, and management was always difficult to achieve and twice as difficult to keep when found, for several flops might drive key people away to find more lucrative employment, but success might equally make them look for greener fields.

Some of these things undoubtedly contributed to the collapse of the Provincetown a year after the end of the New Playwrights. In 1925, James Light had taken over command of the theatre, with M. Eleanor Fitzgerald as business manager and secretary. They were able to keep going for four more years, during which time they were responsible for at least one major explosion, that surrounding the production of *Him*, by the poet E.E. Cummings, in April, 1928.

It is a difficult play to describe, being written in Cummings' customarily opaque style. Perhaps the critic John Anderson, writing in the *Journal*, came closest to explaining it when he pointed out that it was a "shrewd and believable scheme for reducing a 'stream of consciousness' to a dramatic form," and added that it was in the best tradition of James Joyce, Virginia Woolf, and the kind of thing O'Neill had attempted, by means of asides, in *Strange Interlude*. Cummings himself was opposed to its being explained. In a program note, he said, "Relax and give this PLAY a chance to strut its stuff—relax, don't worry because it's not like something else—relax, stop wondering what it's all 'about' . . . this play isn't 'about' it simply is . . ."

That wasn't good enough for most people. In the ensuing uproar, thousands of flaming words were hurled. *Time* called Cummings the author of "a bitter and unwholesome book about the war" by which they meant his gentle and touching prison chronicle, *The Enormous Room*. William Rose Benet wrote a letter replying that the press didn't appear to know of Cummings' high standing as a poet and novelist. Gilbert Seldes assembled, and wrote a preface for, a booklet called "him AND the CRITICS," in which both sides had their say. On the playwright's side were such literary figures as Conrad Aiken, Stark Young, Waldo Frank, Edmund Wilson, and John Dos Passos, while opposed were Alexander Woollcott, WalterWinchell, Percy Hammond, and a number of other newspaper reviewers. In the middle were some like Robert Garland of the *Telegram*, who said, "To . . . those of us who look upon the theatre as a place of amusement, who go with our girl friends to see Mr. Joe Cook and with our boy friends to a good old fashioned burlesque show—the case of Mr. Seldes Against the Newspaper Critics is no more than a fairly diverting show." The publicity kept the play on until May 27th, to full houses, but since there were only 220 seats, and the play was costly, the end result was a loss.

A year later, the Provincetown was appealing for new members and new financial support, explaining that while Otto Kahn had given them some more money, he had other interests and couldn't be more than one backer among others. They moved to the good old Garrick, which was larger than the Macdougal Street headquarters and had a better stage. They presented O'Neill's *S.S.Glencairn*, which was really his four one-act sea plays done in one evening. Soon after came Gold's *Fiesta*, for which a talented young dancer named Helen Tamiris did Mexican choreography that was "lusty and pleasantly lascivious," as one reviewer put it. It wasn't quite enough to keep the play running. One more production followed, *Winter Bound*, by Thomas Dickinson, and then the Provincetown expired. Its theatre on Macdougal Street was to house other rebel plays, but not under its banner.

It must be remarked that there were extraneous factors contributing to the Provincetown's collapse. 1929 was one of the worst years the theatre had ever had, and if it was hard to keep Broadway successes on the boards, it was much harder for smaller theatres. In any case, the Provincetown had lived out a span which was considerably longer than anyone might have expected—for fourteen years they had clung grimly to their position, to be "a laboratory for the playwright and the actor, the director and the designer, a place where they may try out experiments under special conditions."[11] But experimentation is costly. Avant-garde theatres live precarious lives, balanced on the fate of a single season and on the hope of finding a sympathetic audience large enough to subsidize them. The Provincetown had had O'Neill as its major playwright, which was a considerable asset. The Guild had learned to take a careful middle way between experimental plays and commercial ones, and they had been lucky as well. Also, it had been helpful that some of their board members worked outside the theatre and were fairly well-to-do. The Provincetown had won acclaim and respect, but they had been unable to broaden out to catch the bigger audiences. The bizarre nature of many of their plays put off those who liked a bit of fun for an evening, and the social criticism voiced was too vague to suit the revolutionaries.

The problem of finding the right audience had been one of the roots of the New Playwrights' downfall as well. They found themselves under attack from both Right and Left; from the former because of the inflammatory nature of what they said, from the latter because of the unfathomable nature of the forms they chose. Dos Passos, summing up a year after their demise, said, "The American mind of all classes and denominations is too accustomed to keeping art or ideas in separate watertight compartments." After remarking that audiences in general preferred "carefully pigeonholed distinctions of farce, musical comedy, drama," and that they shied away from things that couldn't be so easily categorized, he pointed out that new tools had to be forged with which to work the new content of plays. "This," he concluded, "neither radicals nor reactionaries are willing to grant, nor the fact that the first attempts with new tools are sure to be clumsy."[12]

In fact, "failure" is the wrong word for both the Provincetown and the New Playwrights. Considering the obstacles, their achievements were far from small. The Provincetown had done over a hundred new plays by some fifty American writers. The New Playwrights' record was less impressive but all of their eight productions had been new American plays in a new genre. Both companies had given a showing to the work of interesting new actors and set designers, as had, of course, the Guild. More importantly, all three groups had been instrumental in opening a whole series of new paths which others would follow. They had broken down the proscenium, had departed from the picture-frame stage, had abandoned realism, had tried stream of consciousness, had scrambled separate forms, had set their playwrights poking into the darkest corners of the human psyche or turning the accepted social order inside out. With the greatest zeal and valor they had exploded a dozen mines simultaneously. They may not have started a landslide, but they had certainly caused some shifting in long-established foundations.

1929-1931

It is difficult to remember a New York in which people, leaving the Province-town Playhouse in the depths of the Village or the Guild Theatre on 52nd Street, could stroll tranquilly home along empty streets. At the end of the Twenties, it was in many ways a quieter city, its neighborhoods more like self-contained communities, its crime casting no shadow over its merriment.

Times Square was surrounded by glittering hotels like the Astor, where people met their dates under the clock in the lobby, and by theatres which disgorged crowds in evening dress. There were nine daily newspapers, each with its pontifical drama critic wielding the power to beatify or damn. The signs of dozens of night clubs lighted the side streets; lightless, beyond them, speakeasies lurked. Bootleggers from upstate took rooms in the Hotel Hermitage and sold to favored customers out of steamer trunks, while deliveries in bulk came by truck to the back doors of clubs and restaurants. Short skirts, hip flasks, rolled-down stockings, bell-bottomed trousers, and long sideburns marked the wild youth who felt themselves newly liberated from a more puritanical age. Girls had taken to smoking cigarettes in public and the rumble seat, ideal for necking, was invented. On sultry nights, Central Park was littered with the bodies of whole tenement populations, asleep, or making love, drinking home-made wine, gossiping, sweating. Street cars clanged up Broadway, while along Fifth Avenue the statelier double-deckers ran, and one of the delights of warm evenings was to ride in the top front seat of an open bus. Italian groceries, their windows full of dusty-looking mortadelle, lined Bleecker Street; Yorkville was full of fraternal beer halls cheek by jowl; a vast sea of pushcarts filled the lower East Side; whites could visit the Apollo Theatre on West 125th Street with impunity.

The city looked opulent and carefree, but it festered in a hundred places with poverty. It was, in that way, a mirror of the whole country.

It was a boom time. The war had brought immense profits to many corporations, and the decade that followed saw great leaps in technological development. Motor cars were everywhere, airplanes carried the mail and even some passengers, all sorts of electrically-operated goodies were on the way, from a refrigerator which was to edge the iceman out of business to toasters, ovens, coffee makers, and hair driers. Radio linked the coasts. Coal, steel, oil, textiles, all expanded, and as these industries grew richer and spread still further they brought higher prices and wider employment.

They had also succeeded in drowning out the one possible sour note, that sounded by the labor movement. The unions, which had agreed not to strike during the war, wanted their share of the gravy afterward. It was a modest enough share, being concerned with an eight-hour day rather than a twelve-hour one, the alleviation of Dickensian working conditions in mines and mills, and higher pay to meet the higher cost of living. A wave of strikes rolled over the country in 1919. It was met with ruthless force. Company police beat, rode down and shot pickets in bloody battles in the coal fields and steel towns. At the same time, the cry was raised that the Anarchists and Bolsheviks were trying to seize control of the country, and Attorney General Palmer began his notorious raids on every sort of radical organization. After all, the Reds had taken over Russia, and everyone knew that the richest capitalist country in the world would be next on their agenda. In the panic, hundreds were arrested and jailed, some of them Socialists or Communists, others people who had simply happened to be passing left-wing bookshops when the raiders arrived. The charge, "The Bolsheviks are taking over!" which headlined a Boston paper when the city police force struck for a small pay increase was successfully leveled against all strikers, and by the time the dust had settled the labor movement had been brought to heel.

So, by 1929, everything looked rosy. The Great Red Menace had faded and everyone was making money. The American Federation of Labor had settled down to a mild, old-fashioned sort of guildsmanship, and one of its leaders said, "You can't have Utopia. This is the U.S.A., not the Garden of Eden." If, under the surface, there was still child labor, there were sweatshops, there were company towns patrolled by armed police, there were slums in which four families shared a single flat, it was hardly worth calling attention to amid the general prosperity. At only one point was there a flurry when two anarchists, Bartolomeo Vanzetti and Nicola Sacco, were sentenced to death on a poorly supported charge of murder. Their arrest had come at the height of the Red Scare, and it appeared to many that they were being tried for their radical beliefs rather than their complicity in a crime. Their cause became that of every sort of liberal, and the fight to save them dragged on for seven years until, in August, 1927, they were executed. A year later, Maxwell Anderson and Harold Hickerson turned up with an angry play, *Gods of the Lightning*, a thinly-disguised version of the case. Anderson was already known as a playwright with a punch. *What Price Glory?* which he had written with Lawrence Stallings, had had immense impact in 1924, when it had spoken the authentic language of American soldiers in the trenches. It had been seen as an anti-war play as well, although in fact it contained only one line that could be construed that way, the line from which the title had been taken. *Gods of the Lightning* drew approving reviews, Burns Mantle calling it "splendidly enthusiastic." It also drew police officials to its opening night; they were reported to be considering action against the play for its unfavorable portrayals of the Judge and the District Attorney. It did not, however, draw crowds. It lasted for only 29 performances. Most people did not want to be reminded of a disagreeable interlude.

On Thursday, October 24, 1929, the house that jack built majestically collapsed, timber by timber. The stock market plummeted, bringing down with it most of the economy. The numbers of unemployed increased month by month, and although prices dropped no one had the money to buy anything. Banks began to fail, the most dramatic perhaps being the powerful Bank of the United States, wiping out the savings of thousands of depositors. To cap all, the summer of 1930 brought the worst drought in fifty years, turning the sown fields to deserts and parching cattle to death.

On the windy street corners of cities former businessmen sold apples, but for most people the attempt to salvage something from the wreckage was fruitless. There were nine million jobless by the middle of 1930. Bread lines were set up which distributed rolls and soup which, if they were not very palatable, were filling and free. The soup kitchens were operated in most cases by charitable organizations, for the federal government did almost nothing to relieve the situation. The Republican, Herbert Hoover, then president, speaking for his party, opposed federal aid to the unemployed as a Socialist threat to America's traditional "rugged individualism." All along New York City's Riverside Drive, where a wide grassy park separated the apartment houses from the river, a village grew up. It was made of corrugated iron, tin cans beaten flat, bits of board salvaged from packing cases, bundles of newspapers tied together to form insulation. It was reproduced in a hundred other cities, and the inhabitants of these wretched shacks, surviving by begging, thievery, odd jobs, and the breadline, christened their communities Hoovervilles.

In the débacle the theatre suffered its worst seasons. Those who could still afford the price of tickets not surprisingly wanted romance, nostalgia, amusement that would carry them out of the grim present. Maxwell Anderson's *Elizabeth the Queen* did considerably better than his play about Sacco and Vanzetti had done; *Green Grow the Lilacs* and *The Barretts of Wimpole Street* vied with *Grand Hotel* and *Once in a Lifetime,* while the Pulitzer winner was Susan Glaspell's genteely melancholy *Alison's House,* inspired by the life of Emily Dickinson. But box office receipts were pitifully small, plays closed almost before the second-night reviewers had a chance to get to their seats, and hungry actors were willing to rehearse for weeks without pay in the hope of collecting a salary for at least a couple of nights of performance.

In such unpromising times—indeed, because of them—some new theatrical enterprises were born. One was the Group

Theatre, which will appear in the next chapters. The other was an aggregation of companies falling under the heading of workers' theatres.

The various amateur groups which made up the workers' theatre movement arose largely as a political response to the economic troubles of the day. Some of their organizers were Communists, some Socialists, a great many had no official affiliation with any party although they were generally sympathetic to the Left, but all were united in seeing the theatre, like other arts, as an implement for spreading the message that present-day society was decadent and that only in some profound change could an answer be found. To imagine, however, that their appearance was a stealthy plot on the part of the Communist Party to seize control of the American theatre is the most superficial of conclusions. The idea of Broadway being invaded and conquered by bands of thespian Reds is as deliciously improbable as imagining Mae West ravished by a Cub Scout. The truth is more complex, and rests in much larger part on the need young artists often feel to put their art to some social purpose. There were things wrong in the country that had to be put right. Marxism seemed to provide a satisfactory answer to most of the evils, and in one form or another attracted followers in all the arts. The Soviet Union, its revolution only a little more than ten years old, had all the allurement of a pioneer. It affected American intellectuals as the westward expansion of America had caught the imaginations of Europeans a hundred years before. The Russian theatre vibrated with experimentation. It didn't require orders from Moscow to compel American playwrights to write against poverty, injustice, or war; they did so because they felt a deep resentment against these things. Nor did it take subtle maneuvering to get actors to perform in such plays, since for them it was as much an act of dedication to what they believed in as a chance to perform before responsive audiences. In fact, as we shall see, there was continuous conflict between the more or less official speakers for the Communist Party, who wanted certain political positions emphasized, and the theatre people who insisted on exploring the allurements of their own medium.

There had been an early try at a workers' theatre headed by Michael Gold in the same year the New Playwrights was organized. Called the Workers Drama League, it included among its executives John Howard Lawson, Ida Rauh, who had been secretary of the Provincetown, and Jasper Deeter of the Hedgerow Playhouse. Deeter and Lawson never attended a board meeting. The first production was a ten-minute sketch called *Strike*, written by Gold himself.* He had gone to Europe a few years before and had seen the work of Russian and German mobile companies, which did short propaganda playlets making revolutionary points. *Strike* was modeled on these. It was little more than a simple, antiphonal chant in which employers spoke of exploiting their workers and workers spoke of their dismal plight, and ended with an Organizer calling on the workers to strike for better pay. A more ambitious production, a bit later, was a full-length play, *The Biggest Boob in the World*, translated from the German of Karl Wittfogel by Upton Sinclair, and edited and staged by Gold. The day before it opened there was a quarrel, after which the director walked out. The few flats which were used as scenery turned out to be too dark to see and had to be hastily repainted at the last minute, so there was no time for a dress rehearsal. When the curtain was raised at last before an impatient audience of nearly a thousand people, the players found to their consternation that the acoustics were so bad in the hall they had hired that no one beyond the first two rows could hear anything. However, it was presented a couple of times again with better success, although it was called by one appraiser, "a crude play [with] cruder acting." A few other plays were done, mostly in the style of *Strike*, a form which was to become much more widespread and sophisticated later on. Shortly afterward, the venture disintegrated amid the mutual recriminations of the leadership.

At about the same time, but with considerably more success, some groups were developing which performed only in foreign languages. There were a number of them—Hungarians, Swedes, Ukrainians—but two in particular, one German, the other Jewish, took the lead.

Many of the immigrants to the United States had been far from

*Early in 1931, George Jean Nathan coined the noun "a michaelgold" to describe what he thought of as propaganda playwrights. It never gained any currency.

illiterate. On the contrary, although their English was poor, thus making them objects of derision, their attachment to the literature of their homelands was perhaps greater than that of earlier settlers from England. Swedish amateur groups in Minnesota were performing Ibsen at a time when Broadway was condemning him, Peking opera flourished in New York and San Francisco, and the Jews brought with them an enormous reverence for learning along with an attachment to Heine and Schiller. Especially among those who had fled from Germany, Poland, and Russia, there were many who held radical views on the reform of society and who saw America as a land of free speech in which these views could be aired.

In New York, lower Second Avenue was the equivalent of Broadway, with its own stars, its own theatres, its own press. The Yiddish Art Theatre dominated the scene with performances of the classics. However, there were many left-wing fraternal organizations, women's councils, workingmen's clubs and unions which, although they supported the Art Theatre, wanted to see plays of a more revolutionary nature performed. In the mid-1920s they formed the Workers Theatrical Alliance which was a loose confederation of some two hundred delegates from all these organizations. In Yiddish its name was *Arbeiter Teater Verband,* or Artef for short. For the first three years of its life it was enmeshed in contention without producing any plays, since no better artistic alternative to the Yiddish Art Theatre could be found. However, in 1928, an amateur group, the Freiheit Dramatic Studio, which had been conducting evening classes under a professional director, decided to present its first full-length play. It was sponsored by the Artef. It was a financial flop but the group, undiscouraged, went on to do two others, to appear at cultural evenings, and to continue its training. It acquired a first-rate director, Benno Schneider, who had been one of the founders of the Habima, the Hebrew Art Theatre in Moscow, and who now lived in New York. Under his leadership a more consistent form was developed, rather extravagant in style, relying on exaggerated movement and stylized sets and makeup, but unvaryingly interesting. By 1930, the group, now called the Artef Theatre, rented a small house uptown and began a regular schedule of professional performances. It could manage this because it was partially supported by some three thousand subscribers from the organizations making up the parent body.

The German group, the Prolet-Bühne, or Proletarian Stage, was considerably further to the left. It had been the dramatic section of the German *Arbeiterbund,* or Workers Club, but in about 1928 split off to become an independent company under the joint guidance of a husband and wife team, a tall, energetic man named John Bonn and a tiny, quiet woman named Anne Howe. Bonn, dogmatic and dynamic, directed the group, while Howe, who rarely raised her voice, dealt efficiently with its bookings, finances, and general management. In 1930, the group, which had been doing plays, changed its tack. It began to present purely political exhortations, using a form known as agit-prop.

Bonn had been influenced in Germany as a youth by Piscator, but even more by the mobile theatre groups developed as a sloganeering weapon by the political parties of the left. Agit-prop, from "agitation" and "propaganda," was as basic a form of theatre as can be imagined—not necessarily crude, for it could be done with great skill as Bonn was to show, but elementary. It could if necessary dispense with scenery and costumes and even a stage. Above all, it dispensed with the complexities of human character, being peopled by easily recognizable symbols. In this way it resembled the expressionist theatre out of which it had grown, and which tended to concern itself with types rather than individuals. The purpose of agit-prop was to make certain direct points and to make them as forcefully as possible. It was the forerunner, you might say, of the television commercial, in which a symbolic housewife, Mrs. Everywoman, agitated by the grubbiness of her wash, is shown the way to a better life by another emblematic figure, Mrs. Nextdoor Neighbor. And like television commercials, agit-prop, particularly in its earlier phases, could be persuasive but also boring.

Bonn, however, kept it from that pitfall. Oversimplified his sketches may have been, but they kept audiences awake. They had the virtue of brevity, for one thing, and for another they were performed with great speed and precision and climaxed by shouted slogans. The Prolet-Bühne players wore a basic costume, usually black trousers or skirts and white shirts. They would dart onstage

like Rockettes, moving in unison, chanting together or antiphon-
ally, sometimes reinforced by a drum beat. They performed only
in German but sometimes overcame that limitation. For instance,
in one skit called *Divide and Rule*, which dealt with discrimination against the foreign-born and which they presented at a protest meeting, they mimed their action and held up posters on
which appropriate dialogue was printed in several languages.

Discussing the Prolet-Bühne's work, Bonn said, "Workers'
theatre today is the theatre of the class struggle. Its only purpose
is reflecting (dramatizing) the class struggle, and promoting
(propagandizing) the class struggle. Its only audiences are the
masses of the workers. Workers' theatre is for the exploited, bourgeois theatre is for the exploiters."[13] On this basis, he felt that
nothing could be gained from the bourgeois theatre, that it was
necessary to explain the political issues of the day in Marxist terms
so as to educate a working-class audience and encourage them into
political action, and that to do this effectively only the agit-prop
form should be used. It was more a matter of political expediency
than of theatrical art, although Bonn didn't appear to see this, or
if he did, wasn't concerned by it.

In pursuit of this goal, the Prolet-Bühne wrote its own material,
taking off from such issues as unemployment, poverty, or a strike.
One of their best-known pieces was called *Tempo, Tempo* in
which, through mime, dance movement, and chanted lines, the
speed-up in capitalist industry was contrasted with the Soviet Union's alleged paradise. Even those who could understand no German were stirred by the balletic movement and the continuous,
accelerating drum beat that accompanied it. In addition to such
agit-prop playlets, the Prolet-Bühne's performances might include songs, poems, and rather clumping satirical bits (Bonn was
a man almost incapable of humor). They played wherever Ger-
man-speaking workers got together, in the halls of fraternal clubs,
union branches, at picnics or banquets, and in 1930 appeared on
an average of once every ten days. This was fairly active for an
amateur group whose members had somehow to earn a living as
well.

At just about the same time, and without any contact with the
Prolet-Bühne, a group of young people had been meeting sporadically and talking about starting a little theatre group along much

the same lines, but of course in English. Some of them had worked with the short-lived Workers Drama League. Among them were Harry Elion, a burly C.C.N.Y. graduate in economics, Al Prentiss, an engineer, a would-be playwright named Bernard Reinis, and two brothers, Jack and Hyam Shapiro, who ran a tiny workshop on Second Avenue where they made bronze molds for pot-metal castings.

Talking was what they all did best, having had no experience in the theatre to speak of. The Shapiros had had a little more than the others, for a few years earlier they had been connected with the Chrystie Street Settlement House which had a drama program. They had done some acting and had constructed sets, and Hyam had led a mutiny against the then director which had ended with another member, a thoughtful youth named Lee Strasberg, becoming the director. Strasberg had studied at the American Laboratory Theatre under Richard Boleslavski and Maria Ouspenskaya, accumulating some knowledge of what was later to be called the Stanislavsky method of acting. Some of this had rubbed off on the Shapiros.

In general, however, everything that was done was hit or miss. It was a matter of experimenting with half-understood notions, of trying to formulate a new kind of theatre for which there weren't even any plays. Jack Shapiro, who wanted to write, described one of his early works to a friend this way:

> I started because we needed a play and there were none around. I found a little story in the Freiheit [a Communist Yiddish-language newspaper J.W.] and dramatized it—it was about a poor guy who's starting in business, has no money, is more exploited than a workingman but has dreams of becoming rich. I called it *Steady Work With Pay*. For a set, I had a door I had picked up from a construction site and I used it for the door of the toilet in the factory—the World Knitting Mills—and put a sign on it that read Ladies *and* Gentlemen. That got the audience! The big problem was when we performed the show we had to carry that damn door around with us.

There was, to tell the truth, very little performing. But people began to hear of the meetings of the Pro-Lab, as it was called, and to come to them. One was a boy of seventeen or eighteen named Will Lee. His father had been a book-binder for twenty years and had built a small house in New Jersey, but had lost his job during the Depression, and was forced to rely on chicken farming for a living. Lee had remained in the city, working at one job or another and spending his evenings in the all-night cafeterias in Greenwich Village or around Union Square, where a five-cent cup of coffee bought you endless intellectual discussions with budding poets, novelists, artists, or actors. "I was in the Cooperative Restaurant one night," Lee recalls,

and one of the regulars there asked me if I wanted to join a theatre group. I said, "I have no money." He told me I didn't need any, that they were meeting in the evenings and doing little scenes. So I said yeah, I'd be interested. I went with him up to a room which belonged to a young lady, a large room, where there were a couple of chairs and at one end a neatly made up old-fashioned brass bed—the kind that are worth a hundred dollars nowadays—and a little kitchen behind. We sat on the floor and I was very quiet and reticent. This was a whole new world for me. Jack and Hyam Shapiro were running things. We were doing improvisations, although I don't think we called them that, then. Hymie said to me, "It's raining, you're hungry, you're cold, you're walking on Third Avenue and you pass a bakery. Well . . . go do it." I was broke. The weather was part of my struggle to live through. I was always hungry. I did it. They were all shocked, they said, "Is this the first time you ever did anything like this?" I said, "Yes." I sat down and they started working with somebody else. As my ass hit the floor I said to myself, "This is the work I want to do."

Meanwhile, another amateur company, under the direction of Alfred Saxe, had been formed to do *Gods of the Lightning*. Saxe, a rabbi's son, came from LaSalle, Illinois, and had attended the University of Wisconsin's Experimental School where he had acted in and directed a number of plays. He had come to New York burning to enter the theatre but the Depression was making itself felt and there were too many actors auditioning for even the tiniest walk-on. Like many other fervid spirits he had found his way to the John Reed Club of New York, an organization sponsored by the New Masses to encourage the development of revolutionary writers and artists. Its orientation was openly Communist —Reed himself had helped to found the American Communist Party—and Mike Gold had been instrumental in its development. Saxe asked the club if they would back a production of the Anderson play, and when they seemed interested had found actors and had begun rehearsals.

Some of the actors had gone to meetings of the Shapiros' group. In the end, the production of *Gods of the Lightning* fell through, but the two groups got together and decided to try to develop a new company. An organization called the Workers' International Relief was raising money to help the unemployed obtain relief, food, and clothing, and some of the members of the new troupe put together a sketch called *Unemployed* to be performed at its meetings. Its construction was straight agit-prop, and reminiscent of Gold's early skit, *Strike:*

It began with half a dozen actors walking gloomily about the stage and declaiming:

1st Worker:	I am hungry.
2nd Worker:	My family is hungry.
3rd Worker:	I want to work.
4th Worker:	I want a job.
5th Worker:	Won't somebody give me a job?
1st Worker:	I am hungry, why can't I have food?

After a bit more, by contrast, a Boss—a character as stylized as the Devil in a medieval Morality play—appears onstage carrying a chair and a telephone. He sits down and says, chuckling, into the phone, "There isn't anyone that can have a better yacht than I. I've got to have the best little yacht in the world. I want special attention paid to the bar." Seeing the workers, he snaps, "What's that damn noise out there?" A Servant enters and says, "Master, it's the unemployed complaining." The Boss replies, "What have they got to complain about?"

After going on in such elementary terms to explain the condition of the unemployed, the playlet ends with the Workers' eyes being opened by an Organizer, after which they chant their slogans:

1st Worker:	We must organize!
2nd Worker:	We must organize and fight.
3rd Worker:	We must organize and fight for work or wages.
5th Worker:	Unemployment insurance.
All:	Work or wages—unemployment insurance!

Unemployed was followed by what was thought of as a more realistic play, *It's Funny as Hell*, in which a Welfare Worker, a Politician, and a Manufacturer speak from the stage about their concern over unemployment, but when a Worker, shouting from the audience, tries to present a petition to them they expose themselves in their true colors.

Both these sketches, done without scenery and with the barest minimum of props, relying not so much on acting ability as on simple movement, and performable in a minimum of space, were done chiefly at WIR meetings to begin with, and after a bit the WIR adopted the troupe. They could give it no money but allowed it to use a loft on West 28th Street as rehearsal space. In this dingy headquarters, the company, which now called itself the Workers Laboratory Theatre, set about its training.

They were pridefully conscious of their newness, for there had been no attempt up to then to use the theatre in the political and economic arena. They felt that they were breaking new ground in every way—the forms of their material were untried, the language they used was unfamiliar, and the audience they wanted to play to had never been approached by performers in this way before. They felt themselves filled with a passionate humanitarian impulse: "In a world that was crumbling, we were making something new and exciting," says a former member. "Our getting together to do that kind of theatre was like the beginning of a marriage—it was full of awkwardness and mistakes, but there was a hell of a lot of pleasure in it, too."

They began, as Bonn had done, by rejecting the "bourgeois theatre" altogether. The theoreticians among them, Prentiss, Reinis, Hyam Shapiro, analyzed their position: "The form of a theatre . . . is determined by social and economic conditions. It is a reflection of contemporary society."[14] It therefore followed that "plays written for a bourgeois theatre are written with the aim of amusing, entertaining people for money . . . [But] the workers' play must teach a moral, a lesson for the working class."[15] They told each other boldly that they must and could learn to do anything—write plays, act them, and produce them. "Playwriting," they assured themselves, "may be learned just like any other trade."[16] They believed in the collective effort, feeling that as a group they could gather ideas and strength from each other, and in words that sound a curious echo of Theresa Helburn's, Harry Elion said, "We would rather lose a genius than stifle the development of the group."[17] They formed committees, one to study acting, another to oversee directing, a third to produce plays. Anyone could belong to the playwriting committees, which found basic subjects in news items or current events and then chose certain phases of a subject by vote for inclusion in a sketch. The actual writing of dialogue was assigned to one person. The finished script was submitted back to the committee and finally to the membership. Naive as it seems, the procedure had certain values. As Jack Shapiro later put it, "You're not going to stop playwriting by saying that anybody can write a play. But you may slow down getting plays if you say only one God-ordained genius can write one."

Shapiro also made an important point about audience involvement. He had seen *Beggar on Horseback, Danton's Death,* and Max Reinhardt's production of *The Miracle,* and pointed out that the bond of sympathy between audience, actor, and play was strengthened by the breaking down of the conventional proscenium. One way was to put actors into the audience. "Rather than having stepped through the proscenium, these actors carry the proscenium with them into the audience," he said. "Since we're doing plays dramatizing the economic struggle and the revolutionary aspirations that unite both actors and audience, it is fairly easy for us to break through the proscenium and excite or vitalize or touch audiences."[18]

This was particularly true of agit-prop pieces which might be performed while marching in a May Day parade or on a picket line. On one occasion, when a brand new tactic—the sit-down strike—was being tried by workers in a shop on University Place, the performers, with their props tied up in bundles, were hoisted through a ground floor window, played their show, and were dropped out into the street again. Agit-prop lent itself well to street corner shows. The group would pick a spot on the sidewalk and summon people together by shouting through megaphones. "Kids gathered around us first," one of the members says. "They formed a three sided square. We'd have our back to the buildings; sometimes we even played on stoops. People would hang out of windows, as if those were the balconies." The direct link between actors and audience was emphasized in such performances, and carried on even when they moved to conventional stages. It is perfectly obvious that agit-prop plays could convert nobody who wasn't already at least partly convinced. Their value was to provide that emotional confirmation common to people who watch high school pageants on the Fourth of July. Nevertheless, they *were* theatre. And for working people involved in trade union battles or in the dire difficulties of the Depression, and especially for those who felt a bitter discontent with the political situation, it was theatre that spoke for them and they welcomed it.

The members of the troupe got by as best they could since what tiny donations they received from their audiences barely paid for their few props and bits of costume. Some had jobs, others did part-time work. Those who worked helped out with an occasional dollar or two. Saxe and Lee, who had become very good friends, found a tiny apartment which was used as a dormitory by other members of the company when they had nowhere to sleep. They shared the rent and the limited space with a muscular ex-seaman, Salty Marino, a man with an explosive temper but a generous nature. He used to talk in his sleep, carrying on long conversations with dream people whose answers could be guessed from what he said, and sometimes his co-tenants and their visitors would draw up chairs and listen to him in fascination. Meals were irregular and skimpy. Often, there were fresh rolls and milk for breakfast, and it took Saxe and Lee a long time to discover that Marino was stealing them from doorsteps along the street. Once, they all made what they still remember as "bathtub salad." They chipped in what they could and bought vegetables from pushcarts on Third Avenue; they chopped it all up and, having no bowl large enough, mixed it together with sour cream in the bathtub. "We gorged on that," Lee says, "until we literally ate ourselves to sleep."

Early in 1931, the Prolet-Bühne and the WLT finally got together. The Prolet-Bühne, in the eyes of the WLT, had excellent technicians and an enviable quality of precision. An English translation of *Tempo, Tempo* was added to the WLT's repertory which now included half a dozen other pieces, among them one called *The Big Stiff,* in which several doctors, including President Hoover and William Green of the American Federation of Labor (which, because of its complacency and its failure to organize industrial laborers, was considered to be on the side of the enemy), attempted unsuccessfully to revive a dying Uncle Sam. It was taken from a well-known burlesque skit known as the "Doctor Bit," and in one form or another was to be used by different left-wing groups for the next five years.

Other workers' theatre companies were appearing not only in the New York area but in other cities, most of them in emulation of the work of the WLT or the Prolet-Bühne. The WLT decided that it was time to make contact with these groups, not only to assist them but to encourage the formation of others. The best method that suggested itself was a magazine.

In March, money was scraped together, mostly from those who held regular jobs. People were chosen to write articles, others to type them and then cut mimeograph stencils. These were run off on a borrowed machine. Jack Shapiro cheerfully turned his hand to making a cover, cutting a design in linoleum block. A bottle of ink was bought, a typewriter roller was borrowed for spreading the ink and a tailor's iron for printing the inked block. The loft, for a few days, was a maelstrom of mimeographed pages and freshly inked covers spread out to dry. The whole membership—now about a score of people—met to assemble the pages and staple them, and early in April two hundred copies were ready for distribution at a price of ten cents a copy. The total cost of publication had been about eleven dollars.

Within a few weeks, replies began coming in in answer to the first mailing, which had covered all sorts of progressive organizations as well as unions which had drama clubs. Inspired by the response, the WLT and the Prolet-Bühne took a further step. Under the sponsorship of the John Reed Club, which had many contacts in the cultural field, they called a conference of all interested groups. This was eventually broadened to include film-makers, artists, poets, and writers. It was held in June, and of the 130 organizations which sent delegates, nineteen represented theatre companies which had already been formed. These quickly showed themselves to be the bounciest part of the conference. They exchanged ideas, made speeches, read each other's scripts, and watched them in performance. Above all, they shared a sense of exaltation and achievement.

An observer who attended the conference was Hallie Flanagan, director of the Experimental Theatre at Vassar College. In an article in *Theatre Arts,* the professional magazine which in addition to covering Broadway and the international scene had always given great attention to the experimental and Little Theatres, she appraised the movement which had been launched:

> The power of these theatres springing up throughout the country lies in the fact that they know what they want. Their purpose . . . is clear. This is important because there are only two theatres in the country today that are clear as to their aim: one is the commercial theatre which wants to make money; the other is the workers' theatre which wants to make a new social order. . . .
>
> Unlike any art form existing in America today, the workers' theatres intend to shape the life of this country, socially, politically, and industrially. They intend to remake a social structure without the help of money—and this ambition alone invests their undertaking with a certain Marlowesque madness.
>
> When we shall see, as we probably shall during the next year, their street plays and pageants, their performances on trucks and on street corners, we shall doubtless find them crude, violent, childish, and repetitious. Yet we must admit that here is a theatre which can afford to be supremely unconcerned with what we think of it. . . .[19]

At the conference's end, a Dramatic Bureau was set up to act as a kind of central clearing house for scripts and information, and to provide a national body for keeping in touch with all the member groups. The magazine, christened *Workers Theatre,* grew in pace with the mushrooming groups; within a year there were more than fifty of them, and the magazine was selling at the rate of a thousand copies a month. "We could do more," complained one of the editors, "except that the magazine committee is busy with other things and now has to stay up until late at night mimeographing and putting the magazine together."[20] *Workers Theatre* spread its influence further than the workers' theatre movement, for there were Little Theatres which had become interested in social-conscious plays as their members, too, were affected by the Depression. Vassar's Experimental Theatre, in May 1931, had presented *Can You Hear Their Voices?* written by Hallie Flanagan and Margaret Clifford, a play dealing with the abject condition of dirt farmers and based on a story by Whittaker Chambers which had appeared in the *New Masses*. In the fall of that year a company called The New York Suitcase Theatre had been formed in Harlem to do plays about black people; it was headed by Paul Peters and the black poet, Langston Hughes, among others. Even the summer theatre reflected the mood. *Strike!*—not the play by Mike Gold but one written by a Provincetown founder, Mary Heaten Vorse, parts of which had been printed in the *New Masses*—was done at the Barn Theatre in Provincetown, Massachusetts, where it ran for more than four weeks.

The workers' theatre groups spanned the country, from the Solidarity Players of Boston, to the Chicago Blue Blouses, to the Rebel Players of Los Angeles, some twenty-five or thirty of them in all. Among them were foreign-language troupes; there were no fewer than three Hungarian companies in New York, for instance, doing such plays as Upton Sinclair's *Singing Jailbirds* in their own language. Their greatest lack was scripts since even *Singing Jailbirds* or *Can You Hear Their Voices?* were often beyond their means or their capabilities. Every month, therefore, *Workers Theatre* printed the complete script of a new playlet, simple enough to be done by the most amateurish of the groups. Some of them were incredibly silly:

> *(There is a loud crash offstage. The Workers stop their work and listen. The voice of Dr. Krupps is heard.)*
> Dr. Krupps: Is this the Soviet Union? Who
>   runs this place?
> Annusya: Look, it must be the specialist.

<pre>
Radianova: What a funny looking hat. Just
             like a capitalist.
                    (From *Dr. Krupps, Specialist*)
</pre>

Others, however, had more merit, and one in particular managed a considerable degree of power. It was an English translation of the Prolet-Bühne's *Scottsboro*, as it was performed by the WLT.

The Scottsboro case, which was to become a *cause célèbre* equalling that of Sacco and Vanzetti, concerned nine black youths whose ages ranged from thirteen to twenty, who were accused of raping two white girls. In the face of flimsy and contradictory evidence—it became clear, for example, that the two victims were professional whores—eight of the boys were sentenced to death by a white jury in Scottsboro, Alabama. The case was rapidly becoming a national issue, drawing attention to the plight of blacks in the South and to the viciousness of lynch law. The Prolet-Bühne's piece had been written, rehearsed, and performed all within one week as part of the campaign to give the nine a new trial. The WLT had tried to write its own play on the subject, using the collective method, but when the various bits which had been assigned to members to write were assembled, the result was so obviously bad that they decided to use a rather free translation of the German group's production. Here are some excerpts:

> *(The troupe is lined up onstage facing the audience. As they speak, they slowly move forward.)*
>
> All: Attention. Attention workers. Friends,
>   fellow workers, comrades! Attention.
> 1:   Hear the story of the nine Negro boys
>   in Scottsboro, Alabama.
> All: *(chanting):*
>   In Scottsboro, in Scottsboro,
>   murder stalks the streets.
>   In Scottsboro, in Scottsboro,
>   death haunts the cells.
> 1:   Joy in Scottsboro. Thousands of people—
> 2:   shouting and singing, laughing and screaming—
> 1:   in the streets of Scottsboro.

2: And the sun gleams
3: on the gay Sunday clothes
4: of the wives and children . . .
5: The children with flags—
6: and the men with guns . . .
3: and everyone is shouting—
All *(shouting):* Lynch! Lynch! Lynch!
(Number 3 steps forward, holds up a piece of paper as if he were a clerk of the court, and reads)
3: Eugene Williams, 13 years old. Sentence—
All: Death!
3: Ozie Powell, 14 years old. Sentence—
All: Death! . . .

The playlet ended with the whole troupe advancing to the apron of the stage and, with heightening speed and volume, shouting:

All: Will you let them murder the nine Negro
        boys in Scottsboro?
      No! No! No!
      Organize, demonstrate, protest.
      Raise your voices, raise your fists and scream
      Stop! Stop! Stop!

The difference between the way the piece was performed by the Prolet-Bühne and the WLT was striking, and demonstrated the essential difference between the two companies. The Prolet-Bühne rapped out the lines sharply and at high speed, impersonally, but with rhythmic force. The WLT people were slower, trying to give a certain character to the individual speeches, trying for emotion in their chanting, operating, in short, like actors rather than orators. It was a style Bonn and his followers objected to but it was, in the end, to win out and change the nature of agit-prop performances. In both cases, however, the rhythmically chanted lines, the hypnotic repetition, the grim reading of the names and sentences of the boys, and the burst of shouted slogans made for accumulating theatrical excitement.

In addition to making scripts available, the magazine reported on the work of all the groups, sometimes with blunt criticism—

Help the Miners, presented by the Ukrainian Dramatic Circle, was much too long and seemed like a rather boring debate in spite of the sincere and convincing acting of the central figures. . . .[21]

and sometimes with a certain confusion of purpose as when the Jewish Workers Theatre Group did a solemnly realistic play for which they built an interior set, and the reviewer commented, "Such a hangover from the bourgeois theatre still has a part to play in our theatre." The play was performed in Yiddish and the mood was badly shattered by laughter from the audience whenever one of the characters—a Catholic priest—opened his mouth.

But the most interesting function, perhaps, of *Workers Theatre* was to reflect the controversy that went on among the members, especially those in the WLT and the *Prolet-Bühne* who had started things off. Ben Blake summarized it in a pamphlet written in 1935, *The Awakening of the American Theatre:*

> The "Relationship between Form and Content" was argued back and forth in print with great heat, paralleling the fierce midnight verbal discussions that took place, after rehearsals, over cups of black coffee in smoke-filled cafeterias. Some writers championed expressionism, others pressed for realism, while still others favored vaudeville as "the" only native popular form. One writer advocated the adoption of a single uniform technique by all the workers' theatre groups in the country, for the maximum effectiveness in putting over the particular message of each important play. Another declared, "The workers' theatre cannot adopt a fixed form. It is continuously changing, together with the revolutionary movement . . . we have to experiment with each form we know of. . . . To find the form, we must first study the content." This was the view that soon prevailed.[22]

Another bitter debate arose over how much the workers' theatres could borrow from the "bourgeois" theatre. The early position had been modified as most of the members of the WLT had come to recognize their shortcomings and to feel the need to widen their apprenticeship. Furthermore, they had found that styles of performance which seemed to suit Europeans had very little impact on Americans. In a sense, they had come to the same conclusions as those expressionist playwrights who tried for an essentially American blend of humor, jazz, vaudeville, burlesque to modify the "learning pieces" of the German and Russian initiators. They argued, therefore, that if they wanted to be most effective they would have to learn as much as they could from the long history of the theatre regardless of whose side it had been on. They felt, too, that they could attract talent from the Little Theatre movement, and even from Broadway, to help them perfect their techniques.

The opposition, led by Bonn, argued that "workers" theatre is for the exploited, bourgeois theatre is for the exploiters . . . the only relationship between them is antagonism."[23] But a year of performances interspersed by verbal battle softened his intransigence. It became clear that for English-speaking working people the WLT's method was better. To his credit, he wrote, "I in particular had taken a wrong, leftist [i.e. extreme radical] standpoint . . . I now agree fully with my critics who urged a more active attitude towards the bourgeois theatre."[24] He did not altogether give up, urging that a "readymade style" should not be used exclusively, but it was a victory for those who wanted to spread their wings and investigate some enticing new theatrical regions.

One such—practically a whole new continent—had been opened not long before by the arrival of the Group Theatre on the scene.

1930-1933

It is a commentary on the times that when Walter Pritchard Eaton wrote the official history of the Theatre Guild, in 1929, he felt impelled to refer to the Board of Directors as "soviets." This did not mean that they had fallen into the clutches of Moscow. But many new and stimulating ideas were coming out of Russia, and among them one which captured the interest of artists was that of group, or collective, creativity. It was especially interesting to theatre people because by its very nature a play is the sum of many efforts, from the playwright to the stagehand who raises the curtain. Those who were serious tried to establish greater permanance and cohesiveness in their producing units to improve the quality of their plays. The New Playwrights, the Provincetown, the Guild, Eva Le Gallienne's Civic Repertory Theatre which concentrated on the classics, the Neighborhood Playhouse, and the workers' theatre companies had all understood this concept and had struggled towards it with greater or lesser success. It included the establishment of a permanent company, a program of training, a directorial board with a common point of view, and if possible a permanent house. A sense of purpose, too, helped unify these companies, whether it was simply to do good plays or to experiment with form or to bring on the revolution.

In November, 1930, a handful of people began meeting to discuss these ideas and to talk about establishing a new theatre. But in the minds of the leaders such a theatre had to be founded not only upon superficial agreement in taste or knowledge, but upon a much deeper, almost mystical unity "of background, of feeling, of thought, of need," as one of the three leaders, Harold Clurman, was to put it.[25] Above all, it had to have a uniform technique which went beyond mere surface excellence in solo performances.

> A technique of the theatre had to be founded on life values. The whole bent of our theatre . . . would be to combine a study of theatre craft with a creative content which that craft was to express . . . our interest in the life of our times must lead us to the discovery of those methods that would most truly convey this life through the theatre.[26]

Although Clurman was a long way from the workers' theatre movement, he thus echoed the position which they—and indeed most serious theatre people—were to take with increasing vigor.

Clurman and his colleagues, Cheryl Crawford and Lee Strasberg, had been active in the Theatre Guild. Clurman and Strasberg had played small parts and had acted as stage managers, and Clurman had also served as play reader. Crawford had stage-managed and had been casting director. The idea of a group of their own had been fermenting for some time.

The two men had had long talks as early as 1925, during the run of the first *Garrick Gaieties* which Clurman stage-managed and in which Strasberg acted. They had agreed on some basic points, most notable of which was that a play must be seen as an artistic unit in which all the elements ought to be of equal importance, from the script, which was only the primary expression of an idea, through the direction, the settings, the costumes, the acting, the make-up, the lighting, all of which ought to operate in orchestration to continue that initial idea and further express all its facets. Strasberg, with his training under Boleslavsky and Ouspenskaya, spent a good deal of time then and later directing the Chrystie Street Settlement players, perfecting his understanding of the Stanislavsky method and shaping his own interpretation of it. Clurman and Crawford had been associated with Herbert Biberman in a short-lived studio project which the Guild sponsored, the presentation of a Soviet play, *Red Rust* (a mistranslation—the title was actually *Rust*), which had been much admired for its exuberance and novelty.

They were all three in agreement that the Theatre Guild fell far short of their ideal theatre. The board's taste was good and its standards high, but it appeared to have a respect for culture rather than a passion for creation. "They set the plays out in a show window for as many customers as possible to buy," wrote Clurman. "They didn't want to say anything through plays, and plays said nothing to them, except that they were amusing in a graceful way, or, if they were tragic plays, that they were 'art.' "[27] The three knew that they could go far beyond this approach. They did no more than talk about it for a while, but at last, under Cheryl Crawford's urging, they decided to sound out some actors and others who might be interested.

They began to hold a series of meetings, at first in Clurman's hotel room, then in Crawford's apartment, and at last, when attendance swelled, in a rehearsal room at Steinway Hall. To begin with, they called in actors with whom they had worked or whose performances they had admired, all people who were felt to be particularly sympathetic. They included some Theatre Guild players, Morris Carnovsky, Franchot Tone, Tony Kraber, Sanford Meisner, Phoebe Brand, Clifford Odets, and Dorothy Patten. J. Edward Bromberg and Robert Lewis were appearing with the Civic Repertory Theatre; Margaret Barker in a Broadway hit. Ruth Nelson and Eunice Stoddard had been in *Red Rust*. Stella Adler, by then married to Clurman, was the distinguished daughter of one of the great men of the Yiddish Stage, Jacob Adler. Art Smith had had five years with the Goodman Theatre in Chicago before coming to Broadway. William Challee, Walter Coy, Herbert Ratner, and Mary Morris were all experienced players. And all without exception were youthful, eager for change, and ready to listen.

Clurman had not been much of an actor. Carnovsky, who had first met him in the Guild's *Maximilian and Juarez,* said, "He played an Indian, and for a man who eventually sponsored realism in acting he was the most unreal figure I've ever seen. He squatted in front of a fire and made huge sounds, 'Ugh! Ugh!' " Freed from performing, however, he had a considerably larger vocabulary. He was an eloquent and persuasive speaker, and he did most of the talking at the meetings. Of the three, he had a mind most capable of synthesis, of seeing and grasping the many tendrils that would have to be woven together to produce the new enterprise. Strasberg, more intense, perhaps more obviously brilliant, knew most about the art of the theatre. Crawford was the most practical; more open-eyed than her friends, she was sturdily competent to deal with the down-to-earth business matters that would inevitably face them.

The meetings continued weekly until the late spring of 1931. By that time, there was a reasonable unanimity of feeling, a mutual concurrence of aims, and those who had attended the discussions all winter long had begun to hope that something more permanent might develop. They had already taken to calling themselves *The* Group.

The moment came for decision. The three directors determined to find a refuge for the summer in which, with that nucleus of actors, twenty-eight of them, they could not only rehearse a play for production but complete the transformation of the Group into the Group Theatre. Crawford drew up a report on the company's plans with a proposal that the Theatre Guild subsidize them as a kind of studio. Furthermore she asked the Guild to release the option to a play by Paul Green, *The House of Connelly*, as the new company's first endeavor. It was a drama of the conflict between a decaying aristocratic family and its energetic "poor white" tenants, and like all Green's work was concerned with the new problems of the South. The Guild board, impressed by the potential of the company, gave them the play and a thousand dollars.

A property in Brookfield Center, Connecticut, was rented which contained a barn big enough for a rehearsal hall and an assortment of bungalows and cottages in which living space, meeting rooms, and a communal dining room were provided. Some additional money came in from approving outsiders, among them Maxwell Anderson, who was a close friend of Carnovsky's. At the beginning of June, 1931, the caravan of actors, directors, wives, children, and even a few friends set out for the wooded hills of Connecticut.

That summer was to prove as exhilarating as it was exhausting. They had not only to rehearse the play, but to get to know each other and to learn to work together in a way to which actors were unaccustomed, not trying to outdo each other but subduing their professional egos to the requirements of the play. They had to learn a new approach to acting, which required study, thought, debate, and incessant self-investigation. It was this, more than anything, which gave them the sense of dedication which allowed them to rise above all difficulties.

In later years, the words "Stanislavsky method" were to contain an awful, incantatory power. Perfectly cheerful dinner parties among theatrical buffs were to end in shouting matches, friends were to be eternally divided, and feuds were to begin which have continued to this day. More miscomprehension and dissension, more nonsense, more confusion were to be engendered by the mere invocation of the phrase than at any time since the First Nicene Council wrangled over the word *homoiousias*. The trouble was that many people wanted the method to be a scientific reduction of acting to an infallible system, whereas in fact it was only a method—that is, a more or less orderly way of using certain tools of the craft. It was indeed scientific, in the sense that Konstantin Stanislavsky had thoroughly analyzed many of the things an actor may use to produce the illusion of reality on the stage. During his many years of work as director of the Moscow Art Theatre, starting long before the Russian Revolution, he had concerned himself with the matter of technique, and even after the publication of his books refused to commit himself to a dogmatic assertion that anyone who read them would find any absolute recipe for success.

For most actors, acting rested on inspiration. You learned your lines, you "threw yourself into the part," you walked onstage and a divine frenzy descended on you. If you were good—that is, if your personality was attractive to the audience—you were a good actor. Otherwise, you faked it. Everyone knew certain tricks that could guarantee audience reaction, tricks of understatement, of pausing, of moving in a certain way, of giving emphasis or color to a line or a word. Yet there was more to it than that, for in the case of really fine actors something else was at work, something most of them couldn't put their own fingers on.

Dion Boucicault, in the middle of the nineteenth century, held that acting was not simply a gift from heaven but had principles, like any art, and could be taught. Richard Mansfield urged actors to try to get at the truth of a character rather than look for mere originality. David Belasco insisted that acting was a science as well as an art, and that an actor's job was to reproduce emotions on the stage by means of his imagination, but not to feel real emotion since that would interfere with his interpretation. Yet no one had formulated just what it was fine actors did, and how they did it to produce their results, least of all those actors themselves. Everyone knew the importance of details that reinforced the reality of a character on the stage. Yet for the most part they remained purely superficial, on the level of the famous story about Edwin Booth. Booth, at sixteen, stepped into the part of Tressel in his father's production of *Richard III.* Just before the curtain, the elder Booth looked his son up and down and said, "Who was Tressel?" "He was a messenger from the field of Tewkesbury," said Edwin. "And what was his mission?" "To bring the news of the king's defeat." "How did he make the journey so as to arrive quickly?" "On horseback." "Aha!" said the old man, "And where are your spurs?"

Using Stanislavsky's method, an actor could be fairly sure not only of remembering his spurs but of arriving drenched with sweat, dusty, and smelling of horseflesh.

To describe it in very rough and general form, the approach made by Stanislavsky was to establish the central theme or the point that a play was making, what came to be called its "super-objective," and to derive from that the intention of each scene. A play might thus be scored, like a piece of music, with a series of scenes—not necessarily those set down by the playwright—in which "beats" or lengths of duration of each intention, were established. The actor's work was systematically divided into a variety of attacks both on his own character and on his relationship with the others in the play. These might include the determination of one's own super-objective, or "spine," analyses of one's objectives in each scene and throughout the play (what the Group called *actions*), the re-creation of emotion (under the name of *affective memory* this was to become a major point of contention), exercises in improvisation, a whole range of technical exercises in speech, movement, rhythm, relaxation and tension, and even the perfecting of one's personal relationships with one's colleagues.

The major drive was to find truth on the stage. Toward this end, one sought for ways of making everything one did flow naturally out of real intentions and real emotions. Otherwise, all that would appear would be a mere surface, a facile semblance of the truth.

In *An Actor Prepares,* Stanislavsky has his Director say to a recalcitrant actor:

> Your make-believe truth helps you to represent images and passions. My kind of truth helps to create the images themselves and to stir real passions. The difference between your art and mine is the same as between the two words *seem* and *be.* I must have real truth. You are satisfied with its *appearance.* I must have true belief. You are willing to be limited to the confidence your public has in you. . . . From your standpoint the spectator is merely an onlooker. For me he involuntarily becomes a witness of, and a party to, my creative work; he is drawn into the very thick of the life that he sees on the stage and he believes in it . . . on the stage *everything must be real in the imaginary life of the actor.*[28]

The emotion demanded by a given situation could, it was thought, be reproduced by using *affective memory.* Out of his own memory of past experiences the actor would recall a situation in which he had felt some emotion—fear, tenderness, hatred—and by evoking in detail the circumstances of that situation he would be able to evoke the emotion as well. Each actor was to have a store of such memories—what the Group came to call the "golden box." Group actors, before they entered a scene, prepared themselves emotionally and physically for a moment or two. The phrase, "Take a minute" became their watchword. Under the director's guidance, actors established what goal they wanted to reach or what precise action they wanted to play in a scene, as well as in the whole script, even if they appeared for no more than a couple of lines, and the virtue of this was expressed by Strasberg once when he said, "Stanislavsky gives a very simple example. If you say, 'Hold your hand up in the air . . .' I hold up my arm, but I don't know what to *do* with it. If you say, 'Reach for that light!' well, then everything falls into place because I have a purpose for holding my hand up."[29] Improvisations were used to help the actors establish their spines, or their relationships with other characters, or the mood of a scene, or in a number of other ways. And along with all the technical devices went constant experimentation into ways of gaining even greater proficiency with one's apparatus as an actor, as they set themselves the tasks of being trees or animals, or worked out whole scenes in pantomime. Clurman wrote, "The effect on the actors was that of a miracle. The system . . . represented for most of them the open-sesame of the actor's art."[30]

The days at Brookfield were packed as tightly as a Christmas stocking. They rehearsed for long periods, morning, afternoon, and night. Strasberg, directing *House of Connelly*, was a stern taskmaster, knowing exactly what he wanted and determined to draw it out of the actors. Carnovsky remembers one occasion:

> We were rehearsing a difficult party scene in the course of which I stood on a chair with my glass raised. We repeated it again and again, and something always went wrong. Here was an overhang of the theatre I'd been in where an actor expressed himself through his "temperament"—on the last go-through of this little scene I got angry, dropped the glass on the table as if to say, Damn it, will *they* ever get it right? It was a stupid lapse, an egotistical one. The work went on, and at the end of the rehearsal Lee, with his face white with anger, tore the skin off me. The curious thing is that I remember one thing only, that as he was bawling me out I was afraid he'd have a stroke, and I kept saying, "All right, Lee, all right, don't take it so hard."

Part of every afternoon was spent attending Clurman's lectures which dealt with aspects of the theatre or formulated the Group's aims and structure. Sometimes they were held outdoors, sometimes in the barn where Franchot Tone would absently whittle away at one of the posts and the others would take bets on whether the barn would last the summer. Along with the work there was time for swimming and softball, for listening to music, for an interminable poker game and, late at night, for the perpetual discussion of their work and their goals.

Back in New York, in the fall, the play was shown to the Guild's directorial board. They agreed, after some hesitation, to put up half the cost of production, some $5,000, and to offer the play at reduced prices to their subscription list. The Group, now officially named the Group Theatre, was to raise the other half. Cheryl Crawford found the money, partly from an executive at Samuel French, partly from Eugene O'Neill, and partly from Franchot

Tone. The play opened on September 23 at the Martin Beck Theatre.

Clurman, Strasberg, and Crawford stood at the back of the crowded house, tense and nervous. They need not have worried. When the curtain came down, "the audience," one reviewer reported, "remained to whistle and shout with approval." The cast, along with Paul Green and some friends, went to someone's apartment to wait for reviews. The morning papers appeared at about two a.m., and the company looked at each other with shining eyes. The doyen of critics, Brooks Atkinson, said, "Between Mr. Green's prose poem and the Group Theatre's performance it is not too much to hope that something fine and true has been started in the American theatre." The other reviews were equally flattering, calling it "masterful" and "mighty close to magic." Green was hailed as a playwright second only to Eugene O'Neill. And the Group's labors were amply justified; "I cannot remember a more completely consecrated piece of ensemble work in our midst since the Moscow Art masters went back home," said Gilbert Gabriel of the *American*.

Nevertheless, the Group were still to face a hard road. To begin with, although they approached the Theatre Guild asking for sponsorship, the board was not sufficiently persuaded to commit themselves quite that far. However, they did agree to put up another $5,000 toward the next production. The Group raised $9,500 from sympathetic backers, still hoping that someone— maybe the ubiquitous Otto Kahn—would come forward with a no-strings endowment. No one did. The Depression was still on and biting deeper, the numbers of unemployed were growing, and the theatre still suffered hard seasons. In such times, it took immeasurable confidence to go on. Confidence, fortunately, was what the Group had in plenty, even if they were short of funds.

The House of Connelly had satisfied two of the requirements the Group was to demand of its scripts. It was by an American playwright, and it dealt with a serious manifestation of a real social problem. Their second production, *1931—* by Paul and Claire Sifton, was to be even more pointedly social-conscious. In shortish scenes that sometimes merged into one another, it told the story of two young people—in the best expressionist mode they were called Adam and The Girl—caught in the Depression, trying to find love and self-respect in the face of crushing economic disaster. The play ended on a fiery note with a crowd pressing forward in the face of clattering machine guns to protest against unemployment.

The company began rehearsing while *The House of Connelly* was still running. Not all the Groupers by any means had been affected by the Depression, but they all had the feeling this play was worth doing. Mordecai Gorelik, who had done sets for the New Playwrights and had designed the eye-catching constructivist set for *Processional,* had visited the Group at Brookfield and was greatly taken by their ideas; he was called in to do the settings for *1931—* and produced a brilliantly simple construction which, with the proper lighting, could be transformed in a twinkling into the Sixth Avenue "L" or the entrance to a Park Avenue mansion. Tone and Phoebe Brand played the two idealistic youngsters whose story it was, but the rest of the company took a variety of parts and made quick changes from white tie and tails to the ragged clothes of the unemployed.

The rehearsals became famous among the Groupers for one incident which illustrates the concentration they gave to their art. One of the cast was a man from Illinois, Friendly Ford, a charming, gangling chap without much real talent but as rawboned an American as Lincoln. It was one of the rare cases of the Group's casting to type. A few days before the opening, Strasberg stopped the rehearsal to make a certain point clear to Ford, and since he didn't quite understand, Strasberg gave him an exercise. The authors were sitting in the back of the house waiting impatiently, and as Strasberg went on with his lesson in acting, Paul Sifton yelled, "We don't give a damn about your technical lessons. Show us a run-through!" Strasberg turned white—according to one of the members it was his favorite color for turning—and is said to have replied, in an icy voice, "When it is necessary to develop an actor, that takes precedence over everything, even your play."

1931— was received by the critics with respect and dislike. Percy Hammond of the *Herald* said that there were Emergency Relief Committees with millions of dollars at their disposal taking care of the unemployed, and that there were no breadlines; on the contrary, he said, when he left the theatre he saw "long lines of men at the Paramount, the Rialto, and Loew's. None of them was cold and hungry. . . . No symptoms of destitution were present." He had obviously not noticed one of the largest bread-lines in New York, just off Times Square. Burns Mantle said that it was "either pitifully true or deliberately untrue . . . if propaganda drama is your dish, here you will find it piping hot." On the other hand, the *World Telegram* said, "It has more excitement than any other play in town," while *The New Yorker* remarked that it "is not a piece of graceful writing . . . but it isn't anything to duck either. Go and look at it, and see what you'd like not to."

Most theatre-goers preferred not to. The play closed after only twelve performances. It may also have frightened off some potential backers, for Tony Kraber remembers:

> At the very end of the play, the common people in a mass marched straight downstage and right at the footlights; there's a blackout, and the play's over. On the first night, as we moved towards the footlights I looked down and there was Otto Kahn sitting in the second row. I saw his face, it was like a sheet. The revolution was happening right before his eyes!

But if some people in the expensive seats didn't like it, there were many others in the theatre who did. Harold Clurman recorded the fact:

> We couldn't fail to notice a kind of fervor in the nightly reception of *1931—* . . . uncharacteristic of the usual Broadway audience. . . . Strangers came backstage in a peculiar state of determination, asking what they could do for our organization, for the play. . . . Unions and other special organizations called us on the phone to tell us they would buy blocks of seats for future performances if we kept the play open.
>
> The last night of the play the balcony was packed. Each night the audience had grown more vociferous. But that night there was something of a demonstration in the theatre, like the response of a mass meeting to a particularly eloquent speaker. . . .
>
> The production of *1931—* had made us aware, for the first

time, of a new audience. It was an audience to whom such a play as *1931—* was more valuable than the successful *Reunion in Vienna.*[31]

Unfortunately, the Group did little to draw that audience closer, at any rate not then. It was the audience which was beginning to back the workers' theatre movement, which applauded the Workers Laboratory Theatre's simple efforts, which kept the Artef performing in its little house, and which was very soon to show how it could sustain a professional theatre of its own. The Group made no attempt to develop a subscription list out of its supporters as the Guild and the Provincetown had done. Its directors felt that to undertake to present a fixed number of plays each year would be too much of a handicap, especially as their method of rehearsing could not be fitted into the neat four-week period of the commercial theatre. They proposed a rather vague plan of "memberships" with reduced rates for tickets and "open meetings of the entire Group, audience and theatre," to discuss and criticize productions, but very little came of it.

They had difficulty, as well, unearthing the right scripts. Few plays had come to them, and it was essential that they find something to do to keep themselves occupied and united. The only feasible work was a play by Maxwell Anderson, *Night Over Taos.* Anderson, who had been enthusiastic about the Group from the beginning, had written the play with them in mind. Based on a feverish tragedy by Racine, it dealt with Spanish grandees in nineteenth-century New Mexico and their resistance to American encroachment. Although the directors had some reservations about the play, they felt that Anderson's reputation was probably high enough to carry things off.

Not quite high enough, as it turned out. In spite of the splendid playing of the company—they were learning more and more skillfully how to work together—there was an air of languidity about the play which closed it after less than two weeks.

The Group's first season had been promising but less than successful financially. With people less fervent, it would have been the last. They had no contract with each other, yet there was no question of their holding together. Clurman and Crawford had resigned their posts with the Guild, and with Strasberg determinedly announced that the Group Theatre was an independent, permanent company. Many of the actors, penniless, clubbed together and lived on their collective funds or on borrowed money to keep going. The indomitable Cheryl Crawford went out on a fund-raising tour of the city, and in one way or another money was found for another summer of lessons and rehearsals. Two plays had been selected, Dawn Powell's *The Party* (which they renamed *Big Night*) and *Success Story* by John Howard Lawson.

Lawson had known Clurman since the days of the New Playwrights Theatre. Their relationship was a curious one, part admiration, part misunderstanding. In the Twenties, Lawson had read an article Clurman had written analyzing the art of the theatre and had said, "The art of the theatre? What's that?" Clurman had taken this as frivolity; Lawson had meant only that he was opposed to artifice in the theatre, as was Brecht. Clurman had once said to him that plays should be written about working-class people, but not by Lawson; he had meant that they should come from workingclass writers, but Lawson had taken it as a patronizing remark. Yet Lawson thought of Clurman as "a most perceptive critic," while Clurman, although disapproving of Lawson's outspoken radical views, felt that he was "the hope of our theatre." *Success Story* was by no means a radical play, but it made a serious point about the way in which the drive for power and wealth can corrupt the most idealistic of men. Not only Clurman, the whole Group, when it was read to them, felt great enthusiasm for it. It seemed to say something about society on a wide and deep level. It was seen by at least some of them as an allegory of the self-destructive nature of the goals of capitalism, and in that sense it retained a tenuous link with Lawson's earlier expressionist plays. Quoting Lawson's own words, Clurman wrote a program note which said, "The blood and bones of a living stage must be the blood and bones of the actuality around us'—a view which the Group Theatre fully shares."

The Powell play was a black comedy about the clothing business and the unscrupulous behavior of buyers and advertising salesmen. Powell, whose novels were well known, had begun it, too, as a novel until her next door neighbor on Long Island said it sounded more like a play. She was readier to take his opinion seriously since he was John Howard Lawson. On the day she sold the play to the Group she went to tell Lawson the news, and he brought out a bottle of champagne and said, "This calls for a double celebration. They've just told me they're doing *Success Story!*"

Plans were made for renting some cottages at Dover Furnace, New York. Strasberg was to direct *Success Story,* and for the Powell play he and Crawford tried to persuade Clurman to act as director. But Clurman refused, and in the end Crawford was chosen in spite of her lack of experience.

That summer was in some ways even more inspiring than the previous one, since the members were now more used to each other and more relaxed with one another. Although their fortunes seemed low, the Group had added some members: Roman Bohnen who, like Art Smith, had been with Chicago's Goodman Theatre, Stella Adler's brother, Luther, who had abandoned a good part in another show to join the Group, and Russell Collins from the Cleveland Playhouse. Some playwrights, too, came along as guests, among them Albert Bein, George O'Neil, and Lawson. One of the Group's actors was also trying his hand at playwriting —Clifford Odets, who had already turned out one play which Clurman thought was not very good, and in the course of the summer produced another which he judged very bad. There were some apprentices, as well, who were to pay $20 a week each for their board and keep, and who participated in the classes and lectures. One was Alan Baxter, another Elia Kazan who had acquired the nickname Gadget ("I was a small eccentric object always in motion," he says). Midway through the summer, Kazan ran out of money and begged to stay on anyway, so they gave him a job waiting on table, for which he had plenty of experience having worked his way through both Williams College and Yale Drama School.

In addition to acting classes, rehearsals, and lectures, classes in movement and dance were given by Helen Tamiris, who was to become a sort of unofficial ballet mistress to the company. New acting exercises were experimented with, some initiated by the directors, some by the actors themselves. Strasberg set them the task of acting out scenes based on famous paintings. Clurman had them improvise scenes suggested by pieces of music. Art Smith wrote some sketches based on drawings by the German satirical artist George Grosz, which were done mainly in pantomime to a background of Marlene Dietrich records. They prepared skits or readings for each other and showed them after the working day was done. Carnovsky did a soliloquy from *Richard III* which was his first essay into Shakespeare, and with Joseph Bromberg performed long improvisations in gibberish. Robert Lewis displayed a brilliant gift for comedy with, among other things, interpretations of poems, the best remembered of which was one by Whitman: Lewis would mime waking up, shutting off an alarm clock, staggering out of bed, getting into a shower, and then, as the cold water hit him, shrieking, "I sing the body electric!" This combination of games and exercises became a regular practice among the Groupers, who at least never lacked for entertainment.

Success Story opened with backing from Lee Shubert on 26 September, 1932. As was the case with all Group productions, no stars were listed in ads or on billboards. The company had lost one of its talented members at the end of summer, when Franchot Tone, who had been displaying great restlessness, resigned to go to Hollywood and the movies. He had agreed, however, to open in the play and stay with it for the first five weeks. The question of outside jobs, or more specifically, of people being torn between their real love for everything the Group stood for and their desire to further their ambitions, was to be an increasingly vexing one. Nor was Tone's departure by any means the end of his relationship with the company. He was to help with money for future productions and to return to play the lead in a later play. It was as if, once the initial attachment had been forged, it could never be wholly broken.

The reception of *Success Story* was mixed. It was a play that cut close to the bone, and Lawson had written it with anger and conviction; but that wasn't enough for critics who preferred *Counsellor-at-Law, Dinner at Eight,* or *Another Language.* Not that it was a failure; with 128 performances it stood fourth on the *Daily News*'s Golden Dozen list of hits. But it wasn't filling houses, and when Shubert insisted on taking his money out of the first proceeds at the box office it meant that the actors' salaries had to be cut to keep the show running. The Group had a modest pay scale ranging from $30 to $200 a week, yet even this was too high. The three directors had already agreed to forego their salaries for five weeks; now everyone's pay was cut in half or sometimes less than half, and at the end of the run there was no money for them at all. *Big Night*, which opened early in January, was an utter catastrophe. It was greeted with derision and closed after only nine performances.

Not for the first time, the drama pundits hastened to declare that the Group, an idealistic but hopeless endeavor in the first place, was now dead. And in fact, things looked thoroughly bad. More than half the company had chipped in to rent a large, dilapidated apartment far west on 57th Street, where they set up communal housekeeping, taking it in turns to cook and clean. Odets, in the smallest room of all, sat up until all hours of the night pecking at his typewriter, working on still a third play which he called *I've Got the Blues*. Strasberg and his new wife, Paula Miller, lived in the flat, but he spent most of his time in seclusion, studying. Some of the members who had other income and lived elsewhere helped out with contributions, and now and then Theresa Helburn would bring along a Care package. The actors continued to divert themselves with impromptu entertainments, and once Helburn, watching them do an emphatically scatological improvisation, remarked to Crawford, "If that's the kind of theatre these youngsters are indulging in, Cheryl, then I just don't know. . . ."

After the closing of *Big Night*, some of the actors found work in other shows. Some lived on borrowed money or were sustained by donations from Dorothy Patten and Margaret Barker, who were better off than the others, to a Group fund. By hook or crook they kept themselves going, but there was no doubt in any of their minds that they were going to continue somehow as a unit. Strasberg found an ephemeral directing job. Clurman gave a course in theatre at the New School for Social Research. Meanwhile, he and his two co-directors continued to look for a suitable script for the Group. For a while, they hoped to get Sidney Howard's *Yellowjack*, about the conquest of yellow fever, but in the end, influenced perhaps by the poor showing of three Group plays in a row, Howard refused to let them have it. Clurman liked Lawson's *The Pure in Heart* and suggested that he might direct it, but both Crawford and Strasberg were opposed, and that possibility was dropped. Then, Crawford came up with a play by a struggling young author named Sidney Kingsley. He had written it in 1931, and although several people had been interested it had dangled for over a year while Kingsley supported himself by playing bit parts. At last *Crisis*, as it was called, had been seen and optioned by a new producing team, Sidney Harmon and James Ullman, who had approached Lee Shubert for backing. Shubert agreed and suggested to Crawford that the Group produce it. It was concerned with the life of internes, doctors, and nurses in a big city hospital, and especially with a young doctor's struggle between the girl he loves and his devotion to his profession. It was a theme which on the advent of television was to be mined with the frenzied intensity of the Gold Rush but which in 1933 was practically unexplored wilderness. Crawford brought the script before her colleagues and, although Clurman was not wildly excited by it, in the end they decided that it would do.

For their summer rehearsal period, they were able to make a bargain with the management of an adult summer camp, Green Mansions, in Warrensburg, New York. In exchange for board and lodging for the entire troupe, the company would furnish four nights of entertainment a week. It would mean an enormous amount of labor, for they would have to fit in their rehearsals on *Crisis* and they had no intention of giving up their training classes —they had brought Tamiris with them, as well as a speech coach. They had also brought their set designer, Mordecai Gorelik, for they believed as he did that settings were as important to the development of the characters and the play as the work of the actors and director.

On Decoration Day, the advance guard arrived at Green Mansions to do a hastily put together program for the holiday weekend. The others followed soon after. They had filled Franchot Tone's place with Alexander Kirkland, who was given the lead in the new play, and they buckled down to a busy summer.

The guests at Green Mansions couldn't complain that they didn't get their money's worth. The Group gave them full-length plays like O'Neill's *Emperor Jones*, excerpts from *Success Story* and *Big Night*, one-acters from Chekhov to O'Neill, variety numbers stolen (as was the custom throughout the summer camp circuit) from Broadway musicals or invented over the past year by Group members, and solo material from Bobbie Lewis' comedy bits to Tony Kraber's singing of folk ballads to his own guitar accompaniment. As an experiment one evening, the second act of Odets's *I've Got the Blues* was prepared and shown. Dealing with middle-class Jewish life in the Bronx, it touched a sympathetic chord in the audience, which loved its grim humor, its exuberant and poetic language, and its understanding of the toughness of getting along in Depression times. Clurman directed it, displaying an unexpected capacity in that role, and some of them felt it might make a future production. But Clurman, as the Group's authority on scripts, felt strongly that the first and third acts were still not quite right, and nothing further came of it for the time being.

Meantime, *Crisis* was being readied. One of the most important scenes, the climax of the second act, took place in the operating room of the hospital and would be the first time such a view of surgical procedure had been seen on the stage. Accordingly, it was worked on with special intensity. The staff doctor of the camp was pressed into service as an adviser, and a surgeon friend was brought from the city to supervise technical details. Strasberg wanted the scene played with the stylized rhythm and movement of a ballet, so a record of the slow movement of Beethoven's Seventh Symphony was played while the actors improvised or rehearsed, to give them their tempo and mood. Those who played doctors took to carrying stethoscopes in their pockets to help sustain the proper frame of mind. Later, when they returned to the city and were putting the finishing touches on the play, the actors who were in that scene were taken to see a real operation. Sanford Meisner confessed afterward that he had kept his eyes shut during the whole thing.

Retitled *Men in White*, the play opened in September, 1933. There was some initial confusion among drama reporters when the new title was first announced, some of them being unsure whether the men in white in question were barbers, the Ku Klux Klan, or street cleaners. Everyone was impressed by the Group's insistence that there were no stars in the company. When the house boards went up all thirty-two members of the cast were simply listed alphabetically, and Alexander Kirkland's name came after Elia Kazan's, even though the former had been featured with the Theatre Guild and had starred in movies and the latter was assistant stage manager and had only a walk-on. Just before the curtain rose, Kazan cut his finger. He stood bleeding while the cast of doctors and nurses milled helplessly about. Among all the hospital props there was no iodine, not even a bandage. Finally the wardrobe mistress was called, tore up a strip of cloth and efficiently bandaged the finger, after which the play began.

Not all the critics liked the script, some calling it commonplace or melodramatic, and a controversy even began among doctors who saw it over whether one of the scenes was accurate. Most, however, acknowledged its quality, and everyone was enchanted by the Group Theatre's magnificent ensemble playing. Everyone was relieved that the famous operating scene was neither gruesome nor sickening. The play was romantic enough to appeal to matinée-goers, and so beautifully done as to draw in the most fastidious drama lover. More critics joined the chorus of praise, almost the only exception being George Jean Nathan, who detested the Group, had called them a "fraternal summer camping outfit" and "graduates from the bovine bivouacs and hen-coops," and who dismissed *Men in White* as having "one or two effective theatrical scenes." The climax was reached when the play was awarded the Pulitzer Prize.

The dazed Group found itself with its first really substantial success on its hands, and equally pleasant, a substantial bank account as well. There could be no further doubt in anyone's mind (except that of George Jean Nathan) of the merit of the Stanislavsky method as training and preparation for the actor. And the Group had demonstrated inescapably how stirring a play could be when done by a devoted and close-knit troupe which studied, worked, and performed out of a common impulse.

They hadn't needed to make that particular demonstration for one section of their admirers: the workers' theatres were already committed to collective study and performance. They had followed the rise of the Group Theatre with interest, especially since the production of *1931—*. And for some time, members of the Group had been repaying the compliment, not only following the development of the workers' theatres, and even performing with them, but carrying the gospel of the new approach to acting to the most receptive of their leaders. As a result, some profound transformations had been taking place.

George Abbott as Dynamite Jim, in jail, in the
Theatre Guild's production of PROCES-
SIONAL. *Photo by Vandamm, courtesy New
York Public Library Theatre Collection.*

STAGE LEFT   71

Paul Robeson and Mary Blair in one of the controversial scenes in ALL GOD'S CHILLUN GOT WINGS. *New York Public Library Theatre Collection.*

IN ABRAHAM'S BOSOM. Left to right: Thomas Mosely, James Dunmore, Rose McClendon, Jules Bledsoe, Frank Wilson. *New York Public Library Theatre Collection.*

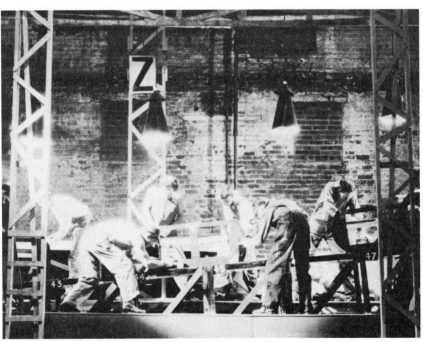

Scenes from two of the New Playwrights Company's productions, top, HOBOKEN BLUES, bottom, THE BELT. *New York Public Library Theatre Collection.*

_1932-1933_

At about the time when Percy Hammond of the _Herald_ was writing in his review of _1931_— that he had seen "no symptoms of destitution" in New York, another reporter for the same paper counted more than 2000 men and women in a bread-line, a "pitiful column of hungry, dispirited people stretched in solid melancholy ranks along the Bowery for a distance of six or seven blocks." While President Hoover was announcing, "Very soon now ... better days will be upon us," the number of unemployed, in 1932, had increased to fourteen million and was to go to seventeen million by the following year. It may not always have been perceptible from the vantage point of a theatrical critic, but the situation was doing anything but improving.

Out of sight of the theatre marquees, things were grim. It was a time of evictions and bankruptcies, of falling production and, in spite of falling prices, hunger so driving that farmers in Arkansas made armed raids on food stores and warehouses. Thousands of young people—one estimate said half a million—hitchhiked or tramped about the country looking for something to do. Other thousands, newly graduated from universities with degrees in science or the arts, were grateful for jobs as busboys or shipping clerks. Irving Werstein, in his book, _A Nation Fights Back_, graphically describes the heart of the matter:

[Statistics] did not mirror the hopeless defeat of a man vainly trudging from factory to factory, office to office, in a fruitless search for a job. The cold figure of 14,000,000 could not show the mounting fear in a man's heart as he used up the money in his savings account, borrowed on his life insurance, sold his possessions piece by piece, took loans from friends and relatives until nothing was left to him except his pride. Then that, too, evaporated as he applied for relief."[32]

Under the circumstances, it was hardly surprising that an insurgent spirit was abroad or that a political organization as essentially weak and ineffectual as the Communist Party should have gained a reputation out of all proportion to its size. The nostrums proposed by the authorities were useless, and for many, not just industrial or farm laborers but professional and small business people, the direction pointed by the Communists seemed worth a try. It was true it rested on revolution, but as the Communists were quick to point out this had been a tested American method of ending tyranny. Revolution, in any case, was the least important attraction. There *was* unconcern in government for the real problems of society, there was unemployment and starvation, there was discrimination against blacks and other minority groups, there was the growing rise of fascism and the imminence of war which, although few saw it then, were both to come to a poisonous head in only another six or seven years.

This is by no means to say that the Communist Party became a major political force. At its peak it probably numbered no more than 75,000 or 100,000 members, and even at that it never had enough power to swing any election single-handed. What it did do, in the words of Arthur Garfield Hays, the blunt-speaking counsel of the American Civil Liberties Union, was to act as a "gadfly." "Whatever their purpose may be," he said, in his testimony before the House Un–American Activities Committee in 1948, "they have been fighting the cause of all mean injustices in the United States . . . and all the way through they have done a job that the rest of us ought to do and, so long as we ignored it, we give the Communists arguments."[33] Whatever was to happen later, whatever real or fancied danger the country ran from the Communist Party and its attachment to the Soviet system in after years, during the Thirties its voice was among the loudest and most unequivocal raised against the wrongs of the time.

It was little wonder, then, that the ideology of Marxism should have attracted idealists, and that the mode of address, "Comrade," should have become as widespread then as, say, "soul brother" is now, as a way of indicating sympathy with the general, if not necessarily specific, aims of a cause. It was not surprising, either, that in such times and under such circumstances the workers' theatres should not only have grown but have affected many people in the professional theatre by their sheer vitality and participation in the movement towards reform. At the same time, however, the trend toward more polished technical performances had continued, brought on in turn by what was happening on Broadway. This trend came to rest more and more on dissatisfaction with the oversimplified forms they had used.

In May, 1932, a year after the John Reed Cultural Conference and the formation of the workers' theatre organization, a National Festival of Workers' Theatre groups was held in New York. It appeared symbolic to the delegates, who came from fifty-three drama groups, that this happened also to be the first time the National Little Theatre Tournament was not held since its inception in 1923. Twelve companies from the eastern half of the country performed in the competition that preceded the festival, and it is significant that while the Prolet-Bühne won first prize with a paean extolling the Soviet Union called *The Fifteen Minute Red Revue*, one of the judges wrote an acerb criticism which appeared in *Workers Theatre* magazine, remarking in part:

> On the spectacular side it lacks variety, on the dramaturgical side it lacks the element of narrative, of suspense, of the dramatic building up of a situation. Its lines ring with the overtones of sectarian phraseology and formulation. . . . A little more variety in its method, a little more attention to dramaturgy, a little less of that stiff, strait-laced manner will go a long way toward perfecting the work of that group.[34]

It was, in fact, to be the last time the Prolet-Bühne appeared in the lead. On the other hand, the Artef was declared out of the competition for "too much dramaturgy," that is, complicated sets and intricate lighting, as well as for the fact that their play was not a new one. What the workers' theatres were after at this point was something in between, something closer to American vaudeville than to either European drama or European agit-prop. The second-prize winner in the competition was *Charity*, written by Jack Shapiro and performed by the Jack London Group of Newark. Although it dealt with the serious matter of handouts by the Emergency relief committees and with workers' self-help, it was done lightly, with jingling humorous verses and touches of comedy. It had not been performed by Shapiro's own group, the Workers Laboratory Theatre, because it was felt by some of them to be too funny and too casual. "It was like being a pious churchgoer," Shapiro later mused. "If it hurt you a little, you could serve God better. Having fun was no good." After the festival and its accompanying conference, the WLT changed its mind. Within another six months, *Charity* was one of their regular numbers, as was another satirical playlet by Shapiro called *The Sell-Out* in which, with a combination of realism and acrobatics, a demagogic politician attempts to sell a worker a shoddy program, in the manner of a carnival quack peddling a cure for constipation.

It was clear that the expanding movement required something more efficient than the clearing house provided by the Dramatic Bureau which had been established in 1931. A national federation of producing groups was set up by the conference, called the League of Workers Theatres. It took over the magazine, *Workers Theatre*, which now had a monthly circulation of over a thousand copies, and made it its official organ. Its second National Festival, held in 1933, was attended by 120 delegates representing more than five thousand members of organizations concerned in one way or another with the development of workers' theatres.

The Workers Laboratory Theatre had naturally been in the forefront of all this activity, and had grown even more rapidly than most of its rivals. Shortly before the festival, it had severed its connection with the Workers International Relief and embarked on its own, a move which gave it greater freedom in the choice of material. It transferred its headquarters first to a loft on West 21st Street, and then, as its membership increased and some contributions came in from organizations which supported its work, to another, larger one, at 42 East 12th Street. The first month's rent was put down, and a never-ending struggle began to meet each succeeding month's bills. The membership fluctuated from month to month, but over a hundred people were on the rolls. The majority, those who had jobs or went to school and could only attend at night, were formed into an Evening Troupe. The others, about a dozen of them, became what was called the Shock Troupe. They constituted the permanent core, devoted all their time to the work of the theatre, and were always available for performances.

There were plenty of demands on both divisions. They added to their repertory until they had about a dozen pieces, among them agit-prop numbers like *Scottsboro*, humorous skits like *Charity* and *The Sell-Out*, slightly more elaborate playlets like *The Big Fight* in which the election campaign was represented as a rigged boxing match between Republicans and Democrats, vaudeville routines like *The Side Show* in which sight-gags and one-line jokes were used for political jabs—Jim the Magician was Jimmy Walker, the dapper and unscrupulous mayor of New York, and the Bearded Lady was a Daughter of the American Revolution—and finally, as fillers, an assortment of songs and recitations. Dozens of union locals, fraternal bodies and progressive organizations asked them to entertain at meetings. A small booking fee was expected to be paid, which was the main source of income for the theatre. The exceptions to the fee were performances for the Unemployed Councils and strike bookings for which the Shock Troupe was always on call, free. During a single month, April of 1933, the WLT performed twelve times, and that was without counting performances on street corners or at strike meetings.

The 12th Street loft was a one flight walk-up in what had once been a handsome building decorated with neo-Venetian twisted columns at the windows, but was by now begrimed out of recognition. The WLT's headquarters filled the complete floor. In the front, partitions had once made two business offices; one of these was now used for getting out the magazine, the other, for the WLT's administrative staff which consisted of a girl called Lucy Kaye. She worked for an interior decorator during the day, but in the evenings she sat in the office and dealt with requests for bookings, typed out scripts, and handled callers. She also provided a valuable source of income. Out of her weekly salary of $25 or so, half went to her family and the other half to the penurious Shock

Troupe. The rest of the loft was open, dusty space with a low stage built at one end out of lumber scrounged or stolen from building sites. This was classroom, meeting place, rehearsal hall and, on occasion, a theatre for shows which were given to raise money for the upkeep of the company. Over the stage hung a tatty red banner bearing the words, "Theatre is a Weapon." It was part of the Marxist canon that the arts were merely instruments, on the one hand for the maintenance of the power of the ruling class, on the other for the education of the working class. Some time later, the banner was taken down as being a little too sectarian.

On the stage, at the beginning, Al Saxe and Will Lee slept, having had to move from the flat they shared with Salty Marino when they became too impoverished to pay even that microscopic rent. Since the loft building was designed for business only, they had to be careful how they entered it at night, keeping one eye open for the cop on the beat. During the day, their mattresses were stored away behind the stage curtains. A couple of days a week they'd go to the public baths, for the lavatory in the loft had a basin that produced only a trickle of brown water. When, at length, the Shock Troupe was formed, it became impossible for them all to settle in the loft, and they cast about for another place to live. Dipping into their treasury, they rented a railroad flat on 13th Street a little way east of Second Avenue. It became their home for nearly two years.

The apartment had few virtues. It was a five-story climb, its five rooms were dark and seedy, and it sheltered several species of bugs which were never successfully rooted out. But it somehow had a cheerful quality. It was always noisy with talk and laughter. There were always a few extra people staying over, tucked up on chairs or sleeping on the floor. And when, at breakfast or dinner, everyone gathered in the long kitchen on benches, there was a cosiness that came as much from the feeling of community as from the lack of space.

Married couples shared one room, single men another, single women the third. When the Shock Troupe grew still larger, the single men spilled over into the living room. In spite of their rejection of bourgeois institutions, they were all rather puritanical and there was no promiscuous bedding. And despite the cramped quarters, they were all punctilious about respecting each other's bit of room. Beds consisted of mattresses laid on the floor, and each tenant had an egg crate or an orange crate on which he kept his personal belongings. It would have been unthinkable for anyone to touch anyone else's shelves. Teams were chosen weekly to do the cooking and cleaning, and on a bulletin board in the kitchen notices would appear: "Greetings! Tell the cooks to stop trying to cook beans without water."

Food was the most pressing problem. It cost about ten dollars a week to feed the whole troupe, and this was stretched by judicious shopping for slightly spoiled vegetables or day-old bread. The girl friend of one of the members used to steal things from home which she thought her mother would never miss, cans of sardines or tuna fish, and contribute them to the larder. Sometimes, instead of payment for bookings they were given food, and once a Baker's Union local donated twenty-six pumpkin pies which seemed to last forever; to this day, some of the former Shock Troupers can't face Thanksgiving. The mothers of some of the boys often spread extra places at dinner for their sons' friends, and one or two at a time would go off to stuff themselves for once. Perry Bruskin's mother was especially hospitable; her oldest son, Bobby, was a tap dancer with hungry friends, and on alternate weeks she would feed Jackie Gleason, Peter Lawford, or Buddy Hackett, and then the younger Shock Troupe colleagues of Perry. After a time, a loose association of outsiders was formed called Friends of the Shock Troupe which not only helped with the making of props and costumes or the painting of signs, but gave money and groceries as well. Prominent among the Friends was Florence Kamlot, a young woman from a well-to-do family, who not only provided supplies from jars of chicken soup to blankets, but drove the troupe to its bookings now and then in a seven-passenger Auburn belonging to her family or in a car belonging to one of her brothers. "He wasn't sympathetic to the labor movement," she says, "and if he ever found out what I was doing with his car, he'd have killed me."

The Shock Troupe kept to a fairly crowded schedule. They were up at about eight, and took a couple of hours for breakfast and housework. Then they walked the few blocks to the loft. The morning was generally given to classes, at first rather primitive ones in acting or dancing, but later, when these were taken over by professionals, mostly from the Group Theatre, they consisted of training on a much higher level. They also spent some time reading and discussing the political news out of which often came the subjects for plays. There were also what they referred to as sessions of self-criticism. These were periods during which they let their hair down and said exactly what they thought of each other, not only as performers but as associates. For people living so intimately these exchanges were extremely valuable outlets allowing them to get their problems into the open. They were sometimes painful and occasionally climaxed in explosions—once, even in a fist fight—but they always ended in even deeper feelings of interdependence and affection.

Lunch was usually nothing more complicated than pot cheese sandwiches. Twenty-five cents bought five pounds of cheese with which twenty-six sandwiches could be made. The afternoon was used for rehearsals of new material or the polishing of old. Not infrequently, there would be open-air shows at meetings, rallies, or picket lines.

We were supposed to go on at 4 p.m., so with our usual promptness we started on our journey at five after four. After going past the wrong station and a heel-blistering walk of fifteen blocks we arrived on or at the scene of our performance. Right at the start we had trouble. A cop . . . approached us and told us that we were forming a crowd and acting disorderly. The leader of the WLT . . . had the crowd sit down. The limb of the law walked away mumbling to himself. The play started. . . . The cop returned. This time it seems we were holding a play without a permit. Why, sure, that guy is on a stage (which consisted of a folding chair) and has on a costume (which consisted of a high hat and a dollar sign). This point was obviated by having the comrade remove the high hat and the dollar sign and stand on the ground. The cop removed himself saying that he was not sure if this was right and he was going to call the station.[35]

They usually tried to get home by six, for dinner, and then back in the loft rehearsed again, worked with the Evening Troupe (which had its own classes and bookings), or filled more performance dates. When they felt flush, many of them rounded off the evening in Stewart's Cafeteria on Sheridan Square or the Cooperative Cafeteria on Union Square, with a nickel cup of coffee and a couple of hours of socializing. If there was a rent party in some other organization's headquarters or a party for the benefit of some political cause in someone's apartment, a few of the Shock Troupe were sure to turn up to entertain in exchange for a couple of glasses of wine. And at least once a month, on a Sunday night, the WLT gave its own rent party for a small admission charge in the 12th Street loft, often parodying its own political sketches and finishing with a dance at which the star performers were apt to be Will Lee, short, agile, grinning like Punch, and his girl friend, Becky Roland, an exotic-looking member of the New Dance Group, an association of modern dancers paralleling the Workers Laboratory Theatre.

The Shock Troupers were far from equal in talent or experience, but that was not always as important as devotion to the theatre or its goals, sheer persistence, or, sometimes the troupe's need for a particular type. In this, it was not much different from a professional company where, no matter how flexible the actors, there is always a need for a good-looking juvenile lead. When Earl Robinson showed up, for instance, having come all the way from Seattle, they seized on him partly because he was a trained musician, but also because he was so clearly an American rustic. "He looked like he had straw in his hair," Lee remembers. "His voice had a Western twang. He had those big round glasses, a typical picture of a rural character." Rhoda Rammelkamp, a tall girl from Massachusetts, was perfect for hillbilly parts or for the rawboned wives of heroic union leaders. She also had a deep voice and excellent diction. "She was a kind of prim Earth-mother," says Perry Bruskin. She taught voice and elocution, and once, in one of her classes, she lost her temper at the incessant larking about and said, "Shit!" "I couldn't believe it," says Bruskin. "For me, the world stopped!" Bruskin himself, at eighteen the youngest member, had been a child prodigy. His father, a brick-layer with a strong taste for culture, had encouraged the boy to recite poems, mainly from the works of Jewish poets. The lad was in great demand at banquets, meetings, and weddings, and at thirteen he took part in a program at Madison Square Garden where he stopped the show cold. "I was short for my age, but strong, and very dramatic," Bruskin explains. "When I came out in a velvet suit and started declaiming, people said, 'Look at that little boy— such a *big* voice!' " His voice and energy helped get him a place in the Shock Troupe, but Saxe confessed to him later, "We really took you because you looked like a workingclass joe." If it was vital to a radical theatre group in those days to have members who looked like Yankees or factory workers, it was even more important to have black members. The Shock Troupe had two, a slender, amiable youth named William Watts and a soft-spoken piano player, Harry Nance. Nance was very reserved and unlike Watts lived outside the troupe's apartment although he was a full-time member.

Some of the group had had only slender experience in the theatre. Harry Lessin had gone from Commonwealth College to acting with the Blue Blouses, a workers' theatre in Chicago. When he arrived in New York he went straight to the WLT and asked for an audition. "You don't have to worry about me, I'm good," he told Saxe. They took him on. Ann Gold and Jean Harper had appeared with workers' theatre companies around New York. Lucy Kaye had no experience at all. Nick Ray, on the other hand, had been torn between a desire to be a theatrical director and a symphony conductor, but, as he says mournfully, "I didn't have much talent in music." After a variety of jobs, he had been taken on as a Master Apprentice in Theatre by Frank Lloyd Wright, at Taliesin, had quarreled with Wright, wandered to Mexico, and returned to New York to work in the theatre. He was a ruggedly good-looking Wisconsin boy, and when he had found his way to the WLT he was snapped up by them. Curt Conway's parents had been vaudevillians. Growing up with the ambition to become an actor, he had written to Walter Winchell when he was about fifteen to ask how he could go about it, and got a letter back consisting of one word: "Don't." Ignoring the advice, he had formed his own amateur group, then got himself accepted as an apprentice under Jasper Deeter at the Hedgerow Theatre. Leaving after a year or so, he had bummed around, had become like so many others convinced that the cure for social evils lay on the Left, and so had come, at last, to the loft on 12th Street.

Towards the end of 1933, the troupe was joined by Stephen and Greta Karnot. Greta was a dancer who had been a Humphrey-

Weidman student and had appeared with Fokine. She became the Shock Troupe's dance and body movement instructor. Stephen had spent eight months studying at the Meyerhold Theatre in Moscow and consequently was thought of as the WLT's theatrical theoretician. He was a lean, moustached man who cut a commanding figure in the leather jacket and boots which he had brought back from Russia and which gave him the air of a visiting commissar from a Pudovkin film. He led discussions on abstruse subjects, something like, "A consideration of the work of directors and actors in the light of the class struggle," which not infrequently turned into monologues. Nevertheless, he acted as a steadying influence since most of the members were younger than he and more volatile, and he was a shrewd and penetrating critic.

It was Al Saxe, however, who by common consent was thought of as the Troupe's artistic and stage director. The bushy-haired, stocky mid-Westerner had a way of winning the affection and confidence of everyone who worked with him. Although he had a fierce temper it flamed out only rarely, and generally he was warm, sympathetic, and friendly. He had had little formal theatrical training but he was imaginative and quick to learn.

Very early, he had argued against the dogmatic view that nothing should be taken from the bourgeois theatre. "Only fools refuse to profit by the experience of the past," he had written.[36] He had met actors from the Group Theatre and was intrigued by their method of acting; he tried to put some of it into classes at the WLT. He was impressed, too, by Karnot's intellectual grasp of techniques. But he himself was an intuitive director, and his taste ran to movement, action, color rather than the long exposition of character or the development of a theme. He believed that political or social points had to be made as theatrically as possible, using every device that came to hand. In his view, agit-prop was the key to a new form which was best suited to the circumstances and aims of the workers' theatre. He wrote:

> Shouting a few slogans is not agit-prop. . . . Where agit-prop groups have gone beyond slogans into a developed field taking in realism, stylization, symbolism, vaudeville, mass chant and so on, it [sic] has succeeded in drawing in professional technicians, and in fact has been responsible for the organi-

zation of our stationary theatres.* Agit-prop . . . must strive
to be as creative as the best of the art theatres.[37]

As a director, he had a lot to contend with. Like almost everyone
in the workers' theatre he was learning as he went along. The
image of Saxe at work presented by Morgan Himelstein, who
never saw him, is imposing: "When Al Saxe . . . started a rehearsal,
his 'comrades' maintained perfect discipline."[38] Unfortunately,
that description was based on a piece Saxe wrote in a hopeful vein
to instruct beginning directors:

> When there is a chief director, he is to conduct all the
> rehearsals without interference from the directing commit-
> tee or the actors group. The director is in complete charge
> during rehearsals. The actors are to follow his directions with
> a thorough discipline.[39]

The reality was quite different. The Shock Troupers were much
given to horseplay and needed only a spark to set them off. Will
Lee had a problem with his speech, his words coming so fast that
they tripped over each other and he sometimes lapsed into gibberish; when this happened, a rehearsal could break up in hysterics.
Since nobody was really an authority, everybody had suggestions
to make and the collective method occasionally extended to directing as well. It was only after some time, through Saxe's patient
coaxing or his flying into rages, and by the occasionally acrimonious "self-criticism" sessions held by the troupe after a rehearsal,
that they came to accept the discipline and submission to a director's guiding hand which is taken for granted in any normal acting
company.

As the economic situation in the country worsened, the labor
movement responded with strikes against pay cuts and other
abuses, and more often than not these were protracted and
bloody. The miners' strikes dragged on and on leaving a trail of
dead and wounded; at Dearborn, Michigan, four strikers had been
shot down in an auto workers' strike; in almost all major industries
there was unrest met with equal violence. In 1933, as a revul-

---

*"Stationary theatre" was the term used to denote a group which performed plays
on a stage; "theatre of action" meant, in general, a mobile troupe which could
perform anywhere. The WLT was both.

sion against the Hoover administration's impotence, Franklin D. Roosevelt had been elected president on a program of social and economic reform, one of the earliest results of which was the establishment of the National Recovery Act to set prices, labor codes and fair practices for industry. One of its sections guaranteed labor the right to bargain collectively with management, and this, too, brought more labor troubles as the attempt to form unions spread, especially in those industrial areas where workingmen had formerly been unorganized. Even the unemployed organized, particularly in New York City, into groups called Unemployed Councils which fought for the expansion of relief measures.

Naturally, the Workers Laboratory Theatre was in the thick of things. Both Shock Troupe and Evening Troupe bustled about, sometimes performing two or three times a day out of a repertory which now included some twenty numbers. They would rehearse on subways on the way to a booking, and would turn their rehearsals into impromptu performances for the straphangers. They appeared at May Day parades and picnics, where they converted the back of a truck into a stage. In one such performance Bruskin, playing a capitalist, had to hold a cigar in his mouth for hours, and, being a non-smoker, was forced to take a couple of breaks in which to be sick. "The fantastic thing about our gang," says Will Lee, "is that we weren't singers but we sang, we weren't dancers but we could move. Nothing fazed me—in pageants I used to slide down a fourteen-foot ladder. It had to be done."

In April, 1933, the League of Workers Theatres held a play competition for the groups in the New York area in which the participants were asked to show their best work. The WLT won hands down with the presentation of the playlet they had once refused to do, Shapiro's *The Sell-Out*, and having thus established their preeminence held the position from then on. They responded to the issues of the day with new material, some of it considerably livelier and more sophisticated than the old.

They had pretty much given up the notion of collective playwriting. They now tried to draw in people who were primarily interested in writing and who were encouraged to work in their own way, at their own pace. "Back in 1931," wrote Harry Elion, "we were in no position to put much emphasis on quality. New groups were being formed, everyone wanted plays, there weren't any professional playwrights who knew or cared to learn about the problems of workers' theatres. . . . Play after play was done with symbolic characters . . . plots always began with discontent and ended with revolution. . . . We forgot about vaudeville, musical comedy, revues. We paid no attention to the problem of adding music and dance to the workers' theatre."[40] It was a lack the WLT had already begun to make up, and they proceeded to go on doing so.

They took Shapiro's *Charity* and turned it into a mini musical comedy, with music and some additional lyrics by Ruth Burke. Retitled *Sweet Charity*, it had so widespread a success that mimeographed librettos at ten cents each sold not only to other groups but to members of the audience after performances. People went out singing its rousing finale:

> Do you want milk for your hungry babies
> Without any ifs or buts or maybes?
> Join the militant workers!
> Do you share with us our firm belief
> That the unemployed should get relief?
> Join the militant workers!

For New York's municipal elections in 1933 they produced *Who's Got the Baloney?* in which the candidates were shown as chips off the same political block:

> In our little voting machine
> We go up, up, up like a feather.
> In our little voting machine
> We will all be elected together.

These playlets and others like them were closer to the kind of thing American audiences enjoyed than was simple agit-prop, but they still weren't the final solution for the WLT. They were all concerned with the search for interesting theatrical forms "pliable enough," as Al Saxe was to write, "to fit any content, to be cast to any mold. . . . By this time it is obvious that no one form will ever solve [our] problems."[41] What emerged, at length, was a combination of forms put together by Saxe with the collaboration and ideas of the rest of the troupe.

Its beginning was a short poem by V. J. Jerome, "Newsboy,"

which appeared in the *New Masses*. Its burden was that the press concealed the true corruption of society under a cloud of gossip, falsehood, and trivia. Saxe conceived of a simple agit-prop sketch in which the lines of the poem would be chanted and mimed. Very soon, this began to be transformed into a more complex piece of theatre. The film concept of montage, used extensively by Eisenstein whose films were familiar to the Shock Troupers, had been gaining some currency and had been tried out by cameramen in the Film and Photo League, a branch of the League of Workers Theatres, which had so far produced two documentaries. As he began fitting action to the poem, Saxe saw illustrative dramatic scenes developing, some of them growing out of the actors' improvisations—a technique they had learned from the Group Theatre—others based on plays he had seen, particularly the production of *1931—*. The Siftons' play had not had conventional acts but short scenes which sometimes melted into one another and which were interspersed with brief mimed Interludes. The technique of dissolving scenes into each other in its turn suggested a montage of sequences, some done in stylized movement, some straightforwardly dramatic, some echoing the old mass chant, some the sloganizing format of *Scottsboro*. It was agit-prop, but agit-prop translated into highly sophisticated theatrical terms.

Newsboy went through several permutations before being crystallized into its final shape. Even then, Jerome, who was considered the Communist Party's solon in all cultural matters, fumed that it did not do justice to his poem, that it was not substantial enough, and that—although it ended with a mild plug for the *Daily Worker*, it did not come properly to grips with the great issues of war and fascism. Another version was prepared by someone named Gregory Novikov for a mass reading at a meeting of the League Against War and Fascism, a version which was on the sluggish side being charged with political slogans and cumbered with speeches. It is this script which is quoted by the researchers who mention *Newsboy*, since it is the only one in the archives of the New York Public Library's Theatre Collection. The version as performed by the WLT, however, is given here:

(The curtain rises on darkness. Voices are heard, chanting in cadence, "Daily News, Mirror; Daily News and Mirror; getcha evening paper here, read all about it; evening paper, evening paper!" *The lights go on. A Newsboy is posed, center, with his papers.)*

NEWSBOY: Evening paper, read all about it. Love nest raided on Park Avenue. Extra! Marlene Dietrich insures legs for $50,000! Yanks take Dodgers 3–0. Getcha paper here, whaddya read. *(Another Newsboy walks across. The first one kicks him.)* Get off my station.

(A girl walks by, crossing a man coming from the other side. He picks her up. A blind woman goes by singing, "Holy, holy, holy," *in a feeble voice. The Newsboy eyes her. A man passes, buys a paper, drops a nickel into the blind woman's cup. The criss-crossing movement of passersby turns into a ballet which is broken into by a Voice, freezing the action.)*

VOICE: Say, boy, how long you gonna stand there, yellin' your guts out under the El because somewhere—

A MAN: In a hotel—

A GIRL: In Frisco—

THE CROWD *(in rhythm)*: A follies girl—shot the brains —out of the old rip—that kept her.

(Two characters pantomime the words as they are spoken.)

VOICE: Don't you get tired, Newsie, shouting all the time about—

ALL *(in rhythm)*: Hold-ups — and divorces — and raids on love nests? *(with a change of pace)* Seventeen million men and women . . . seventeen million men and women . . . *(They form into a bread line and as they shuffle they repeat the phrase, above which is heard)*

VOICES *(in sequence)*: Starving in mines—sweating in mills—tortured in flop joints with hymns about Saviors.

ALL *(shouting)*: Seventeen million men and women!

A VOICE: That's all today. *(The line breaks up grumbling and everyone exits leaving the Newsboy alone on stage without his papers. Two girls pass him, talking. He approaches them to panhandle but they turn away and hurry off. A man enters.)*

NEWSBOY: Say, buddy, can you spare a nickel for a cup of coffee? I never done this before, but I gotta eat.

1st MAN: Eat?
(He exits, dropping a cigarette. A man crosses rapidly. As the Newsboy approaches him, he picks up the butt and goes off with it. Another man reading a paper enters.)

NEWSBOY: Listen, mister, can you spare a nickel for a cup of coffee?

2nd MAN: Oh, no, I don't believe in it.

NEWSBOY: I don't get you, mister.

2nd MAN: I don't believe in charity. Why don't you find a job? A big husky young fellow like you—

NEWSBOY: There just isn't anything, mister.

2nd MAN: Well, don't get down-hearted. Keep trying. Something is bound to turn up.

(He exits. A third man enters.)

NEWSBOY *(fiercely)*: Listen, mister, can you give me a nickel for a cup of coffee? This ain't charity—I'm hungry.

3rd MAN: Why don't you go on the bread line?

NEWSBOY: I said this wasn't charity. *(The man hands him a dime. It drops to the ground.)* Too good to hand it to me, huh?

3rd MAN *(nervously)*: It slipped.

NEWSBOY: Git! *(The man exits hastily. A girl comes on, sees the dime and makes a grab for it. The Newsboy shoves her violently away.)*

GIRL: That's mine! I saw it first.

NEWSBOY: That's *my* dime.

(As he says it, a faint chorus of voices like those of phantoms, begin murmuring, "That's my dime . . . gimme that dime . . . that's my dime." This gradually changes to "Seventeen million men and women!" shouted, as all the figures converge gradually on the News-boy. He backs upstage, holding the dime above his head. All the other reaching hands form a pyramid. Suddenly, his hand drops and reappears holding up a newspaper.) Evenin' paper, read all about it! Lucky Luciano breaks out of Sing-Sing. Extra! Yanks take Dodgers 3–0. Read all about it.

(The crowd breaks apart, laughing.

*Above the laugh-
ter individual
voices are heard.)*

VOICES *(in sequence)*: You hear? He
stands there yell-
ing about—the
Yanks and Dodg-
ers—Lucky Luci-
ano—or a busted
honeymoon in
Hollywood.

A MAN *(pushing his way to the front)*: You hear? Seven
men left to burn
alive in a jail
in Colorado so
that one won't get
away.

2nd MAN: You hear? Scores
injured, one dead,
as cops break up a
picket line.

3rd MAN *(he is black)*: You hear? Seventeen white men
take a black man
for a ride, and
string him up a
tree, and fill his
body full of holes
because a white
woman said he
smiled at her.
*(Four men catch
him from behind
and throw him
to the floor, up-
stage.)**

*The following sequence was adapted from *Merry-go-Round*, by George Sklar and

MEN:	Sit down, God damn you!
BLACK MAN:	Hey, what's the idea? *(starts to rise)*
MEN *(shoving him down again)*:	Sit down!
BLACK MAN:	Say, you can't do this. What's the idea? I ain't done nothing. *(They watch him in silent menace.)* Well say something can't you? I ain't done nothing. Jesus! Say something will you?
1st WHITE MAN:	Why'd you do it?
BLACK MAN:	Huh?
2nd WHITE MAN:	Come on, why'd you do it?
BLACK MAN:	I ain't done nothing.
1st WHITE MAN:	Come on, talk.
3rd WHITE MAN:	We ain't talking about your grandmother.
4th WHITE MAN:	What were you doing down that cellar?
2nd WHITE MAN:	You better come clean and save yourself a beating.
BLACK MAN:	I never done nothing. It's a frame-up.
1st WHITE MAN:	You know you done it.
BLACK MAN:	You can't pin nothing on me. It's a damn lie.
3rd WHITE MAN:	Shut up, you lousy nigger.
BLACK MAN:	You can't do this.
MEN *(in unison)*:	God damn you, shut up! *(As they strike at him,*

Alfred Maltz. The play will be discussed in the next chapter.)

	there is a blackout. In the dark, moans are heard. The following speeches come very rapidly.)
1st WHITE MAN:	You know you done it.
2nd WHITE MAN:	You was down the cellar.
3rd WHITE MAN:	Her husband saw you there.
BLACK MAN:	He owed me money— wouldn't pay—
4th WHITE MAN:	You had her by the arm.
1st WHITE MAN:	Her dress was torn.
BLACK MAN:	Damn lie! *(His voice changes to a shriek. In the dark, whispers begin.)*
ALL:	Tortured. Hanged. Shot. Electrocuted.
A VOICE *(above the whispers)*:	Have you heard of Sacco and Vanzetti?
ALL *(a little louder)*:	Lynched. Murdered. Tortured.
2nd VOICE:	Have you heard of Tom Mooney?
ALL *(still louder)*:	Electrocuted. Lynched. Hanged. Shot.
3rd VOICE:	Have you heard of Angelo Herndon?
ALL *(chanting loudly)*:	Murdered. Shot. Tortured. Electrocuted.
4th VOICE *(shouting)*:	Have you heard of Scottsboro?
ALL *(equally loudly)*:	Have—you—heard? *(Lights. All are crowded around the Newsboy, pointing at him. He is raised above their level on a chair or box.)*
NEWSBOY:	Evening papers. Read all

about it. *(He jumps down and runs around from one to another.)* Here you are—getcha evening paper here.

(They are standing with their backs to the audience. As he touches them, each turns, unfolding a copy of the Daily Worker. The Newsboy at last sinks to the ground. A Man steps forward.)

MAN: Get yourself a trumpet, buddy, a big red trumpet. And climb to the top of the Empire State Building and blare out the news—Time to revolt! Black man, white man, field man, shop man— Time to revolt! Get yourself a trumpet, buddy, a big . . . red . . . trumpet!

BLACKOUT

Short as was its script, *Newsboy* gave the effect of a full theatrical performance, by its variety of scenes, styles, and pacing. Years later, Harold Clurman, who admired it, found it hard to believe that it played for less than fifteen minutes. Some months after its appearance, Saxe wrote a long article in which he analyzed it in complex dramatic and Marxist terms, speaking of its conflicts as expressions of dialectical materialism and comparing its dynamism to the intensity of industrialized American society, but throughout he gives the impression of being slightly bewildered by his own achievement. His analysis was, in any case, pure hindsight, for the production had developed without a cold, diagrammatic plan. "Willy and I liked the poem," he said later, "and we'd sit down and talk about what these lines meant and what we should do. I'd suggest something, Willy'd suggest something else, and we worked things out with our sense of what it should be like theatrically." He was an emotional and instinctive director, and *Newsboy* took most of its shape from rehearsal to rehearsal. For example, Jerome's poem contained the lines, "Seventeen million men and women Starving in mines, etc." The pantomimic Interludes of *1931—* suggested the silent formation into a bread line, and then Saxe thought of going a step further and using a somewhat cut version of Scene VII in the play, in which Adam, driven to desperation, tries to beg from passersby. The scene ends with a youngster, a boy in the original, saying, "That's mine . . . I saw it first!" Adam replies, "If *that's* yours . . . I'll . . . I'll cut my throat." During rehearsal, Harry Lessin, playing the Newsboy, blew his line when the dime fell to the floor, and said, "Hey, that's *my* dime." Instead of correcting him, Saxe said, "Let's leave that in. Jeannie, you pick up the line and say it. Now you, Perry," and so on, until he had built up both volume and tension. The natural movement of the actors was to converge on Lessin, so Saxe let them do it and moved them easily into the pyramidal shape which climaxed the scene.

The play was a success from the moment it was first shown, at a Sunday night rent party in the loft. "Al was groping with it and we were working with him, and nobody knew it was going to be any better than anything else we'd done," says Harry Lessin. "But the first time it was done we saw that it was different." It became the major item in the Shock Troupe's repertory, done wherever there was a stage or a platform and some lights that could be turned on and off. With it, the WLT easily won the Second National Theatre Festival held by the League of Workers Theatres in Chicago, in April, 1934, and on the way to the festival they stopped off to play *Newsboy*, along with some other pieces, in half a dozen towns. When they returned, they took a drafty old mausoleum of a theatre, the Fifth Avenue, actually on Broadway at 28th Street, and did an Evening of Revolutionary Theatre which featured *Newsboy*. A good many professional theatre people came to see it, and few were unmoved by its technical brilliance, whether they agreed with its premises or not. It was performed by many other groups in the League of Workers Theatres, and done by college dramatic societies and university drama schools. It became the most widely performed piece in the repertory of the workers' theatres, making its way as far as London where it was done by the English Theatre of Action. Long afterward, Joan Littlewood, in this country to supervise Brendan Behan's *The Hostage*, told Perry Bruskin, who was directing a road company of the play, that *Newsboy* had been an important influence in her development as a director. It made the WLT the unquestioned leader of the workers' theatre movement and gave it a reputation in much wider professional circles.

While the WLT was engaged in its experiments, a section of it had split off to pursue another alluring goal.

Jack and Hyam Shapiro had kept up their acquaintanceship with Lee Strasberg, from Chrystie Street Settlement days, and through him had met members of the Group Theatre. Jack remembers a performance of *The Sell-Out* at which Elia Kazan shouted, "This is the first time I've seen real theatre!" After some preliminary talking a nucleus of people drew together who felt that a step should be taken beyond the workers' theatres. They wanted to produce more elaborate plays than those of the WLT, for instance, but more strongly oriented to the Left than those of the Group Theatre. They conceived of an acting company trained in the Stanislavsky method, which would present well prepared full-length plays on a professional basis. Among the leaders, along with the Shapiro brothers, were Mordecai Gorelik, who had felt impatient with the Group's refusal to commit itself to a more radical program, and Mary Virginia Farmer, an actress who had been with the Group from the beginning. Early in 1933, they took over the abandoned WLT loft on West 21st Street, along with a number of interested members of the Evening Troupe.

They began by appealing for contributions—what they mainly wanted was office furniture, a bulletin board, and a mailbox—and calling themselves a section of the Workers Laboratory Theatre began, with the latter's blessing and assistance, to prepare a one-act play called *Help Yourself Farmer*. Rose Beigel, one of the executive committee, said candidly that while the group, which named itself the Theatre Collective, would prefer to do full-length plays, there was a shortage of good ones and they would rather work than wait. Very soon, however, they decided to tackle *1931*— which the Siftons agreed to revise for them, updating it to fit the changes that had taken place in the two years since it had first been shown. The play was presented at the Fifth Avenue Theatre for four performances, in June. Its reception was far from earth-shaking outside the left-wing movement—only the *World Tele-gram* noticed it—but it served to launch the Theatre Collective as an independent company. They separated from the WLT, joined the League of Workers Theatres as a full member, and set up shop in another loft on west 15th Street. They planned a repertory for the coming year which would include a play by Paul Peters called *Dirt Farmer*, and a new, original play, *Marion Models*, by Olga Shapiro (no relation to the Shapiro brothers, although a certain amount of confusion was caused when Jack was called in to work with her on the script). The latter play was to be directed by John Bonn, whose Prolet-Bühne was on its last legs and would soon be heard of no more. A program of classes for directors, stage design-ers and actors was started, with Virginia Farmer in charge and a faculty which contained some Group Theatre people as instruc-tors.

The earliest, and worst, years of the Depression had altered the political climate so that the rebel theatre groups could grow and flourish. Their slogan, "Theatre is a Weapon," although intended for the partisan purposes of the class struggle, had its more general application, for the theatre was to be used increasingly as a way of mirroring the concern of many Americans with what had hap-pened to the country and what was to happen. For example, on the day after Christmas, in 1931, a caustically funny musical was unveiled which attacked the hallowed office of the presidency itself, and which was an instant hit. In the elections that followed upon its closing, the country voted out of office that party under whose administration the Depression had begun, and put in a president whose measures for reform were in their own way as drastic as those proposed by the most inflammatory of the workers' theatres. The musical had not been responsible for the change, any more than *Newsboy*, say, was responsible for better press coverage of racial discrimination. A sharp eye, however, would have noted the weathercock turn in the wind.

1930-1934

On October 24th, 1972, the satirical political musical comedy, *Of Thee I Sing*,
was presented on television, just short of forty-one years after its
original opening on Broadway. Nothing could have given a clearer
indication of the differences not only between the stage and television but the two points in time.

The book of the show had been written by George S. Kaufman
and Morrie Ryskind, with music by George Gershwin and lyrics by
his brother, Ira. Kaufman and Ryskind had collaborated on an
earlier musical satire, *Strike Up the Band*, which climaxed with
the United States declaring war on Switzerland. *Of Thee I Sing*
took American politics to pieces in a script which lashed out at
practically every sacred institution in the land, from bathing-
beauty contests to motherhood. Its pleasures were heightened by
a crisp performance from William Gaxton as the president who
takes office on a platform of true love and corn muffins, and the
memorable appearance of Victor Moore, wandering about the
stage like a dissipated baby in the role of the vice-president whose
name no one can remember. The television production cut down
the brilliantly venomous script to about a quarter of its length, put
its emphasis on dance routines, softened its sting to mere good
humor, and left both Ryskind and Ira Gershwin out of the credits,
possibly because neither seemed famous enough. The audience in
1931 would have been taken aback by some obligatory modern
additions, notably the appearance of two black newspapermen

and a black policeman among the cast, and the performance of a strip tease by one of the leading ladies. Significantly, in the line "Can you tear asunder two loving hearts whom God hath joined together?" delivered during a campaign speech, the word "God" was replaced by "Fate," since even at its most iconoclastic television cannot afford to offend anyone.

In spite of the vandalism, however, enough of the frolic and vitriol of the play was left to show why it should have taken audiences by storm in its time, run for well over four hundred performances, and—although competing with Eugene O'Neill's monumental *Mourning Becomes Electra*—received the Pulitzer Prize, which, it will be remembered, was to be given to the play best representing "the educational value and power of the stage." In a historical introduction to *Of Thee I Sing* in *TV Guide*, Brooks Atkinson took pains to stress that the authors were not "political provocateurs" but respectable playwrights who only intended to write a Broadway hit. The reassurance, designed presumably to soothe any fears that Kaufman and Ryskind might have been part of a revolutionary cabal, was meaningless because *Of Thee I Sing was* politically provocative. That it invited audiences to laugh rather than take action didn't change the fact that American politics was about as high minded a profession as pimping for an Amsterdam brothel, and whatever the sentiments of voters in 1972, in 1931 everyone knew it.

It was this truth that gave its edge to *Of Thee I Sing*, and especially during its run in 1932 as the Hoover administration was tottering to a well-deserved grave. Provided that plays were general enough in their indictment and didn't call for too radical a solution, they could avoid being called "only" propaganda and could be seen at their true value, either as good plays on social themes, or poor ones. The next season, that of 1932–33, saw the Pulitzer Prize again given to a political play, this time a deadly serious one, *Both Your Houses*, by Maxwell Anderson. Produced by the Theatre Guild, it concerns a young school teacher from Nevada who goes into politics as a reformer and is outwitted in Washington by tough old hands at the game of graft, conspiracy, and patronage. In his final speech, the hero says, "Who knows what's the best kind of government? Maybe they all get rotten after a while and have to be replaced. . . . It takes about a hundred years to tire this country of trickery—and we're fifty years overdue right now."[42] Even with its Pulitzer the play was only a moderate success; the matinée trade which formed a good part of the Guild's support wanted something a trifle less acid to follow a lunch at Schrafft's.

The Guild was, by then, having other troubles. It had gone through a crisis so severe as almost to disrupt it for good.

After the success of *Porgy*, the Guild had shown a string of European plays, including *Volpone*, the first part of Goethe's *Faust*, Shaw's *Major Barbara*, and a play which foreshadowed the invention of the atom bomb. This was *Wings Over Europe*, by Robert Nichols and Maurice Browne. The former was said to have been the coiner of the phrase "Little Theatre" as a name for experimental and amateur groups. It was a Wellsian fantasy, in which a group of scientists with the unlikely name of The Guild of United Brain-Workers of the World enforce world peace by sending planes containing atom bombs to circle over every capital city. Although one of the authors said that the play was "no more realistic than Mozart's *Don Juan*," he could not know that four decades later reality would catch up with him and that whatever uneasy peace the world had would rest on a very similar threat.

The Guild managed to produce at least one such play, with a political point of view, every year. In 1930, it was *Roar, China*, written by the Soviet dramatist S. M. Tretyakov and originally produced four years before by Meyerhold. It had several distinctions. For one, it was only the second Soviet play shown in America, the first, *Red Rust*, having also been a Guild production, if a studio one. Secondly, it used Chinese actors in the Chinese parts. And finally, it had one of the most powerful sets ever to appear on Broadway.

The play was based on a true incident in which, following the death of a thoroughly unpleasant American trader in a Chinese harbor town, the captain of a British cruiser issued an ultimatum that either the killers be found or two other Chinese be executed in their place, or he would blow the town to bits with his ship's guns. The play was directed by Herbert Biberman, who had done *Red Rust*, and who confided that *Roar, China* was a thrilling piece of theatre but a rotten play. One of the Guild's problems arose over Biberman's appointment. Reuben Mamoulian, who, since his immense success with *Porgy*, had been one of the Guild's directors, demanded to be released from his contract when he was not given the Soviet play. As it was, he escaped one of the major headaches Biberman had to cope with—since many of the Chinese players could speak no English it proved difficult to direct them. In the end, Biberman had to act out everything he wanted done and then have the cast imitate him.

For the setting, Lee Simonson constructed the bows of a battleship which loomed above the action and raised its gun turrets menacingly at the cowering audience in the balcony. Two sampans, floating in tanks of water on either side of the battleship, were towed to or away from the center of the stage, and their large raised sails served in place of a curtain. These, Simonson confessed, were Biberman's idea and they added a great deal to the effectiveness of the set.

Although everyone including the producers agreed that the play was the most blatant sort of propaganda, it won respectful reviews from almost all the critics. "It makes one want to fight oppression," said Richard Lockridge, while John Anderson, calling it "completely engrossing," added that it "surprised the Guild's first-night cucumbers into a veritable ovation." Even Percy Hammond, who disliked it, conceded that "as the world's leading dramatic impresario [the Guild] is interested in whatever happens in the theatre," and that therefore it was providing Broadway with a novel experience, what he called "a lusty and picturesque curio."

The Guild found its way back to American playwrights for the next three plays: Maxwell Anderson's *Elizabeth the Queen, Midnight* by Paul and Claire Sifton, which attacked capital punishment and the power of politics over law, and finally a folk-play by Lynn Riggs called *Green Grow the Lilacs*. Directed by Biberman, and with Franchot Tone in the lead and several professional rodeo riders playing cowboys, it lasted for only 64 performances. One reviewer remarked that it might make a good musical, but his advice wasn't taken until twelve years later when Rodgers and Hammerstein turned it into one and titled it *Oklahoma!*

Green Grow the Lilacs was done in January, 1931. After it, came an elaborate and sentimental anti-war play, *Miracle at Verdun*, by Hans Chlumberg, and then *Getting Married*, by George Bernard Shaw. Although *Elizabeth the Queen* had done reasonably well, the last four plays of the season had totalled only 209 performances among them, a disheartening showing. Before the season had ended, however, the growing tensions in the Guild's Board of Managers had exploded.

The board's members had always exercised supervision over the rehearsals of plays, and had chosen what they thought were works of some theatrical importance—by no means always socially pointed although they had included some of these every year—but usually always with some novel or interesting facet. They had tried to show the works of American playwrights, from relatively obscure ones like George Kaiser to established ones like Maxwell Anderson and S. M. Behrman. They had not been afraid to experiment with costly and complex productions such as *Miracle at Verdun* which, in addition to its many scene changes, used a triple movie screen on which sound films were shown as a counterpoint to the stage action. They had courageously done Shaw plays no one else in America would dare to touch: *Back to Methuselah*, with its fearsome length and verbosity, *Heartbreak House*, which because of its bitter criticism of the First World War aroused some resentment, and *Getting Married*, which was just not very good. They had been O'Neill's producer, since the dwindling of the Provincetown, tackling the ornate *Marco Millions*, the doom-laden *Mourning Becomes Electra*, and *Strange Interlude* with its nine acts running (with an intermission for dinner) from five in the afternoon until eleven. They had even, with another kind of courage, done flimsy comedies like *The Guardsman* and *Caprice* which made a lot of money and won them the contempt of purists. But although they were often attacked, as for instance by Virgil Geddes who said in a letter to the *New York Times* that they were "a commercial organization masquerading under the name of art," they had had the longest life and most consistently good record of any producer in the business. One of the reasons had been the balance of the membership of the Board of Managers. Philip Wertheim and Lawrence Langner were hard-headed businessmen whose major earnings came from outside the Guild but who had been involved in the theatre for more than fifteen years, Theresa Helburn's capabilities as an executive were matched by her theatrical knowledge, Philip Moeller was an imaginative director, Lee Simonson one of the best of scene designers, and

Helen Westley an excellent character actor. Inevitably, however, as time passed, what had been a balance became a division.

Some wrangling had broken out when Wertheim was criticized for not having shown up at supervisory meetings of the board at rehearsals. A little later, Langner complained that Helburn was called "the ruler of the Guild" by the press; a few months later, organizing his own playhouse in Westport, Connecticut, he referred to himself as "the founder of the Theatre Guild," which Simonson said was "invidious, derogatory, and in bad taste."[43] Board meetings began to take on an acrimonious tone verging, occasionally, on downright insults.

In the spring of 1931, Langner made the formal charge that the board had split into two camps. No longer were they a group working together to produce good plays, but three business people and three artists. The artists, said he, had been more concerned with their own careers than with the good of the group; Westley had looked for plays that would give her good parts, Moeller was unable to direct anything but comedy and had alienated some playwrights by trying to rewrite their scripts, and Simonson had kept the Guild from hiring other, equally important set designers like Jo Mielziner or Norman Bel Geddes. Not only had this taken the artistic pleasure out of working for the organization as far as the business people were concerned, it had made for an aesthetic and financial decline, and in fact the past season had shown a shocking deficit.

Soon after, at another board meeting, Wertheim went a step further. Speaking for himself, Langner, and Helburn, he laid down an ultimatum. Either a number of suggested proposals for changes would be adopted, or the Guild would have to disband. There was some parleying that went on for a week or two, and in the end an agreement was reached.

It was settled that a detailed budget should be prepared for a whole season rather than from show to show. A number of economy measures were accepted, including the abolition of percentages paid to board members and, instead, a maximum fee of $100 a week for forty weeks to be paid each member for attending meetings and rehearsals, when called upon, and for play reading. For each play a production committee of two would be chosen; for *Mourning Becomes Electra*, in the fall, they were Helburn and

Wertheim, and in future plays the so-called business members were involved even more deeply—Langner directed the successful Molière play, *School for Husbands,* and Helburn the even more profitable production of Anderson's *Mary of Scotland.* Simonson said stiffly that he had no managerial ability and so wouldn't serve on such a committee. Furthermore, he withdrew from designing Guild shows for the following year, during which time settings were designed by Aline Bernstein and Robert Edmond Jones, among others. Even after he returned, the sets for a good many plays were done by outsiders. Theresa Helburn resigned as Executive Director and that post, now separated from the functions of the board, was given to Cheryl Crawford until she left to throw in her lot with the Group Theatre.

Other points were that no further advance commitments would be made to members of the board for scenic or production work, and that at board meetings, "members were to conduct themselves in parliamentary and gentlemanly fashion, as freedom of discussion does not involve the use of offensive and insulting language."[44]

The Guild had survived, but some of the scars were permanent. Things had been said which could not easily be forgotten. The organization suffered some other blows which, had the board been united, might have been averted. The Lunts, who had been increasingly restless, refused to sign a new contract and left to join with Noel Coward in independent productions. The Group Theatre's separation drew away a number of other talented people. Yet the Guild, licking its wounds, finished its next season in the spring of 1932 with a profit, and was to go on to some even more spectacular successes.

Langner's charge that Moeller had alienated some playwrights may have contained a measure of truth. In 1932, Philip Barry and Elmer Rice, both of whom had satisfactory Guild associations in the past, now had hits on Broadway neither of which had first been offered to the Guild. However, O'Neill and Anderson remained fairly faithful. Both had their ups and downs, but for the Guild's audiences their successes seem to have been their more conservative works. O'Neill's *Ah, Wilderness!* with George M. Cohan in the lead, played for 289 performances; *Days Without End,* an odd theological allegory in which the main character was a sort of

Catholic Jekyll and Hyde, had only 57. Anderson's *Mary of Scotland* ran for 248 performances. *Elizabeth the Queen* had been the only Guild play in the bad season of 1930–31 to make money, but not even the Pulitzer Prize could pull *Both Your Houses* more than a tiny way over the hundred–performance–mark.

Both Your Houses had been one of those equivocal successes to which the Guild was accustomed. Yet there was an audience slowly growing, quite apart from the regular theatre-goers, which would support strongly social-conscious plays; indeed, the stronger the better. For this audience, *Both Your Houses* was too mild a dish. But producers like the Guild could not, or would not, take advantage of its existence. Clurman had noted the new audience when *1931—* was done and the Group Theatre's leadership had shied away from it even while a good part of the company was going out to meet it on their own. When *Roar, China* was produced the Guild had been approached by the radical Yiddish newspaper, *Die Freiheit*, which offered to fill houses for at least thirty performances if it was given special subscription rates; but the board recoiled in horror because "they felt they could not permit themselves to offer one of their attractions solely for propaganda purposes,"[45] although the play was an admitted piece of propaganda by a Soviet playwright—or maybe because of that. There now emerged a producing organization which would rely precisely on this audience. Its problem was going to be that common to all left-wing theatres, to find scripts, and consequently its history begins properly not with its founders but with a pair of playwrights.

George Sklar and Albert Maltz were fellow students at Yale Drama School. Professor George Pierce Baker had by then transferred his famous playwriting class, the 47 Workshop, from Harvard to Yale, and both men were members although in different sessions. Sklar, round-shouldered, round-headed, with a wide, humorous mouth, was in his third year; Maltz, pale, thin, and intellectual looking, was in his second. Their friendship, at first casual, grew stronger as towards the end of that sombre year, 1931, they found themselves more and more in agreement politically and aesthetically. Both wanted to write, but Sklar, aiming for his master's degree, planned to support himself by teaching.

He was working in the library late one afternoon, and Maltz

came to meet him there as they were going to dine together. While waiting, Maltz picked up a copy of a magazine and skimmed through it. His eye was caught by a story about an unemployed man in Cleveland who had inadvertently witnessed a gang murder, and had been locked up by the police as a material witness. However, the gangsters had ties with the city administration, and ultimately the man was found hanging in his cell, an apparent suicide, a not unusual end then or later for an inconvenient witness. When Sklar came out, Maltz excitedly told him the story. They talked all through dinner and late into the night, and when they separated they had the outline for a play. They changed the locale to a city recognizable as New York, where the insouciant Jimmy Walker was mayor and his administration seethed with corruption like an overripe Gorgonzola; they made their protagonist, the victimized witness, a bellhop in a curious echo of *Appearances*, although neither had ever heard of the Garland Anderson play.

During the winter, illness in the family caused Maltz to leave school, but he did a first draft of the play, sending it piece by piece to Sklar. They got together again in February, wrestled the thing into final shape, and titled it *Merry-go-Round*. Sklar showed it to Professor Baker, who read it to the Workshop. When he had finished, he did something unprecedented. "This," he said, "will be our next major production." That was enough encouragement for the collaborators, who promptly sent it off to an agent in New York. Several producers saw it but felt it presented certain difficulties. However, it came into the hands of a trio who shortly before had done a play on an equally touchy theme. They were Shepard Traube, Sidney Harmon, and Walter Hart, and the play, *Precedent*, by I. J. Golden, had been based on the Tom Mooney case, in which a labor organizer had been railroaded to life imprisonment on a framed bomb charge. *Precedent* had been unveiled in the old Provincetown Playhouse and its surprisingly good reviews had kept it there for 184 performances. The producers felt they could take the same chance with *Merry-go-Round*.

The play opened in April 1932 to very good notices, and almost at once offers began to come from uptown producers to move it into a Broadway theatre. Sklar and Maltz were overjoyed, and began trying to decide which one to take. In the two or three days during which they thought things over, they were visited by a man who, without coming right out and saying so, hinted that they might do better to ignore all the offers or they'd be in for trouble. They showed him the door.

"We were naive," Sklar says. "I was twenty-two and Albert twenty-one. We began going down the list of offers. Every one of them said they'd changed their minds." Finally, however, they got to an independent producer who had either not been affected by threats or was just plain stubborn. They had the scenery rebuilt and Hart re-staged the show for the larger theatre, the Avon. Traube and Harmon had dropped out and were replaced by Michael Blankfort, who borrowed his wife's dowry to help back the play. They moved uptown, and on opening night, with the lobby crowded and a line at the box office, the police arrived. The Fire Department license, they explained, had not been renewed, and they padlocked the house.

For the next week the battle to open the show went on. Blankfort and Hart pointed out in a public statement that about a hundred other theatres were operating without up-to-date licenses including the one next door to the Avon. The technicality was that there was always a lag between the official date of renewal and the time the license actually arrived, but this had never bothered anyone before. Mayor Walker, in response to an editorial in the *New York Times,* insisted that he had nothing to do with stopping the opening, that the whole thing was a publicity stunt, and that in fact he knew nothing about the show although, "My friends," he grinned, "tell me it's rotten." The newspapers picked up the case and so did the American Civil Liberties Union, the Dramatists Guild, and the Producers Association, and so great was the uproar that on May 10th the license was renewed—although it cost the owner several thousand dollars to make wholly unnecessary changes in the orchestra pit—and the play at last opened. It ran to the end of June and then the onset of hot weather (there was no air conditioning in those days) and the slump in attendance closed it.

Meanwhile, it had sold to the movies, and Sklar and Maltz were offered jobs as writers in Hollywood. Shortly before they left for the Coast, Sklar was in his agent's office when a man named Charles Walker came in. When he was introduced to Sklar, he cried, "You're the fellow I've been trying to find!" He dragged the playwright downstairs and into the Astor, and there, over drinks, explained.

He and a group of friends were planning a new producing company, to be called the Theatre Union. They included few professionals, but they were all enthusiastic amateurs in the true sense of lovers of the theatre: Walker and his wife, Adelaide, Liston Oak, Margaret Larkin, a writer named Paul Peters, an actress, Sylvia Feningston, who had played a bit part in the first Group Theatre play, a broker who used the name Manuel Gomez to keep his identity as a radical separate from his Wall Street personality, and one or two more. Their aim was already crystallizing in a program from which they never deviated, "To produce plays that have meaning for and bearing on the struggles and conflicts of our time." Some time later, Paul Peters was to make some of the details more exact: "To produce plays that reflect the lives and discuss the problems of the majority of Americans—the working people; to produce on a professional scale but at low prices—30¢ to $1.50 with half the house priced under a dollar; and to organize its potential audience, which includes regular playgoers as well as thousands of people who cannot afford and do not patronize the Broadway theatre." They had, as yet, not gone far beyond the talking stage, but they already knew that the right plays would be hard to find. They had been impressed by *Merry-go-Round* and they wanted to know whether Sklar and Maltz had any other scripts up their sleeves. Sklar said that they'd think it over, and promised to keep in touch.

The partners soon found that they were not really suited to the high-pressure commercialism of Hollywood. They had little success with their first assignment, a film script of a Dashiell Hammett mystery, and by the time the option had expired on their three-months' contract they were spending most of their time talking over an idea they had for another play. At this juncture, Sklar got a letter from Charles Walker. Some backers had appeared, among them John Henry Hammond, Jr., heir to the Hammond Organ fortune and a man of considerable nerve as well as taste. It now looked as though the Theatre Union might be a real possibility, and Walker asked the team to return to New York to be part of it. They needed no further urging.

Back in the East, they applied themselves to their play. It had begun with a situation Maltz had long had in mind, a man standing before a judge who says to him, "You've been found innocent of any crime and I therefore sentence you to be hanged." Working towards a scene which would embody this germ, they wrote a scathing play against war in which a liberal university professor is drawn into protesting against the suppression of free speech when longshoremen refuse to handle munitions, and in the end is executed for a crime he could not possibly have committed. The essential plot was no novelty; the theme of the innocent man being railroaded for political reasons had been used in *Precedent* and *Merry-go-Round,* and indeed life itself had copied it during many of the labor troubles of the Twenties. But up to then, very few plays had struck sharply at the political and economic roots of war. They had been concerned with the camaraderie of men under fire, as in *What Price Glory* and *Journey's End,* fantastical as in *The International,* or vague and generalized as in *Wings Over Europe* and *Miracle at Verdun. Peace on Earth,* as Sklar and Maltz titled their play, pulled no punches. It made no bones about the profit motive as a cause of war, and its only departure from realism came during the last act when, with a touch of expressionism, a series of swift scenes portrayed the thoughts flashing through the hero's brain before his execution.

The play was ready by the end of the summer of 1933. It was read to the Theatre Union's executive board which had expanded to include Hammond, Joseph Freeman, Mary Fox, Michael Blankfort, Tom Tippett, and Sam Friedman, as well as an advisory board which contained such distinguished members as Rose McClendon, Sherwood Anderson, Paul Muni, John Dos Passos, Elmer Rice, Edmund Wilson, Morrie Ryskind, Roger Baldwin, and Steven Vincent Benet. Not only was the play at once accepted as the group's first production, but Sklar and Maltz were elected to the executive board.

The Theatre Union wanted to form a permanent acting company like that of the Group Theatre, but money was too short. They hoped, too, to be able to go away for a summer of work as the Group did, and even got as far as finding an abandoned girls' school in West Virginia, but had to give that up, too, for lack of finances. The executive committee appealed to well-wishers for donations to supplement the original backing, and small amounts began coming in. They were lucky enough to find just the house they wanted. Eva Le Gallienne's Civic Repertory company had had to disband, and her theatre on West 14th Street was vacant. They rented the four walls for a miniscule sum. Its dressing rooms were cramped and dirty, its wardrobe was still crowded with the dusty costumes from *Alice in Wonderland*, but it had a good stage, good sight lines, and good acoustics. It was a long way from the fashionable theatre district being a memento of the days when 14th Street had been nearer the center of things, but the Theatre Union intended to create such a stir that the Broadway theatre-goers would come down to them. In any case, that wasn't what they thought of as their primary audience.

Peace on Earth required a cast of forty, and the board had hoped to use half professionals and half eager amateurs from the workers' theatre movement. Equity put its foot down; the entire cast would have to be professional. This meant that "if the Theatre Union was determined to put on a thoroughly competent performance, it would have to fill some roles with actors chosen solely for their ability,"[46] as one left-wing reporter rather naively put it. In blunter terms, they would have to forego using only people who were committed politically to the Left. However, plenty of actors turned up for auditions, and although a few of them muttered that the play had too many speeches smacking of soap-box oratory, they were soon drawn into the spirit of the thing, and some of them, it was reported, began to read the radical press and to take part in political discussions backstage.

Sklar and Maltz had hoped to get Walter Hart as the director, remembering the fine job he had done on *Merry-go-Round*, but when he read the play he didn't like it. They went, next, to George Kaufman to ask for advice, and he suggested his assistant Robert Sinclair, who leaped at the chance, never having done a full-length professional play before. There was an ironic epilogue. One reason Hart had not been keen to do the job was that Sidney Howard had been considering him to direct *Dodsworth*. Howard came to the opening of *Peace on Earth* and was so struck by Sinclair's work that he finally chose him instead.

The play opened on November 29, 1933, to a capacity house, and when the curtain came down to cheers the authors felt certain they had a hit. The reviews next day changed their minds. Most of the critics found it too admonitory for their taste, and Gilbert Gabriel, often receptive to left-wing plays, observed that far from college professors' being thrown out of work for their socialistic views, they were "being invited to Washington to advise the President," a dig at Roosevelt's "Brain Trust." Even Joseph Wood Krutch, writing in the liberal *Nation*, found it a "plodding exposition of the commonplaces about war and its causes to which we have been treated many times before," although in fact only one play in the past two decades had dealt seriously with the subject —*Spread Eagle*, by George Brooks and Walter Lister, which had been produced by Jed Harris in 1927.*

After the opening [Albert Maltz recalls], George and I got a fascinating lesson in the power of organization. We had an emergency meeting of the executive board Thanksgiving morning and made certain decisions, and then most of the people went off home for Thanksgiving dinner. George and I were both bachelors, and we went around to a cafeteria on 14th Street and had our dinner off a tray, feeling gloomy and certain that the play was going to close. But on the board were people with trade union experience and they had lots of ideas—running leaflets and stuffing mailboxes, sending speakers to unions and other organizations. And after a while, by God, the play began to break even.

The Theatre Union had begun to make its first serious effort to tap the audience they felt sure was ready to support not only this play but the future work of the group. Their speakers—who included the harrassed playwrights—went from end to end of the city reading bits of the play and trying to sell batches of tickets. Once the campaign had gathered momentum, the house was

*It is worth noting that *Spread Eagle*, which concerned a millionaire Wall Street speculator who pushes America into war with Mexico for his own profit, contained some other interesting anticipations. Long before both *Miracle at Verdun* and *Of Thee I Sing* it supplemented the action onstage with film clips. Like another, later, Jed Harris hit, *The Front Page*, it had a final line which relied on profanity for its punch. It was also another of those plays which rested on a political frame-up. Few critics labelled it propaganda; most of them approved of it, and even Alexander Woollcott found nothing to complain of in it, which may be an indication of how woolly its point of view really was.

never empty. Word of mouth helped. One old woman from Coney Island ordered a block of seats every Friday night and brought a different group of friends with her each time. "It was ten weeks before the first taxicab drew up in front of the theatre with the carriage trade," says Maltz, "but then more and more people from uptown came to see it." In the end it ran sixteen weeks.

There had already been some discussions about the second production and Charles Walker had long had his eye on a play called *Wharf Nigger,* by the Kentucky writer, Paul Peters. It had been written in 1928 but had not been seen until the fall of 1931, when it was very briefly unveiled at the Provincetown Playhouse. It had certain structural defects, and Walker finally asked Sklar, who was known as a good technician, if he'd be willing to work with Peters and get the play into shape. Sklar agreed at once.

The collaboration was a smooth one and work went quickly, although they hammered out every line together and felt they had to make every word count. By February, the script was ready and retitled *Stevedore;* Peters had grown more politically aware since first writing it, and he and Sklar would not have a title with the word "nigger" in it. In its final version, it dealt with a black dock worker in New Orleans who is arrested on a false charge of raping a white woman, chiefly because he is trying to organize a stevedore's union but also because he is militantly opposed to white domination. Escaping from the law, he rallies the black neighborhood to barricade a street and fight off a white mob intent on burning down the ghetto. He is shot, but white workers come to the help of the blacks in a stirring final scene which more than one reviewer was to compare to the arrival in the nick of time of the U.S. Marines. This was pretty strong stuff, since it not only attacked Southern lynch law and made a plea for black equality, but affirmed the hitherto unpopular principle of black and white unity in the labor movement.

So powerful was it that when the black members of the cast were chosen—and they included some of the finest Negro actors in the profession, among them Rex Ingram, Leigh Whipper, Georgette Harvey, Edna Thomas, and Jack Carter, as well as some members of the famous Hall Johnson choir—there was head-shaking among the more conservative ones over some of the blazing speeches. There were, however, compensations for them. They found, for one thing, that there was no discrimination backstage at all; they and the white actors got the same pay, shared the same dressing rooms and were treated with utter equality by the director and the production committee as well as the executive board. What was even more to the point, there was no discrimination on the other side of the curtain, for the Theatre Union, from its very first night, sat Negroes everywhere in the theatre—they and the Group Theatre were the only professional theatres which did so and which ultimately changed the policy of seating blacks only in the balcony, if at all. By contrast, it is interesting to examine a play about black people which opened four years earlier to universal acclaim and which won the 1930 Pulitzer Prize, *The Green Pastures*, by Marc Connelly. America's equivocal attitude toward its black population was clearly shown in this Uncle Remus version of the Bible. It was hailed as a great piece of American folk-lore: "Once or twice in the lifetime of every playgoer there occurs an adventure such as that of the first performance of *The Green Pastures*," said Burns Mantle, adding that it demanded "a knowledge of and a kindly sympathy for the Southern Negro and his trusting and childlike religious faith."[47] Richard B. Harrison, who played God, and for forty years had tried to improve the speech of students in black colleges, had to be coached to speak Negro dialect and needed to have his brown skin darkened with makeup. The black cast was paid less than scale, and on tour had to stay in the shabbiest rooming houses and eat at hamburger stands, when they could find any that would serve blacks. In Washington, the play opened at the National Theatre which did not admit Negroes. The theatre was picketed by protesters, as indeed many others had been across the country, and the cast talked of going on strike; but Harrison refused to do so and the curtain rose after all. The cast was too professional to show its bitterness and the Washington reviews were as benign as all the rest. For all the swooning plaudits, it is doubtful if *The Green Pastures* could be shown today without being shot down in flames, whereas by contrast *Stevedore*, although slightly old-fashioned, would stand up fairly well.

For *Stevedore*, the Theatre Union made a doubly determined effort. "After *Peace on Earth*," Sklar says, "we knew we either had to close up shop or make a hell of a fight. The latter meant we had to get enough money to pay for the house for a few weeks until enough people saw the show and spread the word." They began with a reading of the script to the heads of the 158 organizations which had helped to keep *Peace on Earth* running, and offered them tickets at half price which could be resold to their members at full price—and it must be remembered that half the seats in the house were priced at less than a dollar. At those rates the peace groups, the unions, the radical political parties, the political and cultural organizations, the fraternal clubs began buying blocks of tickets, some only twenty-five or thirty, the bolder ones half the house or the entire theatre. Sometimes they used their attendance for fund-raising, benefits, say, for the *New Masses* or the National Student League; mostly, they were theatre parties which gave an opportunity to people, some of whom had never before seen a live play, to go to the theatre with their friends. By opening night, *Stevedore* had six solid weeks of performance guaranteed to it without worrying about what the reviewers said.

However, in the main the reviewers had much that was complimantary to say. Percy Hammond wrote candidly, "Being myself a white man and a capitalist, I ought to resent *Stevedore*. . . . But [the authors] write so theatrically and with such fascinating violence about wrongs and rectifications that I am lost in admiration of their showmanship." "Not for many a theatre-going moon has such vitality come into our showshop," said Robert Garland. Everyone was swept up by the lustiness of the acting and by the fact that the cast seemed to be enjoying themselves to the hilt. Several critics betrayed a blissfully unconscious racial bias. John Mason Brown, for instance, complained that the playwrights didn't "play the game fairly" because they overemphasized the racial antagonisms, but in the same breath he described the Negro dockers as "black bucks." Another reviewer affirmed that he had seen no stevedores in the audience but only "well-dressed colored people," clearly expecting them to arrive in overalls. What was most striking, however, was the behavior of the audience. Both blacks and whites roared their approval of the play's tough language and booed and jeered the villains. It had been the same with *Peace on Earth*—some of the actors had noted that the very speeches they had called "soap box" were most loudly cheered—and it was to be the pattern for most of the Theatre Union's productions, but for the black watchers *Stevedore* spoke most unequivocally. It was not simply the naiveté of those unaccustomed to live theatre which brought so enthusiastic a response, but the fact that actors, director, producers, playwrights had joined to give voice to exactly what this audience wanted to hear, as no one else on the professional stage was doing. One woman, part of a group of twenty-eight Negroes who hired a truck so that they could make the trip from Philadelphia, said, "I'd have walked to New York to see that play." The most dramatic manifestation of involvement came one night when, during the final scene in which the white unionists came pouring in to help the beleaguered blacks, a man jumped up from the second row of the orchestra and leaped on stage to join in the fracas, yelling, "Let's get 'em!" The curtain came down and when it rose again for bows, the actors were embracing him and slapping him on the back. They introduced him to the audience; he was the celebrated dancer, Bill "Bojangles" Robinson.

He was not the only celebrity to show an uncharacteristic support for the play and what it stood for. In an interview with Emanuel Eisenberg, Groucho Marx, noting that the situation was too desperate for wisecracks, said, "Look at that whole business down South. The Negroes have been submitting passively to abuse for almost a hundred years. Fighting is the only thing that can change the situation; fight and protest." And of *Stevedore*, he added, "It's without question the best propaganda play I've seen in my whole life."[48]

Stevedore ran for twenty-three weeks. Even the most carping critics had to agree with Robert Garland that with its production "the Theatre Union arrives quite definitely as a producing organization with which to reckon."

Not that all their problems were solved by any means. Money was always to be a major difficulty, for they refused to raise the prices of their seats. They were proud of the fact that many of those who came to see their shows didn't even know the word "play"—Maltz reports hearing people come out of the theatre saying, "Gee, that was a great picture, wasn't it?" Some of the audience paid nothing at all for their places, for at every performance there was a curtain speech during intermission asking for contributions to pay for the unemployed, and whether any money came in or not, a certain number of tickets was always handed over to the Unemployed Councils for distribution. They kept their expenses as low as they could, paying the flat Equity minimum of $40 to everyone involved with a play whether they were established Broadway names or unknown bit players. The only exceptions were the stagehands, whose union never gave way to anyone on questions of scale. The company also tried a profit-sharing scheme, by which half the profits of a play were to be shared among the actors and production staff as a bonus, the other half to go into future productions. The only trouble was that there was almost never anything that could justly be called a profit.

One of the problems lay in the composition of the executive board. It combined a nice balance of left-wing opinion—some were Socialists, some Communists, and some liberals with no official adherence to any party—and this was one of its strengths. It could draw on a wide spectrum of support, and when it chose plays could do those which had a more general than sectarian appeal. On the other hand, as Maltz put it, the board contained "no brilliantly innovative mind like, say, Orson Welles." There were talented people, but few with theatrical experience to match the leadership of the Theatre Guild or the Group Theatre. This was to prove a serious shortcoming as well as a source of dissension in years to come.

Another problem, never to be satisfactorily solved, was the finding of suitable plays. Paul Peters said that there was "a famine of scripts," and that while many good ones were read by the overworked executive board, there were few suitable for an audience composed mainly of working people. One which was debated at some length, and finally chosen for the third production, was *Sailors of Catarro*, by Friedrich Wolf. The uncertainty stemmed mainly from the question whether the Theatre Union should do a foreign play so early in its career, but in the end it was felt that its dramatic force was great enough to justify the attempt.

Wolf had been a doctor in Germany in the Twenties, and had written plays on revolutionary themes in his spare time. His third, *Cynkali*, advocated legal abortion, and in 1931 he was arrested and charged with practicing abortion himself, the only evidence offered being the manuscript of the play. The following year, he began touring Germany with an agit-prop troupe for which he wrote pieces, but in 1933, when Hitler came to power, Wolf, a Jew as well as a radical, fled to France. *Sailors of Catarro* (pronounced Cát-arro) was his fourth play. It told the story of a mutiny on an Austrian battleship anchored in the Adriatic harbor of Catarro towards the end of the First World War. At first successful, the sailors are weakened by contention, and eventually the rising collapses and its leaders are led off to execution. The English translation had been made by the poet Keene Wallis, who had given it to Paul Peters when the Theatre Union was first organized. It was not until they showed some interest in it that Wallis realized he had never secured Wolf's permission to make the translation. After some frantic letters and cables he unearthed Wolf in France and got his approval, but by that time the Theatre Union was busy with other plans. When they decided, in the summer of 1934, to do *Sailors of Catarro* and wanted to tell Wallis so, *they* couldn't find *him*. He turned up at last in Washington, gave his agreement, and because there were some shaky sections in the script Michael Blankfort was chosen to make a playable adaptation.

Another Yale Drama School graduate, Michael Gordon (then known as Irving Gordon) was selected as director. He had known Sklar and had worked on the Drama School's production of *Merry-go-Round*. After graduation, he had made a few appearances on the stage and had come to the Theatre Union in the summer of 1933 to run the office for ten dollars a week while everyone else was away. He had had good technical backstage training at Yale, although his aim was to be a director, and he had been assistant stage manager for *Peace on Earth*, and stage manager and assistant director for *Stevedore*. He plunged into *Sailors of Catarro* with zest.

To begin with, the play as originally written was not divided into acts, and since it seemed to fall into two parts—the success of the mutiny and then its dissolution—he decided to divide it into two acts, a rather bold innovation then. He also felt that the play ended weakly, when the ringleaders were hauled away to be executed, and he devised a piece of business which gave it a more positive quality; the flag of the rising has been torn down, and one of the sailors scoops it up and hides it under his blouse, repeating an earlier line, "Next time, better." Gordon also had to determine how to present the various scenes played in different parts of a battleship, without losing the unity and pace of the play. In conferences with Mordecai Gorelik, the designer, he suggested that each scene be designed separately so as to see what its requirements were, and then the whole thing be integrated into a single design. The result was one of Gorelik's best constructivist settings, flexible, dramatic, and conveying the sense of a naval vessel without being at all realistic. "No battleship ever looked like this," Gorelik said, and Gordon replied, gently, "But Max, it doesn't have to go on the water."

The cast contained many players often employed by the Theatre Union—as close as they ever came to a permanent company—Howard da Silva, George Tobias, Martin Wolfson, John Boruff, and Abner Biberman, among others. About a week before the opening, John Lytell, who played the lead, fell ill with pneumonia and was replaced by Tom Powers. As a result the first couple of performances were a bit ragged when it opened in December 1934. Notwithstanding, most of the critics applauded it. Burns Mantle noted that there was "a professional quality in the staging . . . the Theatre Union has not previously attained." Although the words "soap box" and "propaganda" still appeared here and there, a note of admiring sympathy was detectable in the voice of more than one reviewer, as if they were growing used to revolutionary sentiments. Indeed, Richard Lockridge of the *Sun* pointed out that there were two plays about revolution showing at the same time, *Sailors of Catarro* and Maxwell Anderson's *Valley Forge,* and that George Washington and Franz Rasch (leader of the sailors) were "a couple of heroes" in a theatrical "era of Mr. Milquetoast."* "Even our best plays," said he, "vide *The Children's Hour* end with the central characters hiding their heads under the bedclothes," whereas these two had "excitement . . . the stir of the heroic."

The atmosphere was slowly but certainly changing. "After *Stevedore,* the social play became acceptable," Sklar puts it. "It wasn't new, God knows; the critics had forgotten their history—Shaw, Ibsen, Molière, and so on. I think we made them realize that we were within a long-standing and great tradition."

*Caspar Milquetoast, the Timid Soul, was the invention of cartoonist H.T. Webster, and became a synonym for meekness.

It was put another, blunter way by Richard Gaines in a long article in the *New York Times* analyzing the state of the theatre. "[There] are two motes in the air—and only two: the Theatre Union and the Group Theatre. They are on the right track," he said. As for the rest of the theatrical world: "By and large, still in the saddle is old Brother Mammon."[49]

1933-1935

At the beginning of 1933, a play opened on Broadway which in one great gulp tried to encompass everything that had been wrong in America up to then. In twenty scenes it dealt with false patriotism, unemployment, the treatment of minorities, the greed of big business, graft in high places, a strike, industrial violence, and the perversion of justice. Its tone was that of earnest, liberal protest, like *Precedent, Merry-go-Round, 1931—*, and its roots were in the early expressionist panoramas of the American scene—*Processional*, for instance, or *The Adding Machine*. It was called, *We, the People*, and its author was the early expressionist and earnest liberal, Elmer Rice. At its end, the protagonist says, "It is our house, this America. Let us cleanse it and put in order, and make it a decent place for decent people to live in!" [50] The customers who paid $3.30 a seat didn't care much for its cautionary tone and it was a failure. But the closing sentiments exactly reflected those of the country and of its new president, Franklin Delano Roosevelt, who was to take office in March.

He had been swept in on a wave of desperation, and he proceeded to clean house with measures that were as radical as they were energetic. Within the first three months of his administration he had pushed through Congress new banking regulations, the National Industrial Recovery Act for industrial reform including the relations between management and labor, the Agricultural Adjustment Act which controlled farm prices and crop surpluses, the Unemployment Relief Act which also set up the Civilian Conservation Corps providing forestry and farm jobs for young men, the Public Works Administration which gave work to thousands in the construction of buildings, highways, bridges and the like, the Tennessee Valley Authority to bring electricity from government power plants to one of the nation's most backward regions, and dozens of other reforms designed to restore the health of the economy. He instituted the policy, which other presidents were to follow, of bringing specialists in economics, finance, and other fields to Washington as advisers—the so-called "Brain Trust," which replaced the fumbling of political hacks. He wanted, he said, to give America a New Deal, and the phrase became the earmark of his administration along with the cloud of initials it raised representing all those bustling agencies which had been created—NRA, AAA, PWA, TVA, CCC, and the like. He was a man who had conquered the ravages of polio in himself and he became the symbol of courage for a sick country. He frightened the wits out of the Right, which saw him dragging the nation into Socialism—"That Man in the White House," they called him—and of the Left which saw him as a kind of quack whose nostrums would keep workingmen away from the surgery of revolution. Nevertheless, the feeling of hopefulness, of fresh beginnings, brought renewed vitality everywhere.

That vitality was reflected in an upsurge of activity in the workers' theatre movement. It can be seen most clearly in the development of the magazine, *Workers Theatre.*

The magazine, it will be remembered, had been taken over by the League of Workers Theatres as its official organ in the spring of 1933. During the summer, the national executive committee made some important changes which illustrate how their base, as well as their outlook, was broadening. They expanded the magazine to deal with everything that went on in the theatre, not simply the workers' theatre groups but art theatres, the Little Theatres, the dance, music, film, and Broadway. To express this wider viewpoint, they changed the name of the magazine to *New Theatre.* They pointed out that the members of the League had all been much too narrow in their plays, and repeated what had been said in the past by people like Saxe and Elion, that they were going to have to break down the cliché of form in which, as one of them put it, "In the first act we suffer, in the second we pass out leaflets, and in the third we go on strike." They insisted that workers' theatres must give up writing and producing plays "which indulge in mere name calling and crude caricaturing of, for instance, Norman Thomas and the Socialist Party, and the individuals who lead the A.F. of L." By degrees, all the political groups of the Left were uniting on more general platforms of action, and these were the first steps. They were reflected soon after in the composition of the Theatre Union's leadership.

The first issue under the new name appeared in October, 1933, but its real bow was made in January, 1934, when it came out as a professionally printed magazine with an austere cover, and an editorial board headed by Ben Blake, with Leon Bloch as managing editor, and a long list of contributing editors, among whom were Em Jo Basshe, Michael Blankfort, Hallie Flanagan, Mordecai Gorelik, Steven Karnot, Al Saxe, Lee Strasberg, John Howard Lawson, and John Bonn. It still cost ten cents and carried no major advertising. It sold a little over a thousand copies. Twelve months later, it could celebrate Christmas by announcing that its circulation had grown to ten thousand. Coincidentally, that was the size of the subscription list of its only real rival, *Theatre Arts Monthly*. It is interesting to compare the two.

Theatre Arts, at first a quarterly, had been launched under the aegis of the Theatre Committee of the Society of Arts and Crafts, in Detroit, in 1916, with Sheldon Cheney as editor. It was in its way a revolutionary organ, the voice of "the progressive group," as Cheney put it, "to hasten the day when the speculators will step out of the established playhouse and let the artists come in."[51] It spoke for the Little Theatres and the few experimentalists, and in its first year it contained articles on "The Dance as an Art Form," "Artificial Lighting for Out of Doors," the scenic art of Robert Edmond Jones, and "Acting and the New Stagecraft" by Walter Eaton, who was later to be the Theatre Guild's biographer. It contained what was perhaps the first appraisal of the Moscow Art Theatre to reach America, by N. Ostrovsky, and a long piece by Zona Gale, "The Colored Players and Their Plays," which considered three one-acters by Ridgely Torrence, the first serious plays about blacks acted by blacks to appear on Broadway. Torrence himself was white, and so were the producer, Mrs. Emilie Hapgood, and the scenic designer, Robert Edmond Jones, but it was "magnificent," said Miss Gale, to "interpret to the public—and perhaps to itself—a race never yet understood, in a land which is not of its own choosing."[52]

By January, 1934, *Theatre Arts* was a monthly which had more or less resigned itself to the fact that the speculators were never going to leave the established playhouse. Its editor since 1919 had been the handsome and indefatigable Edith Isaacs, with Stark Young as associate editor and Ashley Dukes as English editor. It was clad in the familiar yellow and black cover, and sold for half a dollar. The Little Theatres were dying by then, but it still spoke for experimentalism and progress; its voice was moderate, and it contained the best theatrical photographs to be seen anywhere. It had the air of a spirited dowager, concerned and liberal-minded, but a little above taking sides.

For instance, it contained a piece on collective bargaining which described the pressure of theatrical unions against producers for higher wages and greater security. In a prefatory note, the editor held that the magazine ought to stand free of both groups "and bring all of the antagonisms into the open, to show how silly and unsound they are."[53] One can hear the patrician intonation. And indeed, the article, by Morton Eustis, seems to weight the dice against the abuses and high costs brought by the unions contrasted with the risks of being a producer. There is a report by Ashley Dukes on the theatrical scene in Nazi Germany which, with British phlegm, notes that things are much quieter in Berlin now that the political factions have all disappeared. The management of the German stage has changed, says Dukes, adding, "The disappearance of the Reinhardt direction . . . is frankly no great disaster. . . . With him went a number of Jewish producing managers of no artistic consequence, and a handful of young directors of talent." The tone seems to imply that the factions and the Jewish producers have all just disappeared round the corner for a quiet drink. There is an article on radio drama warning of the rise and power of the advertising agencies, a roster of new faces on Broadway including a promising girl named Katherine Hepburn, an article on whirling dervishes reminiscent of the *National Geographic,* some book reviews, correspondence, Mrs. Isaacs's own "Broadway in Review" column, and a lead editorial rejoicing that a recent ruling has freed the Little Theatres from the professional obligations of the Legitimate Theatre Code Authority.

By contrast, the January issue of *New Theatre* is raucous, opinionated, and so dynamic that sometimes both spelling and grammar fly to the winds. "We are Everyman," cries the lead editorial. "Our seal of approval and our roar of censure shall mark the fate of the future American drama. . . . We, as audience, are ready to stand or fall on the incontrovertable [sic] principle that we are part of the production." Other editorials describe the moribundity of the Parisian theatre, and the Hitler Blight: "The Berlin theatre, once the most vital in Europe is empty . . . such complete emasculation of the forces of production of any art has rarely been seen."[54] There is an interview with Kurt Jooss, whose ballet company had been enthralling New York with *The Green Table*, an anti-war satire. The interviewer, Edith Segal, herself director of a group called The Red Dancers, asks such questions as, "Are you a pacifist?" and points out that *The Green Table* is "ineffective as a means of fighting war because it does not show the direction for one to take." There is a discussion on "Scenery: The Visual Machine" by Mordecai Gorelik, written with his customary trenchancy and describing how a Theatre of Action can set its stage using only chairs or platforms or even handy lampposts. Many pieces are couched as reports, a characteristic of *New Theatre* magazine which endows it with a quality at once naive and businesslike: a report on classes to be given by the Film and Photo League, a report of a dance group formed by the cultural department of the Needle Trades Workers Industrial Union, a report on the National Theatre Festival of the League of Workers Theatres to be given in Chicago, in April, and a report on the international scene—not the Comédie Française or the Old Vic by any means, but the entries in the Olympiad of Workers Theatres held in Moscow. There was, too, a continuation of the answers to a questionnaire which had been sent to a number of theatre people under the title, "Prospects for the American Theatre," the first part of which had appeared in October of the preceding year. It eventually spanned four issues of the magazine. The questions were loaded, but there was something disarmingly ingenuous about them: "Do you believe that the American theatre will recover from its present decline? Why?" "Do you believe that the workers' theatre holds any promise for the future of the theatre in America?" "To what do you attribute the tremendous vitality of the Soviet theatre?" To the last, Lee Simonson replied tartly, "To the fact that it was a tremendously vital theatre before the Soviets." As might be expected, those who were already committed to the socially-conscious theatre, people like Paul Green, George Sklar, John Howard Lawson, Liston Oak of the Theatre Union's board, Claire and Paul Sifton, and Mordecai Gorelik, naturally felt that the workers' theatre held the greatest promise of expansion and vigor. What was striking was the sympathetic reaction of those who were not so directly involved, men like Hiram Motherwell, Alfred Harding, Sidney Howard, and Equity president Frank Gilmore. Even more to the point, many on both sides of the fence stressed that good theatre must take precedence over good intentions, a lesson the workers' theatres were having a hard time learning. "Any consistently conscientious outlook on life may be guaranteed to make a bore of any man," wrote Sidney Howard, in answer to "Which outlook upon life offers the greatest creative stimulation for the dramatist today: Conservative, Fascist, Liberal, Revolutionary?" "Revolutionaries and fascists are permitted to be bores," he continued, "but not dramatists."

Whatever else it may have been, *New Theatre* was always lively. And in its pages one sees the evidence of the ever-increasing stir and bustle right across the country: "The John Reed Club Theatre Group of Boston has recently added to its repertoire *Nanking Road*, a play on the far eastern situation, Alfred Kreymbourg's *America, America*, and *Nazi but Nice*, an anti-Nazi revue." "The New Theatre of Hollywood is planning the production of several full-length plays . . . has already produced Em Jo Basshe's *Doomsday Circus*." "The Chicago Blue Blouses are playing every Saturday and Sunday evening for workers' clubs, Unemployed Councils, etc. . . . The Chicago Workers Theatre presented *Marching Feet* to packed houses." Many of the articles were prepared to help the groups that were just trying their wings, so there was a fair sprinkling of elementary pieces on make-up or on how to make spotlights out of coffee tins, but for the professionals there were more advanced treatises, for instance a discussion of the problem of handling crowd scenes by the veteran director Frank Merlin, an absorbing description of Meyerhold's theatre by Lee

Strasberg, and a provocative essay on montage by Peter Martin, one of the earliest American analyses of this technique. And for both beginners and old hands there were announcements of studios and classes in acting, dancing, and film-making.

The best of these were given by the Theatre Union and the Theatre Collective. The Theatre Union began an experimental workshop in which some forty people were enrolled free of charge. Under the supervision of Sylvia Feningston, they studied acting with instructors drawn chiefly from the Group Theatre, foremost among whom was Clifford Odets. He was never more than adequate in a part himself, but everyone agreed he had a way with actors. Most of those in the workshop were in Theatre Union plays, and there were times when their occasionally imperfect understanding of the Stanislavsky method led them into pitfalls. In *Peace on Earth,* one important scene climaxed with a tense moment in which Millicent Green, playing the sister of a strike leader, learned of his death; her scream was followed by a blackout that ended the scene. On opening night, however, another actress, Mara Tartar, in a small supporting role, screamed first. Michael Gordon called her aside later and said in annoyance, "What were you screaming about? *She's* his sister." "She may have been his sister," said Miss Tartar, "but in my preparation for the part I decided that he was my lover."

The Theatre Collective had a much more ambitious studio program, although it began shakily enough as a producer. *Marion Models,* the full-length original play dealing with the garment industry that had been written by Olga Shapiro with Jack Shapiro's assistance, was presented in June, 1934. John Bonn had never successfully adjusted to the shift away from agit-prop and his direction was plodding. Although it was well attended, it was clearly not very good, even *New Theatre's* sympathetic reviewer sighing that "it suffered from schematism and the spouting of revolutionary phrases." The Collective was rarely to be lucky with scripts. But as a training ground it was unsurpassed. By the beginning of 1935, when it found headquarters in a run-down but still fine old building on Washington Square North, its faculty listed some impressive names. Philip Barber, who had been Professor Baker's assistant at Yale, Walter Hart, and George Sklar, worked with playwrights; Lee Strasberg gave a class in directing; Morris Carnovsky, Sanford Meisner, Lewis Leverett, Mary Farmer, and Cheryl Crawford taught acting; and Cecilia Bluestone gave a class with the turgid title, "Fundamentals of Body Development thru Rhythm, Toward Equilibrium." Life in the once grand mansion would have driven its former occupants demented, but provided an unforgettable experience for the Collective's scores of members and students. Maurice Clark, who was the only professional actor in *Marion Models* and became a member of the Collective's executive board, recalls it with nostalgia:

> I get a warm feeling when I picture the teeming life in that building—the hot discussions about acting and politics in our basement restaurant, violent improvisations which would suddenly spill out of a room on to the staircase or even out into Washington Square, costume parties which drew over two hundred people, public performances on a platform in our back yard which drove the neighbors to call the police —a three ring circus.
>
> Classes and rehearsals went on day and night on every floor. It was an amazing and exciting place. At least three hundred applications for membership had to be turned down for lack of space, but around a nucleus of excellent Broadway actors, one hundred and fifty actors were given a thorough training in the Stanislavsky "method."
>
> I recall some aspects of "bringing culture to the toiling masses": the wives of union members drowning out a performance of *The Miners of Peche* by shouting at their husbands, who were having a brawl in the back of the theatre, "Shut up so we can hear the actors"; the exuberant Macy Shipping Clerks attending a party at our studio who poked their fists through all the paintings in an expensive loan art exhibit; the men of the Pocketbook Workers Union, after rolling empty whisky bottles down the theatre aisles while our actors were trying to play *Waiting for Lefty* and then stopping the performance in a rage when an actor used the word Goddamn in front of their ladies. Sometimes we got the feeling that the workers of the world were united against *us*. And yet, such negative experiences vanish when I remember the response of working class audiences to plays about themselves being

made to happen in their presence and in their part of the city by live actors.

A good proportion of the articles and notices in *New Theatre* dealt with the dance, since in addition to being the voice of the League of Workers Theatres, the magazine served the same function for the Workers Dance League. This was an association formed in the spring of 1933, of the groups of young dancers whose development had paralleled that of the workers' theatres. They were offshoots of different studios—some followed Martha Graham, others Charles Weidman, Doris Humphries, or Isadora Duncan, and some were students of Hanya Holm, a disciple of the German dancer Mary Wigman. Their styles were therefore different,* but their aims were the same; they were determined to combine revolution and the modern dance. Their task was complicated by a number of factors, not least of which was the resistance of working class audiences to the curious posturings and symbolic representations of the performers. Emanuel Eisenberg, himself an unusual combination—he was a talented poet, a theatrical press agent, and a dance critic for two New York papers— wrote of the second Festival and Competition of the Workers Dance League, in June 1934:

> The pattern, broadly speaking, was along the following lines: Six or ten young women, clothed in long and wholly unrepresentative black dresses, would be discovered lying around the stage in various states of collapse. Soon, to the rhythm of dreary and monotonous music, they would begin to sway in attitudes of misery, despair and defeat. The wondering observer in every case was brought to the choiceless, if tired, realization that this must be the proletariat in the grip of oppression. . . .
>
> [Then] a vision. Uprising. Revolt. Sometimes it came in the form of a light flooding suddenly from the wings . . . sometimes as a dynamic figure in red, running passionately among the startled tragedians; once it was in the incredible person

---

*The styles of dancing produced corresponding variations in the dancers' figures, according to one former member of the Workers Laboratory Theatre, who insists that all young men quickly learned the art, now lost, of distinguishing ballet, modern, and jazz-modern dancers from the rear.

of a soap-box orator. . . . And always the group would respond with victory: hope had arisen . . . the revolution had arrived.[55]

Mike Gold, who had by this time become the Communist Party's spokesman for culture with his column "Change the World" in the *Daily Worker,* was more indignant. "Is this rattling dance of corpses . . . *our* revolution? Can you inspire the workers to struggle with such a dismal message?"[56]

The dancers defended themselves with spirit. Edna Ocko, who had been one of the founders of the New Dance Group, composed mainly of students of Hanya Holm and the most outstanding of the groups, was continually dashing off bitter replies to these attacks in her capacity as dance editor of *New Theatre.* "Technics do not pop out of a Jack-in-the-box," she wrote.

> They are the product of years of training, and it requires many more years of training to destroy what one has lived by and to build anew. The young revolutionary dancer has neither the time nor the inclination [to plan] an uncharted technical course . . . merely because an artist who has already evolved a complete system of body training happens to be bourgeois. She uses what time and talent she has to compose dances based on those issues she deems to be revolutionary.[57]

The dancers were, in fact, going through their own phase of turning crude agit-prop into new images and forms for the expression of ideas they thought more socially important than the delicately modeled abstractions current in the dance world. To this end, and despite cries of horror from the more conventional critics, they did not hesitate to employ unusual means. They were attempting to bridge a wider gap than that the dramatists faced; they were using a technical vocabulary designed for abstraction to express the most concrete reality, and it was no wonder they sometimes seemed unintelligible. Undaunted, they often reinforced their dances with unconventional accompaniments. They used jazz and folk music—Sophie Maslow performed to the music of Woodie Guthrie, Jane Dudley to that of Sonny Terry. Miriam Blecher did three Negro poems by Langston Hughes. Helen Tamiris tried self-accompanied dance, with cymbals strapped to her knees or holding a drum. For their prize-winning *Van der Lubbe's Head,** a balletic attack on the Nazis, the New Dance Group used poetry spoken by a narrator. They also determinedly clad themselves in sombre leotards decked with what they thought of as the trappings of the proletariat. "We used to wear burlap and put everything together with safety pins," says Edna Ocko,

I also wrote reviews so I used to dance and then run out front to watch, and out front I realized that the safety pins glistened. Trade union halls were always filthy and we were barefoot, so our big problem was splinters and dirt, and we used to end every recital picking out splinters. We had major problems in trade unions when we danced. They all loved tap dancing, and here we came in our rags, in our safety pins, always being starving workers, and the real starving workers wanted ballet dancers in tutus, or tap dancers. We'd come with a tomtom and go through the marching-on-the-barricades department which was not their idea of aesthetics. We did it for nothing, too. We'd drag ourselves out to Brooklyn or Queens, carrying our costumes in brown paper bags on a deserted subway train, nothing like dancers today.

I remember when the shoe workers were on strike. They had a big mass meeting, thousands of strikers. We did *Van der Lubbe's Head* which opens with a foot coming out from the wings. From the other side of the stage another foot appears, then another. When the first one showed there was a kind of groan in the audience, and then when still more bare feet showed, they began shouting, "Why aren't you wearing shoes?" It became a ground swell of complaint: "No wonder we're on strike. They're not wearing shoes!" It went on all through the most dramatic part of the dance. We were all mad, Miriam Blecher was crying, and Becky Roland kept whimpering, "Close the curtain, close the curtain."

The workers were ready to love us, but they said, "At least,

*As a step in outlawing political opposition, Hitler's government used the burning of the Reichstag buildings in 1933 in the same way King James had used the Gunpowder Plot some centuries earlier. Van der Lubbe was the Guy Fawkes, a weak-minded man who was supposed to have started the fire as a tool of the Communist Party.

be pretty." And they were right, we weren't very pretty with our safety pins and burlap.

For all their possible lack of charm, the groups in the Workers Dance League began to make their mark. They appeared regularly wherever the workers' theatre companies appeared. Their festivals and recitals began to draw larger and more appreciative audiences as they themselves became more polished. They presented an all-male program, a great novelty, which included such distinguished figures as Paul Draper, Jose Limon, and Charles Weidman, and in their innocence couldn't guess why the house was unexpectedly packed with a male audience dressed in quaintly extravagant clothes. They felt they had really arrived when Fanny Brice, in one of the Ziegfeld Follies, did a hilarious take-off called Towards the Revolutionary Dance and came out on stage "dressed," as Miss Ocko puts it, "like one of *us!*" Their response was to hand out leaflets in front of the theatre urging people to attend the next recital of the Workers Dance League if they wanted to see the real thing. Their high point was reached when they filled the immense Center Theatre at Radio City for a Sunday night dance recital for the benefit of the *Daily Worker*. They did two shows, both to standing room only. The amount of money they took in, if it did not altogether silence their critics, reduced them to muttering.

It wasn't only the dancers who had trouble with *New Theatre's* reviewers. In the critical classroom where problems of form and content had endlessly to be hammered out, the moral lesson had always to be drawn, the right points—or rather, the Left ones— had to be clearly made, or the most capable theatrical company would find itself in hot water. *Men in White* had "no bitterness against the social system . . . no protest," according to one; another observed that *Ah, Wilderness* was "pretty false," and a third that the satires of Gilbert and Sullivan were superficial because they were the product of the imperialism of Great Britain, but that "a little adaptation" of lyrics and dialogue "would sharpen them and give them contemporary point." Even the Theatre Union found itself being chided by John Howard Lawson, who wrote of *Peace on Earth* and *Stevedore*, "Is it not correct (and necessary) to say that these plays would have been more effective aesthetically if the political line had been hammered out more clearly?"[58] Liston Oak answered sharply, "*The Theatre Union is not an agit-prop theatre. It is a united front theatre . . . functioning as a theatre, not as a political party.*" (Italics his).[59] Not even the Workers Laboratory Theatre escaped, although since the appearance of *Newsboy* they were the darlings of the workers' theatre movement. As their productions became more sophisticated, they sometimes put reviewers in a quandary, for it was clear that their political line was above reproach, but now and then it seemed that the forms they chose might negate it. When, for instance, they did their lampoon on elections, *Who's Got the Baloney?* it disturbed Nathaniel Buchwald, who reviewed it for *New Theatre.* Part of its comedy depended on the passing from hand to hand of an oversized sausage —the "baloney" uttered by candidates in their speeches—which ended up in the hands of the unhappy voter. Buchwald found this incomprehensible and "illogical." He also warned them against fishing for applause from "white collar workers" at the expense of losing their proletarian clientèle. When, early in 1934, a comedy team, Berenberg and Jacobson, appeared from the ranks of the WLT they were taken to task by V.J. Jerome for making people laugh at issues that should be taken seriously. "Revolution is no laughing matter," he scolded, a dictum to which they replied by not taking *him* seriously.

This team had come into the Workers Laboratory Theatre by way of the Evening Troupe. Ben Berenberg, a Brooklynite, had had a number of jobs in each of which his main goal was to save enough money for tickets to vaudeville shows. He had once auditioned for Sue Hastings' marionette troupe, but when they asked him for his address and phone number he was so nervous that he couldn't remember them and had to look them up in his address book; for some reason, he says, this put them off and they never called him. He wanted to go to college, but the family's circumstances made it necessary for him to find work. After stints as a drug clerk, a movie usher, and a salesman, he was told about the WLT and went there to audition. Harold Jacobson, an upstate New Yorker, had show business in his family: one of his grandfathers owned two theatres, the other had been involved with the Grand Street Follies, a great-uncle booked burlesque shows, and his father had had a brief brush with vaudeville. Jacobson himself had worked with a college dramatic company but had been torn between painting, writing, and the theatre. He had found his way to the WLT, too, and both he and Berenberg were cast for an abbreviated version of a Russian play, *Intervention*, by L. Slavin, which the Evening Troupe was planning.

Neither was very happy in the play. Jacobson got the part of a French colonel on the strength of his college French. The role had only three lines, but he had to put on a complicated old-age make-up complete with a moustache for it. Berenberg couldn't warm up to Steven Karnot, who was directing. At one point, Karnot said to him, "In this scene you have mixed feelings." "How do I do that?" asked Berenberg, and Karnot replied, "You're the actor," and walked away. The two found a mutual interest in vaudeville and burlesque, and during rehearsals began working out some routines together for the amusement of the others and sometimes to the detriment of the rehearsals.

One night, the company was to perform for a benefit of the International Workers Order, at Manhattan Center, a meeting-place often used by labor organizations. Carrying their costumes and the scenery for *Intervention*, they went by subway to 34th Street and 8th Avenue. They had a regular routine for such journeys. The flats were hinged so that they could be folded, and while a couple of the players made a diversion at the change booth, the rest slipped through the turnstiles with the scenery, which otherwise would not have been allowed on the trains. When they got to the Center, they found that instead of being booked into a large hall with a stage they were to perform in a banqueting room full of dining tables and with no stage at all. They were fuming with frustration, for the show couldn't be done that way, and they didn't want to disappoint the audience or lose the ten dollar booking fee. At last, one of them said, "Why don't Ben and Jake get up on a table and do that funny stuff they've been doing at rehearsals?" In spite of their protests the pair were hoisted on to a couple of tables pushed together. They had a moment of intense panic and then they began ad-libbing. There was some laughter. It was all they needed. They ran through everything they had worked out, sang whatever songs came into their heads, and began doing old burlesque bits with impromptu political insertions. "We didn't have any real material," Berenberg says, "but the audience wouldn't let us go. We were there for thirty minutes."

After that, the WLT began booking them as a team. Somebody dubbed them Red Vaudeville and the name stuck. By this time Berenberg had been accepted into the Shock Troupe, although Jacobson was living on his own and taking classes at Columbia University, but both were left out of other productions and spent their evenings playing the round of union locals and labor and political organizations, often as many as three a night, and bringing in sizeable contributions to the group's treasury. They worked out half a dozen skits, wrote some songs, and each had a couple of solo numbers in which the political connotations were apt to be nebulous. Berenberg, for instance, did an imitation of Bing Crosby crooning a revolutionary song ("We're marching 'gainst the bub-bub-bub-bourgeoisie.") while Jacobson did a mock Russian tragedy, *Below the Sewers,* which took place "in a hovel with hot and cold running rats," and in which he played seven parts, one of them an old woman with two heads that argued with each other. Their sketches were in the rowdiest vaudeville tradition, and the combination of slapstick and political comment had a quality of familiarity and novelty that made audiences readier to laugh. "The problem of whether an audience will understand disappears," wrote Ben Irwin, in *New Theatre.* "No American audience, workers or otherwise, could miss the meaning of the Red Vaudeville." The team put it another way. "We introduced the double-take into political theatre," Jacobson says.

In one skit, a policeman stops a man selling the *Daily Worker.*

> Newsboy: How can you call me a Red?
> Cop: There it is right there on that button on your lapel. Y.C.L.— Young Communist League.
> Newsboy: No, no. Those are my initials— Yitzchok Charles Lapidus.
> Cop: Yeah? Let me write that down. Now, where do you live?
> Newsboy: I moved.

They were good foils for each other. Berenberg was burly, with a beetle-browed authoritative face and a hectoring manner. He developed a peculiar lope which made him look like a wounded gnu. Jacobson was skinny, with a faintly greenish complexion—once, when he stayed overnight in the Berenberg family's Brooklyn flat, Mrs. Berenberg, peering into the bedroom next morning, said, "Look at him, poor thing, he hasn't got strength enough to sleep." Berenberg was quick at composing songs. Once, on a subway going to a booking, he wrote one aimed at William Green. It was set to the tune of "The Daring Young Man on the Flying Trapeze," and began:

> Bill Green is my name, of strikebreaking fame,
> I'm pretty darn clever at that little game.
> When trouble is started the Reds get the blame,
> The whole thing's cooked up in advance. . . .

They learned it in time to perform it at the booking, and it was later widely sung by many other groups. Jacobson was a trifle zanier in his scripts. One of his pieces, *Life is Just a Bowl of Neuroses*, which was performed several times by the Shock Troupe at their Sunday evening At Homes, contained the line, "I love you, father. How I'd like to run barefoot through your green hair."

One of the team's best showcases—as indeed for the rest of the Workers Laboratory Theatre and all the other groups in and around the League of Workers Theatres—was the Civic Repertory Theatre where, on Sunday nights when the Theatre Union gave no performances, benefits were held, mostly for meeting the perpetual deficit of *New Theatre* magazine. Despite its steadily increasing circulation (by its second birthday it could boast of 20,000 readers and was advertising that among its subscribers were Nazimova, Bea Lillie, Burgess Meredith, and Jimmy Durante), it still carried no major advertising and held its price at ten cents. Its staff was either volunteer or grotesquely underpaid, which reduced its costs. However, it ploughed all its returns back into more text or better pictures, and in consequence it was continually rooting around for money to pay printers' bills and rent. Early in 1934, as another way of raising funds, it instituted a series of New Theatre Nights.

The house was always full, often with a good proportion of professional theatre people from uptown, for those evenings gave a view of the range and quality of the field of left-wing drama and entertainment and could always be relied on for an interesting and diversified program, quite apart from its political attachments. You might see Ad Bates and Irv Lansky, of Edith Segal's Red Dancers, doing *Black and White,* a dance symbolizing the unity of black and white workers, the Theatre Collective performing *Aria da Capo—in Red,* or the Newark John Reed Club doing a mimed and recited version of Alfred Kreymbourg's poem, "America, America." Or you might see the handsome Jane Dudley dancing *The Life of a Worker,* the Workers Laboratory Theatre in its new mime playlet *Free Thaelmann* (Ernst Thaelmann was a Communist leader imprisoned and finally executed by the Nazis), the New Dance Group in a program of folk dances, Berenberg and Jacobson billed, as always, "Positively Last Performance," and Louis and Morey Bunin's puppet theatre in a rousing satire on the Roosevelt administration's National Recovery Act. Sometimes "stars from Broadway shows" would be billed among the attractions. These were often members of the Group Theatre: Bobby Lewis delivering Hamlet's "To be or not to be" soliloquy as a soap-box orator or, with cotton stuffed into his cheeks, parodying Herbert Hoover; Tony Kraber singing folk songs to his own guitar accompaniment or, partnered by Elia Kazan, doing comic routines such as one based on the "Doctor Bit" in which a pair of surgeons operate on a patient and pull an assortment of odd items out of his entrails, ending with the revelation that this patient— Hitler—has no heart. And occasionally, one of the features would be the presentation of a prize-winning play from one of the contests run by the League of Workers Theatres, a method it used to add to its repertory.

Finding suitable plays continued to be a headache. The first contest, announced in August 1933 and concluded the following spring, turned up a number of short plays, most of which were of poor quality. The winner was *Station NRA,* by D. Vivien, which carried a prize not altogether calculated to make a playwright's heart beat faster, a ten-volume set of historical revolutionary speeches. Second and third places were taken by *We March On,* by Mara Tartar, an actor with the Theatre Union, and *Titans of Paris,* a torpid account of the Paris Commune by Irwin Shappin. None of the three was often performed. However, a longer play which was seen at a June New Theatre Night had more promise. It was titled *Dimitroff,* and dealt with the Reichstag fire and the trials that followed it. Its brief scenes alternated between the courtroom and the underground opposition to Hitler outside it, and many of them, although uncomplicated by nuances of character, were forceful and exciting. It had been written by Art Smith and Elia Kazan and was rehearsed and performed on their own time by Group Theatre members who were dividing their lives between their own company's Broadway productions and the equally inspiring activities of the revolutionary stage.

The professional playwrights who were concerned with the upheavals in society also found themselves pulled between Broadway and the Left. John Wexley, who was widely known for his prison melodrama *The Last Mile,* wrote a play about the Scottsboro case, which was still very much in the news.* He took it to the Theatre Collective, feeling that it was far too radical for Broadway, but the Collective was having difficulties organizing its producing staff. After a month, Wexley took the play back and handed it over to his agent. To his surprise, less than two weeks later the Theatre Guild bought it. *They Shall Not Die,* which was set mainly in the courtroom during the tense trial of the nine black youths, opened in February, 1934, to a critical reception keynoted by Robert Garland, who said, "The Guild has once more done a brave thing bravely. I don't say you'll like *They Shall Not Die.* But, as one American to another, I dare you to try to lump it. For you are apt to carry it in your mind's eye for many a livelong day." Broadway had finally caught up with the Workers Laboratory Theatre, whose Scottsboro had been part of its repertory for three years.

John Howard Lawson, by now established as a movie writer and president of the Screen Writers' Guild, had two plays done on Broadway, *The Pure in Heart,* which the Guild had tried out with sad results on the road and which lasted less than a week in New York, and *Gentlewoman,* which had a brief run for the Group

---

*Eight of the defendants had been sentenced to death and one to life imprisonment, but owing to public pressure the executions had been stayed. Later appeals, which went all the way to the Supreme Court, resulted in the ultimate acquittal of all but one, Heywood Patterson, although the various indictments and retrials dragged on until 1942. Patterson escaped in 1948, to Michigan, which refused to extradite him, but two years later he was convicted of manslaughter and died in prison.

Theatre. Neither was more than mildly socially-conscious. But in the summer of 1934 Lawson made a journey to the South to see for himself what was happening in the long-drawn-out strike against the Tennessee Coal and Iron Company. In Birmingham, Alabama, he was arrested for asking too many embarrassing questions, kept in jail overnight, and forced to leave the state the next day. He added the experience to his other observations and by the following year had written an indignant labor play called *Marching Song*.

Albert Maltz, too, had gone out to see what was happening around the country. He had started in May for Toledo, Ohio, where there was a strike of miners, and then went on into the soft coal district of Pennsylvania where he lodged with a miner's family and lived for a time in a mining camp. From there, he headed west, now and then writing articles for the *New Masses*. In a town in South Dakota, he spoke at a large meeting of the National Farm Workers Union and was invited to attend a dance they were giving the following night. However, he decided to push on and left the next morning. It was as well for him that he did. The dance was attacked by vigilantes from the American Legion who dragged several men out of the hall and clubbed them murderously. "As a Jew from New York," he says drily, "I don't think I'd have come out of it alive." He did, however, come out of the trip with the scheme of a play fully formed in his mind and got to work on it as soon as he was home again. It was based on his studies in the coal fields and was called *The Pit*.

Art Smith and Elia Kazan, who had been responsible for *Dimitroff*, were devoting themselves more seriously to playwriting. The Group Theatre was rehearsing a new play by Melvin Levy, *Gold Eagle Guy*, a kaleidoscopic view of the rise of a young man to riches and infamy. They worked on it during the summer of 1934 in a large house they had rented in the Catskills, and part of the extracurricular activity consisted of classes in the technique of playwriting given by Harold Clurman. In them, along with Smith and Kazan, were Alan Baxter, Roman Bohnen, and Clifford Odets. The sessions continued when they returned to New York, and were given sporadically when the Group went to Boston for a season during which they presented *Men in White, Success Story,* and the premiere of *Gold Eagle Guy*. In September, another contest had been announced in *New Theatre* for revolutionary short plays—this time with the unashamedly bourgeois bait of a fifty dollar first prize. In Boston, the members of Clurman's playwriting class discussed the possibility of another play like *Dimitroff*. An idea of Odets's was chosen.

Odets was the only one of the five who really thought of himself as primarily a playwright. Some time before, he had revised and finished *I've Got the Blues*, which, since Strasberg and Crawford were still cool towards it, had been recommended by Clurman to an agent and had been optioned by Frank Merlin. With the option money, Odets had been able to move out of the flat he shared with Strasberg and into one of his own, where he began work on another play, *Paradise Lost*. In the fall, he read an article in the *New Masses* by Joseph North about a strike of taxi drivers in New York which had taken place earlier that year. It had been distinguished by the unity and militancy of the hackies in the face of a union leadership riddled with gangsters affiliated with the fleet owners. Odets met with North and pumped him for information, and by degrees a play began to take shape in his head. In Boston, he showed the outline to Clurman and then to his fellows in the playwriting class. They were enthusiastic about it, and wanted to try the workers' theatre method of writing it collectively. From this point on, everything disappears in a cloud of apocrypha. According to some of the Group people, Art Smith did much of the writing. Others say that much of the play was developed in improvisations. Some insist that Odets did it in three days, or in two, or in twenty-four hours during which he was locked in a hotel room. Kazan, who was one of Odets's closest friends and one of those involved, says, "Five of us were supposed to write it, but in the end Cliff wrote it out of inertia."

However much others may have contributed to it—and there are lines which certainly sound as if they had come out of improvisations—*Waiting for Lefty* rings throughout with the kinds of speeches and scenes which came to be Odets's trade-mark. When it was read to the Group actors in a basement room of the Majestic Theatre in Boston, it filled them with excitement. Odets had chosen a form well suited both to the Group's talents and to the exigencies of the workers' theatres. The play was short, running some forty-five minutes. The only scenery required was a row of chairs, for the theatre itself became the set—a union hall, with the audience the union members.

It is clear from the beginning that the union is controlled by gangsters, and there are armed thugs scattered around the hall in an attempt to intimidate the members. In defiance of its corrupt leadership, the union has elected a committee to consider the possibility of a strike, and everyone is now waiting for the arrival of the committee's chairman, an ardent young Italian-American called Lefty. While they're waiting, the union is addressed by its president, Fatt, who is interrupted by heckling from the floor, and then the committee members speak. As each one begins, the lights fade on stage, a spot comes up, the speaker steps into it, other characters appear, and his own story is acted out—or rather, that crucial point in it in which he became militantly aware of the evils that make a strike necessary—in brief scenes which are moving, grim, or powerfully dramatic. In one, a hackie's wife accuses him of having lost his manhood and urges him to "Get wise . . . get your buddies together." In another, which contains one of Odets's tenderest and most characteristic love scenes, a young couple realize they can't afford to marry and are forced to part. Another, which has faint echoes of *Men in White*, deals with a Jewish doctor who loses his patient and then his job to a political appointee; another concerns a young actor who can't find work; still another shows a young chemist refusing to accept an assignment to develop a poison gas. All are forced to take jobs as cab drivers. As each scene ends the lights come up and we return to the union hall where the tension is growing. At one point, Fatt introduces a union man from another town who argues plausibly against the strike. He is exposed as a labor spy and racketeer by a member from the audience. When Fatt demands proof, the man from the audience says, "He's my own lousy brother!" Lefty, like Godot, never arrives. At the end, a stirring speech in favor of the strike by Agate, one of the committeemen, is interrupted by the arrival of news that Lefty has been found dead with a bullet in his head. Agate calls for a vote, voices from the audience shout, "Strike!" and on this note the play ends.

Nearly all the Group actors were by now keenly interested in workers' theatre and even those who weren't enjoyed doing extracurricular work. The cast of *Lefty* was a large one and there was room for many of them, although some had to be content to be voices from the crowd or silently menacing toughs. Odets himself shared the direction with Sanford Meisner, and they began rehearsing the play after hours with an eye on a New Theatre night that was scheduled in January, 1935. "We had all played together and could work scenes out," says Kazan. "We were used to each other and had the habit from classes, so Sandy and Clifford guided the scenes rather than actually directing them." Clurman, Strasberg, and Crawford kept away from the production. Clurman rather approved of it as an exercise, but Strasberg's only reaction, when he saw a final rehearsal, was a shrug. "He didn't say anything, but he said a lot with that gesture," says Meisner.

Gold Eagle Guy moved to New York where it opened at the end of November. Although its reviews were good, attendance wasn't quite strong enough to keep it going for more than about eight weeks, and the Group's leaders faced the dilemma of closing down for the rest of the season or finding another play. Strasberg, supported by Crawford, argued that everyone was tired and that since no other good vehicle offered itself the actors ought to be released to find work, especially since many had already been offered outside jobs. Clurman reminded them that they had a playwright in the Group itself; Odets's *I've Got the Blues*, retitled *Awake and Sing*, was now free since Merlin, who had had trouble casting it, had dropped his option. Strasberg, however, had always disliked the play and vetoed it once again. Some weeks before the closing date of *Gold Eagle Guy*, therefore, Clurman, on behalf of the directors, announced to the whole company that the season was going to end with the final curtain of the play.

The response was loudly indignant. The actors rejected the idea, beginning with Stella Adler, who said, "As long as we can find something to act in, let's act." Everyone wanted to continue somehow, and Odets got up and pointed out that *Awake and Sing* was available, and that in fact the Group had performed the second act in Green Mansions with some success. Strasberg said stiffly, "How many times do I have to say it, Cliff? I don't *like* your play." In the end it was agreed that the next week or so would be given over to play reading. One of those read was *Awake and Sing* which, in its revised form, was new to most of the company. After the reading, there was general agreement that it was perfect for the

Group. Furthermore, Clurman, who had only directed summer performances, now felt himself ready to try his hand at a Broadway production and was encouraged in this decision by many of the actors.

Late in December, after a Saturday night performance of *Gold Eagle Guy*, the Group assembled on stage. In an expectant silence, Clurman declared that *Awake and Sing* would be the next production, that he would direct it, and that it would go into rehearsal at once. The company burst into cheers.

Meantime, they had gone on whipping *Waiting for Lefty* into shape, and it had been entered as part of the program for the New Theatre night on January 6th. There had been one difficulty. Robert Riley, who booked entertainment for the League of Workers Theatres and was stage managing the New Theatre nights, had arranged the bill for that particular evening. In addition to *Lefty*, it included one of the courtroom scenes from *They Shall Not Die* done by Theatre Union actors. There was also a suite of dances by Anna Sokolow, and Riley, thinking she should be coddled, had put her on last. The Group people were furious. They had no intention of having their final curtain anticlimaxed by a dancer. To placate them, Riley changed the order of the program, opening with the excerpt from *They Shall Not Die*, followed by Sokolow, and finishing with *Waiting for Lefty*. "It was one of the luckiest things I ever did," he remembers.

A further complication took place on the night of the performance when, a few minutes before the show began, the Civic Repertory's electrician, Gus Lynch, tapped Riley on the shoulder and handed him a piece of paper. "Look at this, for Christ's sake," he said. "These Group Theatre guys have a light-plot!" It was essential to the performance of *Lefty* that the main lights be dimmed and spots come up in which the individual scenes were played, and this was the first Riley had heard of it. During the intermissions, he and Lynch hurriedly worked out the cues, finishing just in time for the start of the play.

That performance turned out to be a new and hair-raising experience for both cast and audience. From the beginning, the actors could sense that that rare electricity was being generated which comes very seldom in the theatre; every word, every speech, every scene seemed to develop a mounting excitement which, for those who were there, became almost unendurable. Tony Kraber, who played the young chemist, Miller, says, "At once, you felt the audience was with it like no audience you ever saw before. . . . When Ruth Nelson said something like, 'Grapefruit—my kid never saw a grapefruit,' you could hear the whole audience gasp in sympathy." Harold Clurman was in the audience. "The actors no longer performed; they were being carried along as if by an exultancy of communication such as I had never witnessed in the theatre before . . . Line after line brought applause, whistles, bravos, the heartfelt shouts of kinship."[60] At the final scene, when the actors planted in the audience began calling "Strike!" the entire audience took it up. They began a few at a time, and suddenly with a surge they rose and began shouting in unison, "Strike, strike!" The actors on stage stood frozen, staring open-mouthed. In the balcony, people began cheering and stamping their feet, and those in the back rows of the orchestra looked up apprehensively as plaster and dust came filtering down on their heads. Morris Carnovsky, who played all the villains' parts in *Lefty*, says, "When the curtain finally came down, forty-five minutes later, we talked among ourselves backstage and then we went out on the street and there were knots of people everywhere standing and discussing the play instead of going home. Even now, when I talk about it, I get a catch in the throat." The Shock Troupe of the Workers Laboratory Theatre was there and, along with many others, they never went to bed at all that night but stayed up talking, profoundly shaken by the experience. It was to prove a turning point for them, as well.

By chance, there was one reviewer there from a daily paper. Henry Senber wrote for the *Morning Telegraph*, which in those days carried a good-sized theatre section and was almost as widely read among show people as *Variety*. Whitney Bolton was the regular critic, but Senber sometimes doubled for him or wrote general pieces. He was on space rates, which meant that the more he wrote the more he was paid, so he used to spend time looking for out-of-the-way theatrical material and had long been in the habit of checking on the New Theatre nights. He was no stranger to off-Broadway theatres. He had been a bit player with the New Playwrights—in *Hoboken Blues*, he played the wrong end of a horse—and had gone from there to the Provincetown, where he was in the controversial Cummings play, *Him*. Nor was he unfamiliar with the Civic Repertory Theatre for he had been a hanger-on in Eva Le Gallienne's junior group. It was most fitting, therefore, that his review of *Waiting for Lefty* should have scooped the field. He wrote with prophetic accuracy:

One left the theatre Sunday evening with two convictions. The first, that one had witnessed an event of historical importance in what is academically referred to as the drama of the contemporary American scene. The other was that a dramatist to be reckoned with had been discovered.

 **1935**

It was to be some weeks before the regular critics saw or reviewed *Waiting for Lefty,* but not because it wasn't there for the seeing. Almost every Sunday night for the next six weeks it was shown somewhere. And at every performance, it received the same emotional response, cheers, shouts of approval, even tears.

At its second performance, given at the dank old Fifth Avenue Theatre, which was being used more and more often by the workers' theatre groups, the balcony was jammed with taxi drivers. Before the play started, they were addressed by Joe Gilbert, the secretary of their union, who reminded them of the real strike meeting they had all attended in the Bronx in March, a year before. At the end of the performance they yelled, whistled, and applauded and were only stopped—and then only for a moment or two—by Tony Kraber asking whether there was a doctor in the house. There had been an accident in the scene in which Kraber, as a chemist, turned down a shady offer made by Morris Carnovsky, as an industrial tycoon. The scene finished with Kraber taking an angry punch at Carnovsky as the lights blacked out. This time, however, the fist which was just supposed to miss Carnovsky's face connected with it. There was a crunch, and in the darkness Carnovsky gasped, "Tony! What have you done?" They hurried him offstage, and he had presence of mind enough to tell the stage manager to reverse the order of the next scenes until he could staunch the bleeding. He finished the show, somehow. By an odd chance his own family doctor was in the theatre and, after Kraber's announcement, came backstage. Carnovsky's nose, famous for its perfection of line, was broken, and the doctor set it on the spot before the dressing room mirror so skillfully that no mark ever showed. However, Carnovsky had to be replaced by Roman Bohnen in *Gold Eagle Guy*. "I played handsome Will Parrott," he says, ruefully, "and with a splint on my nose I wasn't handsome enough."

He didn't need to be handsome to continue playing all the villains* in *Waiting for Lefty,* and no further mischances marred subsequent performances. Some of the critics finally saw the play on February 10th, when it was done at the Civic Repertory Theatre as part of a benefit for the Group's experimental fund. The first half of the program consisted of variety numbers: comedy routines by Bobbie Lewis, Tony Kraber's folk songs, a dance by Helen Tamiris, Carnovsky and Joe Bromberg doing gibberish improvisations, and Sandy Meisner and Florence Cooper in a Shakespeare parody. Brooks Atkinson was there, laughing heartily. He remarked next day that this part of the bill was "winningly good-humored," although many years later he was to write in his book, *Broadway,* that the Group people "had little humor and no gaiety." Of *Lefty,* he said that the Group gave "its most slashing performance." John Anderson joked, "Comes the revolution we need not ask 'Odets, where is thy sting?' " but added more seriously that the play revealed "a fresh and probably influential talent in the revolutionary theatre."

Gold Eagle Guy closed on January 26th, and on February 19th the curtain went up on *Awake and Sing.* It had a small cast, only nine people, among them a forceful young actor named Jules Garfield who had come to the Group from small parts with the Theatre Union. The versatility of the Group's actors was shown to striking effect. Morris Carnovsky, fresh from "handsome Will Parrott," played a weary old grandfather, while Stella Adler, whose last part had been that of the ravishing Adah Mencken in *Gold Eagle Guy,* now appeared as a middle-aged Bronx housewife.

*A note on production, published when the script was printed in *New Theatre* in February, says, "Fatt, of course, represents the capitalist system throughout the play."

Since so few of the members were in *Awake and Sing* the Group had wanted to do a second play and had been considering either Lawson's *Marching Song* or a play by Philip Barber. However, as a result of the success of *Waiting for Lefty*, they decided to transport it to a Broadway house. Odets quickly wrote another short play to go with it. Based on a letter in the *New Masses, Till the Day I Die* was the tragic story of an underground leader in Nazi Germany who commits suicide rather than betray his comrades. The tandem bill opened on March 26th, and the prices of tickets reflected the Group's realization that there was a special audience ready for these plays: $1.50 top, with balcony seats as low as fifty cents.

Between the two theatres both Odets and the Group gathered a harvest of reviews that showed how important a place they had taken. Most critics agreed with Robert Garland that "of all the young men . . . writing for the contemporary theatre [Odets] is the most stimulating," and with Percy Hammond that the Group members "are among the best the stage affords." But perhaps the most surprising thing about the reviews was the tone most of the critics adopted towards what had formerly been their bugbear, the propaganda drama. Burns Mantle said of the double bill, "The workers' theatre blows off considerable steam. . . . It is, I think, a healthy explosion," and of *Waiting for Lefty* itself, that it was "the more vivid type of proletarian drama projected with magnificent dramatic force." John Anderson called it "an evening of iron-fisted and exciting stuff," while Brooks Atkinson said, "The progress of the revolutionary drama during the last two seasons is the most obvious development in our theatre." And Richard Watts, Jr., went a step further and warned that "the critics who are telling [Odets] that he should outgrow his propagandist purposes are giving him bad advice. It is to his enthusiasm for the radical viewpoint that almost all his finest qualities, from his fire to his sense of pity and terror, can be attributed." The ice had broken, at last. Within another decade the use of the word "propaganda" as a form of polemic would be as outmoded as the word "immoral" is today.

For the workers' theatres, Odets became the most important revolutionary playwright in sight, and the prestige of the Group Theatre, already high, soared still further. Their standards of performance became a goal for all the left-wing troupes to shoot at, while *Waiting for Lefty* lent new strength to those who wanted to do away with sloganeering and speechifying on the stage. Herb Kline, the new chief editor of *New Theatre,* wrote that worker audiences were complaining, "We're tired of plays with wooden heroes and soapbox speeches, we're tired of 'agitprops,' give us plays with real people in them, people like us." Odets, he said, had answered this plea. "By combining the best quality of 'agitprop,' direct appeal to the audience, with realism, Odets succeeds in involving us completely in the lives and struggles of his taxi-driver characters."[61] It was in some ways a mixed blessing. "You can't dodge it," wrote Ben Irwin some months later. "Consider one act plays for the new social theatre and inevitably you find yourself thinking in terms of *Waiting for Lefty.*" And as usual, there was a dichotomy on the Left in the matter of realism. The theatre people approved—Kline's only objection was that Odets sometimes sacrificed character portrayal for the sake of dramatic situations—but the political critics sulked. Nathaniel Buchwald, in the *Daily Worker,* growled that *Awake and Sing* was "cluttered up with messy naturalism," and Michael Blankfort, considering the play in the *New Masses,* objected that although it was well done its characters did not draw the correct social conclusions, with the exception of "Ralph Berger who takes the rebellious word from his grandfather—unfortunately this development arises out of some mystical unity between the two and not also, as it should in a revolutionary play, out of the understanding of the social forces which have made the Bergers a cursed family." Nevertheless, everyone was in agreement when *Waiting for Lefty* won the $50 first prize it had originally aimed for. Within a few months, it was the most widely performed piece in the workers' theatre repertory, edging out *Newsboy.* Odets made special concessions about his royalties, allowing the play to be done free by amateur groups in the movement and for minimal payments by the semi-professional ones, and it was shown, sometimes with *Till the Day I Die,* more often alone, from one end of the country to the other. It won the George Pierce Baker Cup at the Yale Drama Tournament; it took the Samuel French Trophy in Pittsburgh, in a city-wide tournament of Little Theatres. It was done by theatre workshops in Harvard, Johns Hopkins, Michigan State, and dozens of other colleges, and by the drama clubs of many unions. It also became, according to Alice Evans of the Chicago branch of the New Theatre League, the most widely suppressed play in the history of the American theatre. In Newark, Mayor Ellenstein, who had previously sanctioned a grant by the city council to promote a Nazi club's song festival, issued an injunction against *Waiting for Lefty*, saying, "In times like these we cannot have plays that incite," and the authorities banned, or tried to ban, its presentation in a score of other cities from Hartford to San Francisco.

Waiting for Lefty, along with the increasing prestige of the Group Theatre and the penetration of its members into the workers' theatres, hastened the transformation that was taking place. In the February issue of *New Theatre*, the League of Workers Theatres announced still another change of name and organization.

> The original program and forces of the LOWT, designed primarily to build theatres of action, was not wide enough to embrace and coalesce the manifold forces now at work in the professional and amateur theatre. What became necessary was a new and broader organization to coordinate all the constructive, socially conscious elements in the theatre and to rally the vast masses of the audiences as yet unaware of the dangers which confront us.[62]

The new organization was to be called the New Theatre League, and it was open to all who would accept a simple platform: "For mass development of the American theatre to its highest artistic and social level. For a theatre dedicated to the struggle against war, fascism, and censorship." There were few progressives in the theatre who could find anything to fault in so wide an affirmation, and the membership and activities of the League increased accordingly. The League sent out organizers to help in the formation of New Theatre companies in many cities. Although the charge had been made, and was to be several times repeated, that there were no left-wing theatres anywhere except in New York, there was ample refutation in the representation at New Theatre League conferences during the month of October, 1935, in Chicago and New York, to which several hundred groups sent delegates and performers. They ranged from highly polished semiprofessional units like the Artef or the Chicago Repertory Theatre, to the Y.M.C.A. Negro Players of Columbus, Ohio, and the tiny New Dance Group of Washington, D.C. The midwestern meeting, which was addressed by *Esquire*'s literary editor, Meyer Levin, among others, included important theatre groups from Chicago, Cleveland, Minneapolis, Duluth, Des Moines, Los Angeles, and San Francisco; the eastern conference, with a larger number of black and foreign language theatres, included Philadelphia, Boston, Newark, New Haven, and all of New York City's five boroughs. There also sprang up miniature Theatre Unions and Group Theatres in imitation of the originals, which performed *Stevedore* or *Till the Day I Die,* sometimes at great risk. When the Hollywood Group Theatre did the latter play, its director, Will Geer, was kidnapped by members of the Friends of New Germany and beaten so badly that he had to be hospitalized.

The Workers Laboratory Theatre had been, as usual, in the vanguard of the forces working for change. In the latter part of 1934, they had done an abbreviated version of Molière's *The Miser,* an old favorite of Saxe's in which he played the title role, and which led Herb Kline to ask in *New Theatre* why more scenes from famous plays could not be done. He listed as possibilities Molière's *Le Roi S'Amuse,* Elmer Rice's *The Adding Machine,* Gogol's *Inspector General,* and "by changing the words of the narrator ever so little, make a fine revolutionary play of the animal satire, *The World We Live In.*" The WLT had also put its own staff playwrights to work, and had come up with two short realistic dramas, *Jews at the Crossroads,* by Oscar Saul and Lou Lantz, and *Daughter,* an adaptation by Peter Martin of an Erskine Caldwell short story. The latter contained some plot elements that were beginning to look a trifle shopworn: a tenant farmer kills his starving daughter, and is offered his freedom by the rich landowner if he will say that the black organizer of a sharecropper's union raped the girl. The other play, dealing with Jews under the Nazi regime, was criticized for its draggy opening in which everyone talked like mad for several minutes to establish situation and character. Ben Berenberg, taking some time off from Red Vaudeville, played the boss of the factory, a part which whetted his taste again for acting. Although both plays had weaknesses, they also had tensely dramatic moments, and both were competently done and were given regular performances, although neither had anything like *News-boy*'s success. Their polish was due, in large part, to the classes in acting, now no longer hit or miss but given by friends from the Group Theatre, who in addition to all their other work managed to sandwich in a few hours of instruction every week for the Shock Troupers.

It must not be supposed, however, that the WLT had given up its other activities. On the contrary, 1934 had been its busiest year, with a wider range of work and more members than ever, both in the Shock Troupe and the Evening Troupe. So much so, that the company had had to institute a much more formal arrangement of bookings and fees. In its early years, things had been fairly casual. A union local might have its own business meeting to go through and would keep the troupe cooling its heels for an hour or more so that if they had accepted a second booking for that night, they stood a good chance of missing it. Also, fees had been uneven, the troupe accepting whatever the organization they played for felt it wanted to pay. Now, however, things were different. The WLT had stature, it had won competitions, it had made its reputation as the leader of the workers' theatres, and it had formed an audience which not only enjoyed everything it did but spoke fondly of it as "*our* theatre." The WLT leadership worked out set fees for performances depending on the length and composition of the program. They also insisted on a deposit and a specific time of performance, and once or twice, when the organization they played for failed to put them on on time, they left, keeping the deposit. It didn't take long for the message to get across.

Their repertory now spanned the realism of *Daughter, Jews at the Crossroads,* and *Intervention,* which the Evening Troupe occasionally performed; the mime-dance-recitation of *Free Thaelmann* and similar pieces; satirical playlets like *Who's Got the Baloney?* (changed after the elections to *La Guardia's Got the Baloney,* with Perry Bruskin as a dead ringer for the aggressive little mayor, a role he repeated some years afterward in Billy Rose's Diamond Horseshoe) and *Hot Pastrami,* a kind of commedia dell'arte by Oscar Saul; out-and-out burlesque, represented by the Red Vaudeville team and by pieces like *Hollywood Goes Red,* in which Will Lee, as a movie Bolshevik, seizing the heroine, cried, "Just watch me, folks, and I'll surprise her, I'll take her out and nationalize her!"; and of course, *Newsboy*, which remained the strongest of their productions although, as time went on, it was shown less often. Nor did they altogether abandon old-fashioned agit-prop. They still did *Scottsboro* from time to time, and during the summer they gave a series of sidewalk shows on the waterfront, where the newly-formed Marine Workers Industrial Union was attempting to organize seamen and longshoremen. For these appearances, the Shock Troupe developed a skit called *Dr. Mixemup and Dr. Fixemup* which in simple language gave the arguments for joining the union. And with the arrival of Earl Robinson as a member of the troupe, music and songs began to play an increasingly important part in their programs.

Robinson, who had a Washington State College music degree, had hoped to study composing at Juilliard or the Eastman School of Music. "I was equipped to become a music teacher," he says, "but the depression was on and the one thing the country didn't need was another music teacher." He had worked as a pianist on a boat going to the Orient and had then made his way to New York where, while waiting for another job on a ship, he met a girl who brought him to the Workers Laboratory Theatre. They were eager to have him, as much for his countrified looks and speech as for his musical training. Against his will, he accepted parts in some of the playlets, but before long be began to compose songs and then to teach classes and direct the company's musical numbers. The WLT's writers, Oscar Saul, Lou Lantz, and Peter Martin, all tried their hands at lyrics for him and several songs were written, among them one which became a staple throughout the labor movement: "Flying Squadron." A strike of textile workers began in the east in which groups of pickets calling themselves flying squads sped from one factory to another until the strike had spread to involve nearly 400,000 workers. The same tactic was then used on the waterfront. Robinson wrote a pounding, driving tune to which Martin first set words, and to which more lyrics were added by other people in a spontaneous song-fest one evening at the WLT's headquarters:

> The flying squadron's coming through,
> The seamen and longshoremen, too,
> Make way—for the flying squad!

We'll tie the city fore and aft,
They'll have to ship their freight by raft,
Make way—for the flying squad!

The song was soon picked up by union men across the country and was heard at innumerable strike meetings. Robinson played musical accompaniments on the piano for *Newsboy, Sweet Charity,* and other playlets, while for open-air performances or strike halls he used a guitar, losing at least one in a fracas at a picket line. Like his friends, Woodie Guthrie, Pete Seeger, and Josh White, he pioneered the use of folk songs with topical—usually political—lyrics added, and later composed new songs in which the American folk quality was blended with a modern musical idiom; in later years, *Joe Hill, Ballad for Americans,* and *Lonesome Train* were to be nationally known examples. He also met and worked with Huddie Ledbetter, known as "Leadbelly," and once got into difficulties because the latter's notions of folk song differed from those of some left-wingers. "I brought Huddie to a progressive summer camp for adults," he recalls,

> and I was so interested and excited by his work that I failed to screen his songs. After an evening of him singing "Ella Speed," "Frankie and Albert," and songs of gun-toting gamblers and bad women, the camp was in an uproar. Arguments raged over whether to censure him or me or both of us. By next day, things had calmed down and that evening when he sang his "Bourgeois Blues" and the ballad he had composed about the Scottsboro boys, the air cleared.

Robinson's singing classes were part of the expanded courses of instruction which were giving the WLT a higher professional gloss. Greta Karnot, who had been a pupil of Doris Humphries and Charles Weidman and had studied with Fokine, gave regular classes in dancing and bio-mechanics. Harold Jacobson, who had been a college fencer, brought along his foils and masks, and Perry Bruskin said later, "Fencing was an aristocratic sport, it was what Douglas Fairbanks did. That our theatre could have something as elegant as that—you can't imagine how it impressed me!" Rhoda Rammelkamp's speech classes were supplemented by long critical sessions in which everyone's problems were carefully analyzed:

"Greta ought to have more jaw exercises so she'll be able to open her mouth wider and bring out the words. . . . Willy needs speech exercises, he speaks from the head rather than the diaphragm." Most valuable of all was the training in acting technique given mainly by Robert Lewis, Sanford Meisner, and Lewis Leverett, although others helped from time to time. Straight from the horse's mouth came sense memory, affective memory, improvisations, the "golden box," and all the rest of the drill into which the Shock Troupers plunged with zest. Improvisations especially enchanted them, and these sometimes released so much emotion that they were apt to end in free-for-alls. "I used to say Curt Conway was a shirt actor," says Perry Bruskin. "He was very physical and he always tore your shirt off in improvisations." On one occasion, Will Lee and Al Saxe, ordinarily the closest of friends, almost came to blows. "One day," says Lee,

> Al swung and hit me in an improvisation. I said, "Don't you ever do it again or I'll kill you." Sandy gave us an improvisation another time where Al was an army officer and I was his batman, cleaning his shoes. He says, "Not clean enough." So I did them again. He said again, "Not clean enough." I said, "I did the best I can." And he hit me. I froze. I was going to give it to him, and then I said, "Oh, hell," and relaxed. Sandy said, "That was brilliant!" Later, I heard Sandy say that now I understood what acting was about—the whole process going through your mind, all your emotions and reactions to a moment reflecting on you physically—that was what I had learned.

Similar classes in dance, acting, and choral work were given to the Evening Troupe whenever possible although the sheer size of the company sometimes made things difficult. There were about a hundred people on the rolls, but fortunately the only time they ever turned up simultaneously was for a party. They were divided into groups which performed the various playlets and songs in the repertory and they had their own schedule of bookings. However, because most of them had day-time jobs or attended school, their performances were confined to the weekends or evenings and were further limited by the time spent on classes, discussions, and rehearsals. A young, scholarly Hawaiian of Korean ancestry, Peter

Hyun, who came to the Workers Laboratory Theatre late in 1934, took on the labor of managing the Evening Troupe and kept it running with astonishing smoothness. Some of the people from the Theatre Union school or the Theatre Collective's studio were drawn close to the WLT and helped out with directing, teaching, or acting now and then, among them Peter Frye, David Kerman, and Edward Mann, while some of the Evening Troupe's steady performers like Johnny Topa and Gil Laurence, spent almost as much time with the company as the members of the Shock Troupe did.

Another newcomer was Charles Friedman, who joined the Shock Troupe around the end of the year. He was to be the catalyst of one of its most profound changes. He had worked with the Theatre Union, at first as a technical assistant and then as general manager. He had seen the WLT do *Newsboy* and other pieces and was greatly impressed by them. From a first meeting with the group's leadership at which he offered some suggestions for work and organization, he came eventually to a much closer relationship which ended with him becoming a member and then, with Saxe and Karnot, one of the executive directors. He was something of an anomaly in the Workers Laboratory Theatre. Balding, although he was only in his early thirties, he was a natty dresser and among the casual clothes and unkempt heads of the rest he looked, in his neat neckties, clean shirts, and business suits, as if he had just dropped by to inspect them for a Rockefeller grant. In fact, as he explains, his wife had to work as a waitress to keep him in clean collars. Before going to the Theatre Union he had held jobs on Broadway, and brought some of its tough efficiency with him, and one of the earliest things he did was to find new lodgings for the Shock Troupe. It was almost a form of self-protection since he and his wife, Robin, had moved into the collective apartment on 13th Street and had been taken aback by its squalor. Friedman found a manufacturer of lamp shades who was sympathetic to the radical movement and got him to put up the money for a few months' rent on a house on 27th Street east of Second Avenue. Into this, the Shock Trouple, now grown to more than twenty people, moved. Stephen Karnot supervised the decoration, having a good eye for color and a way with decorator's tape strips that made for neat edges, and everyone pitched in to clean up and paint the place. There was a large basement room for which an upright piano and a wind-up phonograph had been donated by friends, a big kitchen looking out at the ruins of a garden, and three floors of bedrooms and bathrooms. The married couples—or those permanently living together—got their own rooms, and the others lived two, three, or four to a room, which was luxury compared to the 13th Street flat. There was still a shortage of furniture and many people had to be satisfied with mattresses laid on the floor, but the big basement room, full of chairs from the Salvation Army and, naturally, supplied with plenty of lamp shades, made a comfortable lounge. They even found a cook who would work for his board and lodging and an irregular $5 a week. He was a slender, sad-faced black man and, although it seems hard to believe in these knowledgeable times, the Shock Troupers were never more than slightly puzzled at the fact that he had a great many male overnight guests and that the cigarettes he smoked gave him an unfocused look. At last, there came a night when the company was giving a big dinner party for some uptown guests. The cook, from too many of his odd cigarettes, was unable to stand up by himself, and Greta Karnot and Rhoda Rammelkamp prepared everything except the main course, fried chicken, which they didn't know how to make. They propped him up, one on each side, and held him while he did the frying. The next day they fired him, and got a nice motherly woman with a daughter named Proletta, in honor of the proletariat.

Although their quarters had improved, they were as poor as ever, for the money that came in from bookings went right out again on rental for the 12th Street loft, costumes, props, scenery, transportation, food, and many other expenses. Florence Kamlot, one of the most active of the Friends of the WLT, helped by Curt Conway's father, used to canvas the west side markets every few days and beg rejected vegetables or other foods. Once, it was a wheel of cheddar cheese which had become a little overripe. After three days of cheese sandwiches, cheese omelets, and macaroni and cheese, someone in the troupe purloined what was left and got rid of it. No one ever seemed to have any money of his own, although the directors, urged by Friedman, in an attempt to make everything very businesslike, voted to pay everyone a dollar a week. Perry Bruskin recalls wearing hand-me-downs from his brother-in-law: "The shirt didn't fit, the jacket was too tight, but I got dressed up and went for a walk down 14th Street. There was a wonderful smell of luncheonettes, bars, meat sandwiches. It was an adventure!" At Christmas, Nick Ray hadn't enough money to send cards to his family. Looking through his belongings, he found a matchbox in which were some pretty stones given him as souvenirs by friends in Mexico long before. He sent these to his relatives, and got back letters thanking him for the star sapphires and fire opals. "I had been toting these things around all that time," he says, "and there was enough money there to have supported the WLT for years." Everyone, however, remembers the warm, comradely, family feeling of that time of communal life and work, and the sense of high purpose and exciting accomplishment that made such obstacles as poverty seem trivial. They were the acknowledged leaders of the workers' theatres, and in their basement living-room could be found theatre people of all sorts who were drawn to them by their artistic reputation as well as their passionate idealism. Marc Blitzstein came to a party one night and entertained them at the piano with some pieces he had written for the New Theatre League in Philadelphia; among other things, he had set a section of the National Guard manual for civil disorders to music. Moss Hart came several times and agreed to act in an advisory capacity. European visitors appeared, among them Kurt Weill, Bertolt Brecht, and Hanns Eisler, as well as members of London's newly-formed Unity Theatre, to rub shoulders with actors, directors, and playwrights from Broadway.

The Workers Laboratory Theatre's singular combination of poverty and prominence was shown in one particular booking early in March, when they were invited to perform at Bennington College. Eight members of the Shock Troupe went, to do *Newsboy*, *Free Thaelmann*, and some songs. They were driven to Vermont by Florence Kamlot. She had been married that afternoon to Gil Laurence of the Evening Troupe, who insists that he first decided to marry her when he found out she owned a car. "I moved into the flat on our wedding night," he says, "and then found out that she was leaving to drive the Shock Troupe to their booking. There wasn't room in the car for me. I was a little annoyed but she had made that arrangement before we arranged to get married, and I knew my duty." At Bennington, the company was given dinner at the dean's house, then played their show, and afterward stayed overnight as the guests of several staff members. "The food tasted like heaven," Harry Lessin sighs. "And that stage—it was so clean, no dust, a place for everything. Later, I shared a room with Perry in somebody's house and the towels were so white and clean we were afraid to use them." Their performance was received with as much applause as if they had been playing at a strike meeting. Soon after, two of the Bennington seniors were released from college work to spend a month or so with the WLT and write a thesis about it. "They came as if into a foreign country," Kamlot says. "They loved it! They even got their conservative parents interested, and one of the fathers, who had a factory that made uniforms, made some costumes for us. They were caught up in the feeling of love and friendship they found in our theatre."

Inevitably, the WLT was affected by the movement towards expansion and professionalism which was spreading throughout the New Theatre League. Friedman was particularly pressing that the company should change its structure and orientation. A series of debates began, at first among the directors, then involving the whole Shock Troupe. Everything was brought to a head by the fact that all at once it appeared they had a full-length play.

Its history had begun some time late in 1934 when a young Californian who wasn't particularly interested in the theatre walked into the headquarters of the WLT looking for a girl he'd met at a party. His name was Arthur Vogel. He had come East looking for work, and after a spell in a Civilian Conservation Corps camp had gone on to New York City where he just managed to support himself by sticking advertising leaflets under the windshields of parked cars. The girl he met said she was going to audition for a play so he went along to the 12th Street loft and waited for her. After quite a while, he pushed into the audition room to find that she had long since finished and had left by another door. However, the three men who were there began chatting with him, and one of them asked him what he'd been doing. Vogel began to explain that he had been in the C.C.C. and before he could go further, the man—it was Friedman—asked for details of what it had been like. Flattered by this interest, Vogel told them. The C.C.C. camps had been set up to give healthy, outdoor work to unemployed youths. They did a considerable amount of tree cutting and replanting, ditching, road mending, and forestry work, most of it of lasting value. But they lived in barracks under the command of army officers and subject to quasi-military discipline, and for the youths from cities this was often hard to adjust to. Vogel described a strike in his camp of some two hundred boys against their officers. One morning when the trucks were lined up to take them to work they showered the officers with hard-boiled eggs they'd saved from breakfast, and then walked back to the barracks and stayed there until their demands for better food and treatment were met. At this point, Vogel was interrupted as the three listeners stared at each other and exclaimed, "A play! A playwright!"

They persuaded him to try to put his experiences into a one-act play and told him to come back when he had something to show. He knew nothing at all about the theatre, but they had been so eloquent he felt sure he could do it. He went to the library and read all the one-act plays he could find, and then got to work. When he returned with what he had done, it became obvious to the executive board that he really couldn't tackle the job alone. They asked him if he'd accept a collaborator, and assigned Peter Martin to him.

Martin was a witty, bear-shaped man, a graduate of New York University, who had been drawn into the WLT as a writer some time before. Vogel was greatly impressed by his self-assurance, and for nearly a month they worked together in Martin's tiny room on Second Avenue. Vogel was by then on relief, but Martin had a little money and they sustained themselves on masses of delicatessen he brought in. It became clear that Vogel's material would never fit into one act. The play grew to two acts, but they were awkward and unsatisfactory. The story was rich, complex, and interesting, and too much for the pair to handle without help.

At this point, Friedman introduced them to John Howard Lawson, who had become the doyen of left-wing playwrights, and who agreed to take Vogel and Martin as house guests in Long Island and give them what help he could. The experience was an eye-opener in the ABC's of playwrighting for the pair as Vogel remembers it:

Lawson gave us rooms overlooking the water and every day we worked. In the evening, we'd read what we had written and everybody would listen, Lawson, his wife, the kids, and a giant Airedale. After a couple of weeks we weren't getting any reactions, not even from the dog, when Lawson burst out, "You're not getting character! You've got a Polish kid in your play, a guttersnipe from the streets, and look at the fancy dialogue you give him." He started to act out the part, talking the way such a kid would really speak: "You the captain? Cut my t'roat, lemme tell you sompin'—!" It was like daylight. The next day I dictated a whole scene to Pete, a short one, about four minutes. When we read it that night everybody laughed, and Lawson shouted, "Now you've got it!" That's when I began to understand—dialogue follows character. It seems so simple. That's what Lawson had shown me.

The news that work was proceeding and that the play would be a full three acts had been reported to the Workers Laboratory Theatre. And there, the long discussions about their future had finally flowered into decision. The transformation would be far from superficial. It rested on a great many considerations, among them the need to prove themselves in a larger arena, the growing association with professionals in the theatre, the successes of their mentors the Group Theatre and the Theatre Union, the restless desire to reach larger and less parochial audiences, and the practical fact that the play—*The Young Go First,* as it was now titled—could not be done properly without a real theatre, sets, and some more advanced guidance than could be given by the Shock Troupe's regular directors.

New Theatre magazine carried the announcement of the transformation in its March issue, in which Al Saxe, speaking for the company, said, "The Workers Laboratory Theatre is emerging from a lusty childhood into an equally vigorous adolescence." It was now to be called the Theatre of Action, implying that it had at last left the laboratory stage. It would have an advisory committee which included Paul Peters, Lee Strasberg, Moss Hart, George Sklar, Albert Maltz, Charles Walker, John Henry Hammond, Jr., and Edward Dahlberg. Its executive board would consist of Saxe,

Karnot, and Friedman, Herb Kline of New Theatre, John Howard Lawson, and Jack Renick. It would present not only *The Young Go First*, but another new play, *My Dear Co-Workers*, a one-acter by Edward Dahlberg. It would not altogether abandon its original purpose but would modify it. "Although the Theatre of Action is primarily a mobile theatre," wrote Saxe, "it is intended to present new plays for a run of a week or two at some mid-town theatre before giving them in workers clubs, union halls, etc." The phrase "a week or two" was a hedge against disappointment; in fact, nearly everyone felt committed to an all-out invasion of Broadway.

Although the script of *The Young Go First* was in a very rough state, they began their preparations for production, hoping that they might actually go into rehearsal in March. Elia Kazan, who had become very friendly with many of the Shock Troupers, and had long been an admirer of the group's work, was asked if he would help Al Saxe with the direction. By the latter part of March, Kazan had a schedule calculated to demolish a less energetic person. He had stage-managed *Awake and Sing* at the Belasco Theatre, and understudied Meisner, at the same time playing a hair-raisingly effective Agate in *Waiting for Lefty* at the Longacre, dashing back and forth between the two theatres. He was also working on short experimental films with Ralph Steiner, then active in a movie offshoot of the workers' theatre movement called Nykino, which was housed in another floor of the 12th Street building along with the WLT's props, costumes, and scenery. However, he had always yearned to be a director and since the newly-christened Theatre of Action would be rehearsing during the day he at once consented.

Vogel, out on Long Island, got his first indication that the play was to be a major production when he opened a Sunday paper and read a feature story saying that the Theatre of Action was to present *The Young Go First*, by George Scudder and Peter Martin. With a sickening feeling that he had been cheated out of his work, he ran to the phone and called Friedman. "Who's this fellow Scudder?" he asked. "You, you nitwit," Friedman replied. They had had to get the information to the paper in a hurry, and Vogel had told them long before that he wanted to use a pen-name so they had picked one for him at random out of the phone book.

The script was brought to New York at last, and read to the Shock Troupe. Ragged as it was, especially in the third act, and without a satisfactory ending, it seemed to them that they did indeed have a play. The authors were told to get to work and finish it. By then, Martin and Vogel had begun to bicker a good deal, so Friedman was assigned to them as a mediator. The three worked every day in Martin's apartment. Meanwhile, using what there was of the script, Kazan and Saxe began rehearsals.

The play dealt with a group of tough city youngsters in a C.C.C. camp. At first they find some enjoyment in the outdoor life and unusual circumstances, but bad food, poor sanitation, and military discipline increase their resentment. They protest and at last get up a petition to the camp commander, but this only gives them a reputation as trouble-makers and in the end they are split up and sent out to different camps. However, they vow to carry on their fight and to continue to apply the lessons of organization they have learned. Beneath its simple story, the play made the point, harped on by the Left, that the camps were dominated by the army and were consequently a preparation for war. Hence, the play's title.

The play could not be cast out of the Shock Troupe alone, but there were plenty of actors eager to work with the Theatre of Action. Seven of the nine boys were Shock Troupers, and for the other two Edward Mann and David Kerman were chosen. Mann had had small parts in *They Shall Not Die, Panic,* and several other Broadway shows; Kerman had gone from Eva Le Gallienne's company to the Theatre Union. Two girls from the Shock Troupe, Jean Harper and Rhoda Rammelkamp, were given roles, and three outsiders, Roslyn Harvey, Catherine Engels, and Joan Madison, were brought in. The parts of the army officers, all older men, were filled by Philip Robinson, one of the original Group Theatre members who had just come back from a year in Hollywood, Mitchell Grayson, another movie refugee, Joseph Lerner, who had been in stock companies and on Broadway, and Lou Polan, a professional of twelve years' standing, who had just returned from touring with Jane Cowl and whose sister had introduced him to this new and intriguing young group. Of them all, Polan was the only one to whom the method of acting used by the directors was an absolute and puzzling novelty.

Kazan quickly became the dominant partner because of his

knowledge and experience as well as his driving energy. He used a lot of improvisation which, he said, "the Group Theatre talked about but never did much with. I tried in *The Young Go First* to advance this technique somewhat—in that play, which was about a group's crisis and activities, it seemed to fit in." Many of the exercises were designed to help the boys function together in terms of the characters they were to play. Many were designed to get them to play actions emphasizing their solidarity, and they played them to the hilt, often carrying them to extremes. In one, for instance, they were prisoners in a concentration camp and were supposed to try to escape; Jacobson, who was guarding them, was hit with a sandbag and knocked cold. "Many of the improvisations the Group people gave us were intended to isolate you in extremely dramatic situations inside limits where you couldn't get help from anyplace else," says Perry Bruskin. "Lew Leverett used to give us islands. Bobbie Lewis put us on a sinking ship. For *The Young Go First*, Gadge gave us one in which we were on a dirigible." In that particular exercise, Curt Conway was a spy who, when he thought he was going to be unmasked, decided that he had to escape and ran for a window in the back of the loft with some confused idea of climbing out on the outside of the dirigible. Lou Polan, who had been told privately to act as a storm trooper in command, had to stop him. Polan, unaware of how this sort of exercise was meant to be played, first cried, "Stop!" and then, when Conway started out the window, pointed a finger at him and yelled, "Bang!" To Polan's bewilderment, everyone collapsed with laughter. Kazan explained that improvisations were not meant to be make-believe but should be carried out to the bitter end, physically and emotionally. "You've got to go and physically stop him," he said. After a time, Polan began to grasp the concept and to draw lessons of real value from it. "These youngsters were so involved," he says—he himself was then in his early thirties. "I was used to seeing actors like Walter Hampden who'd kid around during emotional moments in rehearsal. These kids were serious!" "We played for real in those days," Curt Conway agreed. "In Lou's school, if you got mad you shook your finger in somebody's face, but with us, tell us to escape and all you had to do was blink twice and we're on top of you."

Kazan's ability to penetrate the personalities of actors and to impel them into dramatic action won him the respect and affection of most of the Shock Troupe and of his co-director, Saxe. "I liked him," Saxe says. "He was a down-to-earth guy." Nick Ray, who became a close friend and colleague of Kazan's, compared the two. "There was an analysis of character which Gadge was able to peg down. Al's method was less articulate, more loving, more fanciful; he helped me use affective memory correctly. But Kazan —I made notes about him in my journal during rehearsals, I said, 'This man will become the greatest actor's director in the American theatre.' " Perry Bruskin remembers "the kind of spirit and dedication we had towards Gadge. If he had said to me, 'Perry, for the sake of the next scene, jump off that ten-foot platform. You'll probably break your leg but it's got to be done,' I'd have done it without a second thought."

Because the script was still incomplete, Kazan and Saxe took to improvising more and more scenes, and this was particularly easy to do because of the episodic nature of the play. By degrees, these improvisatory scenes became fixed and as a result the gaps between what was being written and what was being performed widened, and the authors, especially Vogel, began to feel persecuted. This unhappy and chaotic state continued even after a theatre had been found. It was the Park, on Columbus Circle. It had originally been called the Cosmopolitan and had been built by William Randolph Hearst for Marion Davies. It had been empty for a long time, and they got it for a minimum rental. The set was built onstage, a construction which could be barracks, offices, or hospital, and rehearsals began there with Vogel at a typewriter in one aisle making line changes which were argued about right up to opening night. Friedman's soothing intervention had given the play an ending, and in the programme he was listed as a co-author. With two directors and three authors, the thing was beginning to look a little top-heavy.

They had had a few strokes of luck. The stagehands' union, the International Alliance of Theatrical Stage Employees, normally very uncompromising to deal with, had allowed them to work with a crew of four, and an affectionate relationship had been established between the men, all leathery veterans, and the youthful cast and directors. Indeed, shortly before the play ended its run the stagehands gave a party for the cast in Marion Davies's private

apartment, a once-elegant boudoir at the top of the theatre looking out over the park. It was the first time in the history of the
I.A.T.S.E. that such a thing had been done, and it's unlikely that
it has ever been repeated. The sets had been designed by Mordecai Gorelik, one of the most distinguished of designers. Theatre
parties sold in advance brought in nearly enough money to open
the show, and the rest was put up by Herman Shumlin. And one
day Vogel was called out to the front of the house by Friedman,
who said, in a voice full of emotion, "I want you to meet someone."
"I saw a tall, gray, tired woman in her seventies," Vogel says, "and
I couldn't understand his reverence." She was M. Eleanor Fitzgerald, who had been the business manager and secretary of the
Provincetown Playhouse, and who had undertaken to manage the
box office for the company.

The last few days before the opening were particularly hectic.
At one moment a bitter argument between Kazan and Vogel over
one scene ended with Kazan rushing the playwright up the aisle
and throwing him into the lobby. Vogel went home—he was living
with a sister in the Bronx—and was only persuaded to return when
Friedman went after him and reasoned with him.

Opening night was May 28th, and the theatre was full. The
actors ran up and down the iron staircases to the fly gallery, building up energy. "We came on strong," Nick Ray says. So did the
audience, which was composed mainly of long-time friends and
supporters of the workers' theatres, and when the play finished to
numerous curtain calls the Theatre of Action was sure it had a hit.

Unfortunately, it hadn't. The harshly competitive world of
Broadway was to prove too strong, almost from the beginning. A
new comedy, *Knock on Wood*, drew most of the critics and of the
first-stringers only Burns Mantle and John Mason Brown went to
The Young Go First. Both recognized the quality of the acting, but
both felt the play was poorly written. It was an opinion most of the
other reviewers shared, even the most friendly ones. John
Gassner, then the Theatre Guild's play reader, who wrote long
percipient analyses of each season for *New Theatre,* said rather
sadly that *"The Young Go First* squandered its dramatic effect by
dragging in the labor movement and vigilantism by the heels
instead of fusing them with the main body of the drama, marked
time, and otherwise betrayed its triple authorship." John Howard

Lawson wrote a letter which appeared in the *Times*, saying angrily that the Theatre of Action had an impressive record of five years of work but the press had ignored it and gone, instead, to a trivial farce. Robert Garland agreed that it was "a pretty startling revelation that a deep-rooted prejudice against the theatre of social expression exists," but never reviewed the play himself. *Knock on Wood*, by the way, lasted for only eleven performances.

Unqualified praise might have kept *The Young Go First* running longer than it did, but serious criticism, flattering though it might be to the acting and production, was no help when taken along with all the other problems. The weather began to grow warm, and the lack of air-conditioning, which always spelled doom in those days for all but absolute successes, kept people away. Theatre parties after the pattern of the Theatre Union let them play to good-sized houses, but as summer arrived with its precious vacation time for working people few organizations could commit themselves much beyond the end of June. The Park Theatre, neither actually on Broadway nor in the cultural belt around 14th Street, was thought of by New Yorkers, with their curious sense of geography as a long way uptown. And cheap though the play was to run, the house rental and the salaries of those who were not members of the Theatre of Action couldn't be met, especially since the prices of tickets were kept very low. *The Young Go First* went, after six weeks of gallant struggle.

There was a party at the 12th Street loft, the night of the closing, given by friends of the Theatre of Action from other groups in the New Theatre League. The props used in the show were auctioned off as souvenirs, and in spite of the drinking and dancing and impromptu entertainment there was an air of gloom that went deeper than mere mourning for the closing of a show. They had hoped that this would be the beginning of a new career for the group, but it seemed, instead, to be the beginning of the end.

Looked at objectively, *The Young Go First* had not done so badly. By comparison with some other plays that season, 48 performances was by no means shameful. Maxwell Anderson's *Valley Forge* had played 58, and George Bernard Shaw's *The Simpleton of the Unexpected Isles,* with Nazimova in the lead, had done only 40. If the Theatre of Action had been a brand-new company, they might have had the resiliency to build on what had been successful in the venture and to disregard its shortcomings. Or if they had been an established professional company, they would have been able to shrug and bear their losses. As it was, they felt that they had staked everything and failed.

They had run into debt for nearly three thousand dollars, a staggering sum for a theatre which was used to computing its costs in small bills. They had let their ordinary bookings, their mobile work, slide—some of it had been taken over by the Evening Troupe—and had got into the habit of thinking of themselves as what they called a stationary theatre; it was incredibly discouraging to contemplate going back to street corners and union halls. At least one advantage had come of *The Young Go First,* most of the boys now held Equity cards; but this, too, made them think of themselves as professional actors and had altered the shape of their ambition. But it was neither easy nor practical to begin again looking for a full-length play, then launching a campaign to raise the money to produce it. Their energy had begun to flag. They were much different from either the Group Theatre or the Theatre Union. They had begun with a different premise: they had worked together for five years as a political theatre, and that very commitment had worn them out. *The Young Go First* had brought to a head tensions in some of their relationships which were difficult, or impossible, to heal. For instance, Berenberg had played one of the boys, and wanted to go on acting, while Jacobson considered himself a comic and was almost totally uninterested in being an actor. The play separated them. They performed together desultorily afterwards, but the Red Vaudeville team had been irreparably disrupted. Harry Lessin's girl friend, Basha, had grown tired of living between her mother's flat and the collective apartment and had given him an ultimatum: either he married her and they settled down together somewhere or she'd leave him. He capitulated. He continued to work as a member of the Shock Troupe but lost the close connection he had had with the others. His move was regarded with envy and unease by some other couples. Worst of all, a thin but distinct rift divided the whole group. Some felt that the move towards professionalism was inevitable and right; others now felt that they had been pushed rather than led into more than they could manage, and harbored some resentment towards Friedman who, they thought, had tried to commercialize their theatre. The truth lay elsewhere. Will Lee, considering the matter a long time afterward, said, "We seemed to have all grown to a certain height together, creatively, and now we all leveled out. We all knew we needed stronger creative leadership and it wasn't around. During the five years or so we lived together we never had any rest, or any time off, and we only slept a few hours a night for months. We were broke, hungry, and exhausted. We started to run out of steam, but more important, in those five years we had gotten older and our lives were changing."

There was a touching postscript to *The Young Go First.*

About a week after the closing, Arthur Vogel came wistfully to the loft. He had no more play ideas, nor was he an actor, but he hoped there might be something for him to do. The executive committee was meeting, and they told him they were busy. "Come back some other time," Friedman said, dismissively. Vogel said, "Sure, sure," and left, his face burning. "I never went back," he says. "I rode on the subway back to the Bronx, and finally I said to myself, 'You've got to accept it. You have no right to think of yourself as a playwright, you just stumbled into one play.' I cooled down and decided to study the craft." He got himself some books and tried writing seriously, and did in fact finish several plays which were eventually given off-Broadway productions. About a year after *The Young Go First* closed, he desperately needed work, and went back to the C.C.C., which was now looking for educational advisers who would teach courses in reading and writing, and organize entertainments. One day at lunch, the commander of the camp he was assigned to told him that a directive had come from Washington asking that the writing of short plays about the work of the C.C.C. be encouraged, affirmative plays to overcome the pernicious influence of works like *The Young Go First.* "I never heard of that one," said the commander. "What about you, Vogel?" Vogel said he'd never heard of it, either. The commander looked up at the boy who was waiting on their table. "What about you, Rubinoff?" he asked. "You're from New York. Did you every hear of a play called *The Young Go First?*" To Vogel's astonishment, the boy said, "Sure. It was great." He then began to tell the story of the play, acting it out with gusto. Vogel sat with his mouth open, listening to the familiar lines. For perhaps the first time it was born in on him that there had been an audience on which his play had had a great impact and a lasting effect. When the boy had finished, the commander pushed his chair back from the table and shrugged. "I don't know what all the fuss is about," he said. "It sounds pretty good to me."

The Newsboy (Harry Lessin) chases a competitor (Will Lee) off his beat, in the Worker's Laboratory Theatre's NEWSBOY. *Photo by Alfredo Valente.*

Left: The Captain of HMS Europe (Edward Cooper) looks broodingly over the dock covered by sleeping coolies, in ROAR CHINA. *Photo by Vandamm, courtesy New York Public Library Theatre Collection.*

Bottom Left: A scene from ARIA DA CAPO—IN RED, done by studio members of the Theatre Collective.

Below: The black neighborhood prepares for a siege, in STEVEDORE. Left to right: Ray Yeates, Georgette Harvey, Alonzo Fenderson, Leigh Whipper, Rex Ingram, Jack Carter, Carrington Lewis, I. Peters. *New York Public Library Theatre Collection.*

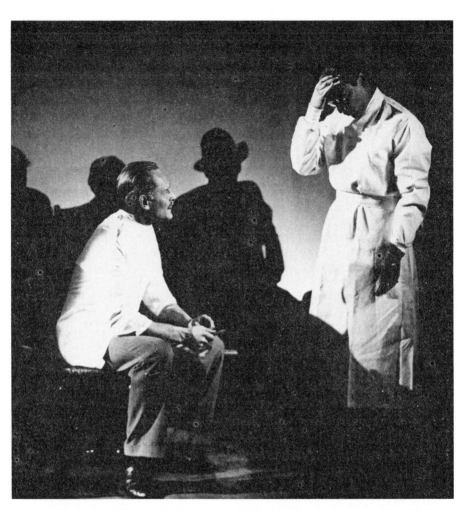

Dr. Barnes (Roman Bohnen) breaks the bad news about a patient to Dr. Benjamin (Luther Adler) in the Group Theatre's WAITING FOR LEFTY. *Photo by Alfredo Valente, courtesy Queens College Library Theatre Collection.*

9 *1935-1937*

Like the Forty-niners, theatrical producers are incorrigible optimists. They sink every cent they can raise in a stake and set out doggedly in the face of unbelievable difficulties to find gold, even though every statistic proves that ninety-nine out of a hundred will turn up nothing but mud or iron pyrites, while the hundredth is likely to find just enough pay dirt to buy another try. Obviously, those who set out on their own have only themselves to feed and can travel light. A group is more vulnerable; keeping everyone together in the face of trouble can be more, sometimes, than the goal is worth. For the three leading prospectors in the field of socially-conscious drama—the Group Theatre, the Theatre of Action, and the Theatre Union—the years between 1935 and 1937 seemed to offer almost insuperable obstacles. The Theatre of Action, by a combination of mischance and the wrong play, was left sundered and exhausted. The Theatre Union, riding on the success of two out of three plays, started 1935 with rosy hopes. In almost no time, they had a stroke of bad luck and had followed it with a mistake in judgment, either of which would have settled the hash of any organization less determined.

The first blow rested on the special nature of their audience, which was both right and wrong for the first play of the year, Albert Maltz's *Black Pit*. Originally called *The Pit*, it had been inspired by a meeting Maltz had had in the summer of 1934 during his visit to the coal fields with a once-militant miner who had lost his courage after serving a jail sentence on a faked charge. "I extended it further," Maltz says, "into a man's finally turning stool pigeon. I tried to show how a decent human being can be led down a path by the pressures on him. Stool pigeons weren't born that way." The play, as finally written, told the story of a Polish miner who is jailed for three years for picketing. Out of prison, he is blacklisted by mine owners, and at length, when his wife has a baby, is driven to turn informer on his comrades. It was a poignant and well-written attempt to probe, for once, in a purely working-class drama, into a complex character and situation, and it was marred only by Maltz's over-zealous attempt to get the Polish-American dialect down on paper and into the actor's mouths. However, even before the play opened, rumors began circulating that it was an attempt to justify betrayal. "The mood of the Left —or at least a section of it—in New York, was heavy," Maltz explains. "To introduce any complexity was abhorrent to them."

As a result, advance bookings suffered, and when the play did finally open, on March 20th, the reviews reflected a certain ambiguity of feeling. Richard Lockridge felt that it was "harshly effective as drama, if not altogether convincing as propaganda." Robert Garland called it their "most theatre-minded, the least obviously propagandistic." The *Daily Worker,* while loyally urging people to see it, did so rather glumly. The *New Masses'* Joseph North disliked it. Even with the evidence of the play itself before them clearly making the point that for a man to become an informer was wrong and tragic, many labor people could not understand it. Mildred Harris, a newspaperwoman and playwright, reported that she had listened for hours to a battle that raged between producer Herman Michaelson and his wife, Clarina, who had helped organize a union of shopgirls at Ohrbach's. Mrs. Michaelson had brought a group of her girls to see *Black Pit,* and she cried furiously that it had undone all her work. "But listen," said Miss Harris, at last, "was it a good play?" That was unanswerable, being precisely the hub of most of the debates over the social-conscious plays; their excellence of form could not be separated from the political rights and wrongs of their content. It had been a sticky problem from the start, and was to continue being one to the end.

Black Pit managed to run for a little over ten weeks, although not to full houses. Early on, the executive board began considering material for the next production. They had several choices. George Sklar had written a lively, slashing satire called *The Life and Death of an American*. He and Paul Peters had also put together a revue called *Parade*, with music by Jerome Moross, the first time a long, complete work of this kind had been attempted in the workers' theatre. The board was uncertain about both. *Black Pit* had been an unconventional play for the Theatre Union, and these two, mixing comedy and politics, seemed even more so. Most of the board members were people for whom the theatre was chiefly a vehicle for their social and economic convictions, and in consequence they lacked the dash and imagination that would allow them to expand into wider fields. In the end, they settled on something that seemed politically unimpeachable.

Bertolt Brecht had produced a play in Berlin based on Maxim Gorky's novel, *Mother*, the story of a woman whose son is a revolutionary leader. Worried lest he get into trouble with the authorities, she keeps an eye on him; by degrees, this brings her into participation in his activities, and when at the end he is killed, she takes his place. The play, which had incidental music by Hanns Eisler, had run for sixty performances. On the sixty-first, the German police had arrested several members of the cast, and soon after Brecht and Eisler, with the eye of the secret police on them, had both been forced to flee from the country, Brecht to Denmark, Eisler to the United States. Paul Peters had done an adaptation of *Mother*, and this, after Brecht's permission had been secured, was selected for the first play of the fall season. Victor Wolfson was chosen as the director, Sylvia Regan, the Theatre Union's audience manager, started the mechanism of booking benefits and theatre parties, and Mordecai Gorelik, always a strong partisan of the expressionist theatre, was hired to design the sets.

At least two of the board members, Maltz and Sklar, had some reservations about the play, feeling that Brecht's form of expressionism might not be altogether suited to American audiences. While it is hard to simplify it, in essence it was based on a concept which Brecht called "alienation." Where ordinary theatre attempted to evoke an empathic response from its audience, an emotional involvement with the characters and their situation, Brecht's theatre attempted to disrupt this involvement so that the audience could watch what was unfolding before them with objective detachment. Drama was to be the presentation of events on an epic scale, from which the spectators ideally should learn lessons to be applied to their social condition. Emotion, in such a case, would only becloud the intellectual acuity one should bring to bear on a play—indeed, the word "play" itself was too frivolous, and Brecht preferred the term "learning piece." He mustered a great many devices to further his aims, among them music, song, dance, or symbolic pageantry. Many of these, by their sheer theatricality, defeated his purposes, and indeed in the opinion of some theatre people, Brecht was at his best when he was contradicting his own theories in practice, as for instance in *The Threepenny Opera*, where whatever allegory might be intended on the excesses of the capitalist state is swallowed up by the lusty exuberance of the staging.

Paul Peters's adaptation seemed to overcome some of the artificiality of *Mother* and to give some dimension to what were flat characters. If that was calculated to ease any of Maltz's worries, it was exactly what Brecht might have been expected to object to and, in fact, did in indignant correspondence. One of the board members, Manuel Gomez, who spoke German, was sent to Denmark to discuss the matter. He reported that Brecht absolutely vetoed some scenes Peters had written in, and insisted that the original manuscript must be strictly adhered to. The board met worriedly. They had already spent the money which had come in from advance theatre parties, and since the Theatre Union operated on the slenderest of shoestrings they had to have a play ready for the fall. Everyone but Maltz voted to go ahead on Brecht's terms. "I thought that without Peters's changes it was not playable," Maltz says. "I said, 'Rather than put on a play that's sure to fail, let's shut up shop.'" He was overruled, but the board decided to invite Brecht to America to supervise the production, in the hope that they could work with him and persuade him to accept some compromise.

When Brecht arrived, there began for Maltz, who was the head of the production committee for the play, what was very possibly one of the worst periods of his life. "There were three of us on the production committee," he recalls.

We would sit in the theatre watching the rehearsal, and practically daily, Brecht would yell *"Sitzung!"* [Meeting]. We'd march out and have to endure an argument lasting an hour or two which had to go through a translator. One peculiar feature of dealing with Brecht was that he was a man who didn't bathe. He wore a leather coat and cap, and a gray shirt like a worker's, only of silk. He never washed it. To sit next to him was an ordeal. . . . In spite of the fact that he was a slender, small man he'd let out a voice that made the walls rattle. When rehearsals first began he'd jump out of his seat and run up on stage and try to move the actors around physically, yelling in German. We put a stop to it and told him we'd bar him from the theatre. We told him to discuss his criticisms at conferences, so after that came the *"Sitzungs."*

One of the problems was Brecht's insistence on having a burlap curtain, exactly seven feet high, which was drawn by hand along a wire. Victor Wolfson and the members of the production committee wearily argued against it. They pointed out that although it was fine for the people in the orchestra, those in the balconies could look over the top of it and watch the stagehands running about. Brecht replied that to expose the machinery of production assisted objectivity. His position that the audience was there to learn seemed extreme to some people. Michael Gordon remembers Brecht showing him a photograph of an enraptured audience taken from the footlights. Brecht said, "Look at them. They're intoxicated! It's disgusting. How can you teach them anything?" Gordon says, "I looked at it and all I could think was, *I* should only get that kind of response!" Another distraction, or so it seemed to the committee, was the stage direction requiring that explanatory captions be projected on a screen before each scene. The captions, however, did no more that describe what the audience was about to see. For instance, the sentence might appear on the screen: "Pavel Pavlovitch does not recognize his own brother," and then there would follow a scene in which two brothers met and sure enough, one didn't recognize the other. "It seemed meaningless," Sklar says.

Matters came to a climax at a final run-through before an invited audience, many of whom were modest backers of the Theatre Union to the tune of a hundred dollars or so. They got little enough return on their money, and an important dividend was watching a preview. In the middle of the performance, Brecht leaped to his feet and began roaring, *"Das ist Dreck!"*—"That's shit!" So obstreperous was he that he was at last told to leave the theatre, which he did, incoherent with rage. Ten minutes later, Eisler, who had been rehearsing with Jerome Moross and Alex North who played the pianos used for musical accompaniment, jumped up. He was a rotund man with an egg-shaped face, usually genial enough, but now furious; he ran onstage shouting that the tempo was all wrong. Moross, *his* temper frayed, got up from his piano, walked over to him, and said, "I won't play your God damn music, it's a steal from Wagner anyway." It took all the tact the production committee could summon to soothe everyone and finish the run-through. Maltz confessed later that he conferred with a friend who was a doctor to see if they could somehow administer knockout drops to Brecht so that he wouldn't be able to picket the opening, as he had threatened. Luckily, neither the conference nor the threat came to anything. "The trouble between us, I suppose," Maltz says, "was a basic lack of understanding. We undertook the play in the first place because he gave us permission to adapt it. But he probably thought we meant 'translate' so that he was shocked by what was done to the script. From his point of view he was trying to create something new and we were a group of Philistines who were trampling on his work. His whole effort was to restore everything to the original. It came out, finally, neither his play nor ours and it was a flop."

It opened on November 19th, and it was indeed a flop. Not all the hard work of Sylvia Regan and her booking office could keep it on for more than 36 performances. Oddly enough, no one was more disappointed in the play than the Broadway critics who chided it for being dull and elementary. Burns Mantle said that he had expected "when those earnest propagandists set their minds and their hearts, their enthusiasms and their workers' zeal at the business . . . I should have an emotional urge to stand in the aisle and shout a bit myself," but alas, most of the drama took place offstage and far from shouting he had only felt the urge to yawn.

It had been a mistake for the Theatre Union to have rejected

Parade and another for them to have had a *Mother* fixation. As if to prove that there was no monopoly on mistakes, the Theatre Guild, back in the spring, had determined to do the Sklar and Peters revue.

After the dispute between the "artistic" and the "business" members of its board, the Guild had made a good recovery. But they had developed some weaknesses. The relationships between the board members had become more distant, and in some cases their relationship with the Guild itself had relaxed. Hollywood began to beckon irresistibly. Theresa Helburn went there in 1933 and became involved in the film industry, Helen Westley paid a visit there the same year, Moeller went in the spring of 1934, and Simonson in December. Some of these visits were directly advantageous to the Guild; for example, Helburn got movie money for both *Valley Forge* and *Mary of Scotland*. The board also became more cautious. They tended to think twice about new or controversial plays, and their behavior towards playwrights in general was shabby. It may have been the result of nervousness, irresolution, or the division within the board, but they often took months to read scripts and, having passed on them, months more before determining whether or not to produce them. They insisted that their original option on a play entitled them to the playwright's making revisions without the security of a contract or further money. During January, 1935, two playwrights, Paul Sifton and Virgil Geddes, picketed the Guild Theatre, where Margaret Kennedy's *Escape Me Never* was playing, calling themselves the Provisional Committee of Unproduced Theatre Guild Playwrights and informing passersby that while the Guild held options on no fewer than eight plays which they had written between them, only one had been done. As for the socially-conscious play, after the poor showing of *They Shall Not Die* and the even poorer one of a strongly anti-Nazi play, Anton Bruckner's *Races*, which was tried out on the road and never was brought to New York at all, the board developed a certain wariness which in subsequent years made them turn to exceedingly milk-and-waterish material or, for a long stretch, nothing that could seriously be called social-conscious at all. Before that, however, of the six plays in the season 1934–35, the longest-running was S.N. Behrman's *Rain From Heaven*, which did voice some opposition to the Nazi regime, although in so genteel a tone as to be hardly audible, while the shortest-running was *Parade*.

When it went into rehearsal, *Parade* included, in addition to the basic material by Sklar and Peters, sketches by such expert comedy writers as Frank Gabrielson, David Lesan, and Kyle Crichton. Most of the music was by Jerome Moross, but there was also a number by Marc Blitzstein, "Send For the Militia," which had grown out of the song he had once let the Theatre of Action hear. There was also a song poking fun at liberals, "My Feet Are Firmly Planted on the Ground" by Emanuel Eisenberg, with music by Moross, and, as a specialty, *Newsboy*, which was leased from the Theatre of Action. Al Saxe was borrowed to stage it. It was an imposing list, and even on a mere reading nearly forty years later much of the comedy stands up pretty well, although some of the Sklar-Peters sketches seem a trifle heavy-handed. Certainly, by comparison with other revues of the same period, *Parade* makes a good showing. Furthermore, it had a fine cast: Eve Arden, Avis Andrews, Charles D. Brown, David Lawrence, Ezra Stone, and the wistful clown, Jimmy Savo, one of the most deliciously funny men then on the stage.

What it did not have were, firstly, the right audience, and secondly, the courage of the producers' convictions. In some ways, the latter was the greater snag.

The Dramatists' Guild agreement with producers gave playwrights absolute control over the text of a play or the book of a musical. In the case of a revue, however, when there was no story, the producer could substitute or eliminate numbers, and as *Parade* came closer to its New York debut, the Guild board members supervising the show, Simonson and Moeller, began to get cold feet and took to chopping and changing so rapidly and so often that the whole production began flickering like an old-time bioscope. *Parade* was unveiled in Boston, and from the time its curtain went up there was trouble. During *Newsboy*, at the line, "Have you heard of Sacco and Vanzetti," Governor Fuller, who as a judge had sat on the bench during that case and who was in the audience, got up and stalked angrily out of the theatre taking a score of other people with him. Next day, *Newsboy* was deleted from the show. In the days following, more numbers which seemed too politically hazardous were removed, and Sklar and

Peters, watching their material dwindle, became increasingly frantic. "The stuff they pulled out in Boston would have made a whole other show," Sklar says. He and Peters decided there was a minimum beyond which they wouldn't go, and this was reached when it was announced that a song, "Letter to the President," one of the two numbers sung by Avis Andrews (and with a dance accompaniment by Miriam Blecher,) was to go. "I got up," Sklar says, "and made a little speech saying that if they took that out we'd repudiate the show and picket it. Lee Simonson got white and said, 'Please, don't threaten. Let's talk like civilized people.' We said, 'That's it,' and went out and took a long walk. We went back to our hotel and we were being paged; Simonson wanted us. He said, 'I've called the rest of the board in New York and persuaded them to keep the number in. But please don't resort to threats again. I know you, George, you're a very serious man. But you're really just a nice, sincere Jewish boy who wants to be loved.' "

In a somewhat tattered condition, *Parade* began its New York run on May 20th. It was the sixth presentation in a season which had included plays by James Bridie, S. N. Behrman, Maxwell Anderson, George Bernard Shaw, and Margaret Kennedy, and the Guild's subscription audience was baffled and resentful. There were some walk-outs on opening night. Jimmy Savo was as funny as ever, but was handicapped to a certain extent by an inability to grasp the social criticism implied in some of the parts he played. In Eisenberg's song he was supposed to be a befuddled liberal, and to make the point was to come out on stage carrying a copy of the New Republic. At the dress rehearsal, he appeared holding the Saturday Evening Post, and when Sklar grabbed him and said, "What are you doing with that?" he replied, "What's the matter? It's a magazine, isn't it?"

The confusion of purpose was reflected in the reviews, which displayed a singular similarity of phrasing. Robert Garland called it "neither fact, fancy, nor good red propaganda," Brooks Atkinson said that it was "neither fish, flesh, foul [sic] nor Jimmy Savo," and Gilbert Gabriel, himself in some political confusion, wrote, "It manages to be neither fish nor fowl nor even good red Goering." What was obvious to everyone was that the Theatre Union should have done the show, and Atkinson summed matters up by remarking that the Guild's heart was not really in it, and that on 14th Street it might have appeared to greater advantage. There was not to be another serious try at a left-wing revue until some two years later when the International Ladies Garment Workers Union produced *Pins and Needles,* which continued for more than eleven hundred performances and demonstrated how successful such a show could be when done with singleness of purpose and for a properly receptive audience.

The Theatre Union was not yet done with blunders. The next came on the heels of the production which followed *Mother.*

Grace Lumpkin had written a novel called *To Make My Bread* about the "lint-heads," the workers in the Carolina cotton mills. It was dramatized by Albert Bein, whose talent as a writer had flowered during a long period of enforced leisure; when only twenty-two he had been sent to jail for five years after what he called "a slight misunderstanding" when he had tried to rob a Kansas City bank. The poems and stories he had written in prison had come to the attention of Clarence Darrow who, along with the novelist Zona Gale, encouraged Bein to continue his writing. *Let Freedom Ring,* his adaptation of the Lumpkin book, was his second play, the first having been *Little Ol' Boy,* in 1933, in which Burgess Meredith had been widely admired.

Bein put up his own money for *Let Freedom Ring* and produced it in association with Jack Goldsmith. It was a hard show to cast, since it required among others seven actors to play the hillbilly McClure family, all of whom had to be large-framed, had to look like mountain people. and speak with reasonably authentic accents, and one of whom, Pap, had to be able to sing ballads and play a wire-strung square dance fiddle. Rounding them up put gray hairs on Bein's youthful head. At lunch one day, in a restaurant frequented by actors, he spotted a tall young woman with a southern accent. He jumped up and went over to her, exclaiming, "You're Ora McClure!" "You're wrong," she said. She was Norma Chambers, a Virginian who was working as general understudy in *The Children's Hour.* He was right, however, and she got the part. The role of Kirk, the McClure who becomes a union organizer, was given after some hesitation to Robert Williams, a former Dartmouth football player. "How can a college boy play a working-class type?" Bein asked, and Williams replied belligerently, "John Reed went to Harvard, didn't he?" The part of Pap was a poser. However, into Bein's office came a rangy middle-westerner with a guitar. His name was Will Geer. "I heard you're doing an uprising play," he said. "I like uprising plays. I'll sing you an uprising song." He launched into one he had written himself, called, "The Ballad of the Wives and Widows of Presidents and Dictators." The wire-strung fiddle presented no problem to him, nor did the fact that although he was only thirty-one he had to play a man of seventy-one. Geer had worked on a Mississippi riverboat, had studied acting in Russia, had performed all over America with a road company, and had helped organize a Hollywood version of the Group Theatre. He was to specialize in playing tough old men on the stage and in films and went right on doing so after he had actually become one.

Let Freedom Ring began on Broadway on November 6th, 1935, and held out for three and a half weeks. By that time, the Theatre Union, with *Mother* running but in a shaky state and no other production in view, has been alerted. Some of the board members had originally urged Bein to write the play but had wanted revisions which Bein had refused to make. Now, with *Let Freedom Ring* beginning to falter, the Theatre Union took over the play and brought it downtown. Since *Mother* was in the Civic Repertory Theatre, the Bein play was put into the Provincetown Playhouse. The reviews were good, labor audiences turned to this animated and colorful production with something like relief, and it ran for ten weeks more, putting it well into the success class.

At the end of 1935, the Theatre Union faced the problems of the coming year with a kind of Monday-morning weariness. As always, the basic hurdles were finances and plays, and the very nature of the organization both created these difficulties and made it almost impossible to solve them. Mike Gold, analyzing the situation in his column in the *Daily Worker*, expressed the fear that the Theatre Union was going the way of the New Playwrights Theatre. He hinted that the executive board was limited and ingrown, that there ought to be a permanent acting company, and that scripts could be found if they searched hard enough. With an echo of the parochialism that had long ago been rejected by the workers' theatres, he exclaimed, "Go out and create playwrights!" Albert Maltz, on behalf of the harried board, replied at length with some hard facts. The annual deficit of the Theatre Union was $15,000. This was because although five of the six plays they had done had made enough to pay their running costs and three had shown real profits, none could quite manage to pay off the total original cost of opening. Not unless the price of tickets was increased, and if that were done the working people who supported the company wouldn't be able to afford to come. Maltz pointed out that *Let Freedom Ring* was a perfect example. When it had opened on Broadway its running cost was $6,500 a week, which meant that tickets had to be too expensive for its natural audience. The Theatre Union's own productions, on the other hand, cost about $3,500 a week and brought in about $3,650. Even though their initial nut, with all the economies they practiced—Equity minimums for everyone connected with the show, relatively small casts (in *Peace on Earth*, twenty-nine actors took seventy-three speaking parts), and a small overhead—might be only $6,000, they could not cover it with a weekly profit of under two hundred dollars. This meant, too, that a permanent company was only a dream. "Last spring . . . six actors were designated members of the company," wrote Maltz. "This meant . . . that they would always be on call for our plays and that we would always cast them unless absolutely impossible. Well, three months later, two of those actors were forced by personal, financial problems to take jobs on Broadway."[63] As for the finding of plays, the trouble was that the Theatre Union was not simply looking for socially-conscious scripts but for good plays with a revolutionary point of view. Maltz declared that "Committees from the Theatre Union are constantly reading plays, seeing playwrights, corresponding, searching. Remember that our revolutionary literature is new. Writers develop—they don't burst out like a flower overnight." The Theatre Union, he went on, was nothing like the New Playwrights. The latter had not been a working-class theatre. "Its reason for existence was primarily to revolt against the bourgeois theatre and it was a revolt more of form than of content. Its plays were not clearly revolutionary plays and its audience was not a revolutionary audience." He finished bitterly, "The Theatre Union is a working, living, workers' theatre. It was created where nothing existed before. It has brought five hundred thousand people* in to see revolutionary plays. . . . It needs criticism, yes. But it can be wrecked by slander."

The Theatre Union launched a fund-raising campaign for $15,-000, which they hoped would cover the costs of three more plays. As usual, part of the money was raised by Sunday night benefit performances, through the first months of 1936, sometimes of plays which had won the perennial New Theatre League contests or those sponsored by the Theatre Union itself. The search for scripts went on steadily, as Maltz had indicated, with the Theatre Union scanning dozens of submissions and the New Theatre League canvassing established playwrights for shorter plays suitable for its membership; as a result of the latter action, Archibald MacLeish, Dawn Powell, John Dos Passos, and Lynn Riggs all promised the League to write one-act plays on social subjects. Some very good short plays did, in fact, emerge from all the ferreting, notably Maltz's *Private Hicks,* Paul Green's *Hymn to the Rising Sun,* and Philip Stevenson's *God's in His Heaven,* as well as a touching monologue by Clifford Odets, *I Can't Sleep,* which was a little beyond the ability of most workers' theatre actors but was performed several times very effectively by Morris Carnovsky. For its part, however, the Theatre Union was looking for full-length plays, and this induced a myopia which was responsible for its next error of judgment.

Late in 1935, the New Theatre League and the American League Against War and Fascism, sensitive to the increasing belligerence in the world, sponsored a contest for anti-war plays. One of the entrants was a twenty-three-year-old radio writer named Irwin Shaw. He wrote his play at white heat in something like a week. Its idea was not altogether original—it resembled *Miracle at Verdun,* being concerned with a half dozen dead soldiers during "the second year of the war that is to begin tomorrow night" according to the stage directions, who refuse to be buried in spite of the pleas of their wives, their sweethearts, their commanding officers, and the politicians, and who climb out of the grave and set off to deliver a message to the world against the evils of war.

*The actual figure, calculated by Sylvia Regan on the basis of the first five plays, was 523,000.

Shaw had unfortunately mistaken the date of the contest and by the time he sent in his play, the deadline had passed. However, he had been spending a lot of time around the New Theatre League office and the Theatre Union, and he showed the play to George Sklar. Sklar was wildly enthusiastic about it. He had only one reservation. The title was *Bury Them, They Stink*, which he felt lacked in polish whatever it may have had in bluntness. He suggested *Bury the Dead*. He arranged a reading for the Theatre Union board and did his best to persuade them to take it, but it had a grave defect in their eyes. It ran for seventy minutes and could not be broken into by an intermission without damaging its continuity. It would have to be shown with another play to make up a full evening, and that somehow seemed unsatisfactory. In the end the vote went against it. "That was a major mistake," Sklar says.

There were others who were interested, however. The Group Theatre considered it, but they had already contracted with Milton Shubert to do a play called *The Case of Clyde Griffiths.* They said they would think things over, but according to Harold Clurman, Shaw was "very young and impatient," and insisted on an immediate production. The Theatre of Action saw a copy of the script and clamored for it, but Shaw felt they were not professional enough and perhaps too committed to the narrower field of workers' theatres. He had already been approached by a group representing the cast of *Let Freedom Ring*, all professionals and eager to try their hand at an independent production. Ben Irwin, then at the head of the New Theatre League, was as excited by it as Sklar had been and offered to put up some of the League's money for expenses if the play were presented as a benefit for them. Shaw agreed. While *Let Freedom Ring* was still playing, the cast began rehearsing *Bury the Dead,* under the joint direction of Worthington Minor and Walter Hart, both of whom had commitments elsewhere and so had to alternate with each other. There was little sleep for anyone during the four weeks or more of preparation, but at last, on March 14th and 15th, they displayed it at the Forty-sixth Street Theatre along with a curtain raiser *Prelude*, by J. Edward Shugrue and John O'Shaughnessy. Some of the critics, by now alert to the appetizing possibilities of those New Theatre League Sunday nights, were there and praised it. Backing appeared in the person of Alex Yokel, whose pockets were jingling from the success of a comedy called *Three Men on a Horse*. *Let Freedom Ring* had closed by then, and the cast joyfully formed itself into a new company which they called The Actors Repertory Company, with every intention of finding further plays and continuing to work together. *Bury the Dead* opened uptown at the Ethel Barrymore Theatre on April 18th.

It was hailed as another *Waiting for Lefty*. Gilbert Gabriel spoke of it as "a tremendously stirring piece of imaginative and argumentative drama," and there was no dissenting voice. The play, said Robert Garland, "says in one scene what *Miracle at Verdun* failed to say in seven." Its appeal lay in the fact that while it was a condemnation of militarism it did not attempt to make a case for the Marxist thesis that all wars stemmed from the nature of capitalist society. Furthermore, it was far from mere sentimental opposition to war; in Shaw's own words, "I am not a pacifist and *Bury the Dead* is not a pacifist's play." He was, he said, arguing that men should go to war only for the things they personally held dear, and "not for the leaders of the Democratic Party or the owners of Bethlehem, Pennsylvania. Don't go to war unless you have something to gain." It was a position few could oppose.

The play ran for nearly a hundred performances, at the end of which time Shaw had been summoned to Hollywood where he began to write a football film. By then, it may be presumed, the Theatre Union was well bruised from kicking itself for having passed up its chance. It had followed *Let Freedom Ring* with a play which was timely, cogently written, and handsomely produced, but which had nothing like the impact of *Bury the Dead*. It was called *Bitter Stream*, and it was the first full-length drama in America to deal with Italian fascism.

In the light of the world war which was only a few years away, it is astonishing how little reaction was stirred in most Americans by the rise of Hitler and Mussolini. For the majority, Hitler was a strong man remaking Germany, leading a party similar to the Communists and Socialists, and to be applauded for the speed with which he dispatched them along with all other opposition. The very word "dictator" was so new as to have the quality of a curiosity. As for Mussolini, there was something quaintly comic about his posturing, and in any case, as everyone knew, he had made the

Italian trains run on time. Nowhere was this unconcern more evident than in the theatre. It will be remembered how casually Ashley Dukes, in *Theatre Arts Monthly*, had dismissed Hitler's purge of all Jewish and dissident elements in the German theatre. Nearly a year later, George Jean Nathan, having great fun at the expense of theatrical refugees, wrote in *Vanity Fair* that they had been banished to Austria or Switzerland where they had to "eke out a meagre existence in million dollar palaces, with nothing to subsist on but eight or ten meals a day."[64] Although plays dealing with what was wrong in America might be accepted and even do well on Broadway, anti-Nazi plays were thin on the ground. Before *Till the Day I Die* (which, after all, had been hitched to *Waiting for Lefty*) three plays, *The Shattered Lamp, Blood on the Moon,* and *Kultur,* had had very short lives, and a fourth, *Races,* had never even made it to New York. The world had to burst into war before, in 1941, Lillian Hellman's *Watch on the Rhine* could grip a Broadway audience.

Yet the threat had been clear enough. In the spring of 1933, after the Reichstag fire, Hitler's government had suspended all individual liberties in Germany. Almost as soon as the Nazi Party took control by the barest and most suspect of majorities, Jews had been banned from the professions, the government service, and the universities. Shortly afterward dissenting Catholics and Protestants found themselves under attack, and death by beheading was restored as the punishment for opposition to the government. The army and air force were openly brought to a pitch of readiness and tested their weapons and tactics in Spain when the Civil War began in July, 1936. In Italy, Mussolini's Black Shirts had introduced for political heretics a modern version of the Inquisition, featuring large doses of castor oil followed by beatings on the stomach with rubber truncheons. As early as 1932, the Italian war machine was furbished and ready, and in October, 1935, was sent against the tribesmen of Ethiopia. In defiance of the valetudinary League of Nations and in the face of utter passivity by the other powers, Italy demolished the Ethiopian resistance (an Italian Air Force commander spoke lyrically of the beauty of his bombs bursting among the tiny, black, running figures below) and annexed that country in 1936 in time to join Germany in further military try-outs in Spain. But if you had scanned the alphabetical listing of what was playing on Broadway at the beginning of that year, you would have found no indication that anything of the sort was going on. Theatrical producers by and large were concerned with love and murder on safe, home ground rather than the hate and murder that were abroad elsewhere in the world.

The Theatre Union's play, then, was something of a novelty. It dealt with the impact of fascism on the Italians, and especially with the risings of farmers against crippling taxes and the loss of their lands. It was based on Ignazio Silone's widely applauded novel, *Fontamara*, and concerned an oafish farmer who is sucked into the rebellion against Mussolini and in the end volunteers as a substitute for a leader of the underground, letting himself be executed in the other's place. The dramatization, at first called *Sons of Rome* and then, when this seemed misleading, retitled *Bitter Stream*, was written by Victor Wolfson. Wolfson, with his brother Martin who was one of the Theatre Union's regular actors, served on the production committee which also included Sylvia Feningston, the versatile Michael Blankfort (then in his late twenties, he had been an actor with the Hedgerow Theatre, an assistant director for *Stevedore*, a director for *Peace on Earth*, a producer for *Merry-go-Round*, a play adapter for *Sailors of Catarro*, a playwright for *The Crime*, and was currently a drama critic for the *New Masses* and a member of the Theatre Union's executive board!), and Charles Friedman who, after the Theatre of Action drew in its horns, had returned to the Theatre Union where he served as production manager. Jacob ben Ami had been chosen to direct, but after disagreements with the committee and the playwright over interpretations of some characters withdrew, and Friedman took over that job as well. Albert van Dekker had the tricky leading part with its subtle combination of cloddishness and heroism, and in the cast were a number of Theatre Union stalwarts, among them Lee Cobb, Hester Sondergaard, Vincent Sherman, and Frances Bavier. Bavier was to suffer a disappointment in this play. In nearly all the previous productions she had appeared in parts that called for rags or old clothes, but in *Bitter Stream* she was cast in a role that required her to wear a chic evening gown. However, soon after rehearsals began she was re-cast in a better part, but it was that of a blowsy inn-keeper which sent her right back to shabbiness.

In general, for Theatre Union productions, costumes were not too much of a problem since any old clothes would do for downtrodden workers. This play, however, required uniforms and Italian peasants' clothing, and the Theatre Union as always had a skimpy budget. Eleanor Fitzgerald, then subscription manager, recommended two girls fresh from Yale Drama School, Barbara Guerdon and Harriet Richardson, to do the costumes. They turned out to be experts at fabricating and improvising. From a tiny costume rental shop they bought old Brink's Security Corps uniforms and by various ingenious additions turned them into fascist uniforms. They found boots in Salvation Army depots. They bought yards of cheap materials and set up dye-pots in the grubby basement dressing rooms, where for hours they dipped and sloshed, cut and stitched. Once, when Albert Maltz incautiously dropped by to see how they were getting on, they pressed him into service as a dyer. They had a few trying moments. This was their first professional job, and they were shy about measuring the inner seams of men's trousers. They tossed up, and Richardson lost and had to hold the top of the tape measure. They also had no money or facilities for properly cleaning clothes, and when one of the actors complained of athlete's foot they swore with wide-eyed innocence that they had disinfected the boots. "We paid for it later," says Guerdon, "by itching ourselves for days."

The executive board may have been feeling a little desperate over the fate of the play, for they took two measures to ensure a longer run than *Mother* had had. They lowered their top ticket price from $1.50 to $1.05, and added a nickel to the cost of the other seats bringing them up to fifty, sixty-five, and eighty cents. They also formed a committee of thirty trade union and labor leaders to sponsor *Bitter Stream*, and thus rally greater support for it. All this helped some, but not enough. The production had suffered from its change of directors, and while most of the reviews were at least commendatory some of the critics felt it was not quite up to the Theatre Union's usual standard. It closed at the end of May, after sixty-one performances.

As if it had not enough to contend with, the Theatre Union now lost its home. The bank which owned the Civic Repertory Theatre felt it wasn't getting enough money and determined, if it couldn't increase the rental, to tear the old place down and turn it into a parking lot. Maltz was a member of the delegation that went to plead with a bank officer. Explaining that they couldn't increase their payments, Maltz said, "We're a non-profit organization." The officer stared at them. "Why do you work without profit?" he asked in bafflement, and turned down their plea.

The board searched all through the summer for another house. The company had become identified with Fourteenth Street. They had made good the boast expressed at their inception to bring the carriage trade downtown. Now, some of the board felt they should move uptown, more especially as no suitable theatre seemed to offer itself in the old neighborhood. In September, they found a delightful small house, the Nora Bayes Theatre, which was tucked above a larger theatre on West 44th Street. However, they still had not settled on the next play, and worse, there were ominous signals of contention within the board.

Charles Walker, whose exuberant drive had started the whole thing, had been losing interest. A would-be playwright, he had always hoped the Theatre Union would some day produce one of his plays. In 1935, he and his wife, Adelaide, had made a trip to the Soviet Union, and like many others with a somewhat romantic conception of revolution had been disillusioned. Soon after, he had submitted a play to the board dealing with an idealistic American who tries to introduce American technological methods into Russia. Although in response to criticism he revised it several times, it never worked out properly and was rejected. From that point on, his enthusiasm noticeably waned. He was not the only one to feel some political disgruntlement. When the Spanish Civil War began, its complex roots and factional ramifications threw many people on the Left into confusion. The fragile United Front in Spain, made up of anarchists, Socialists, pro-Stalinists, anti-Stalinists, anarcho-syndicalists, national minorities, and splinter groups, was reproduced among the left-wingers abroad; charges and counter-charges were hurled back and forth, and whatever clarity of purpose there might have been was quickly obscured by the hail of polemic. The Theatre Union's board had originally gained strength from its diversity of opinion. Now it was divided.

Matters were not helped by those who should have given it unqualified support. Left-wing critics continued to snipe at it. Early in 1937, when it was trying to raise funds with a drive for ten thousand subscriptions, an article by Ben Compton in the Daily Worker criticized it for not having paid sufficient attention to the wants of its audience. It should, he said, have conducted forums, say on those Sunday evenings which had been frittered away on shows, so that it could have heard from its audience what they expected of a labor theatre. It should have had a permanent company, maintained a mobile troupe, and continued its studio which had dropped by the wayside for lack of funds. All this advice was about as practical as furnishing a man dying of thirst with a set of maps for avoiding the desert, instead of giving him water.

By the beginning of 1937 the board had a play in rehearsal, John Howard Lawson's *Marching Song*. It had finally been turned down by the Group Theatre, Harold Clurman feeling that it was rather cold and artificial. What may have disturbed him was the contrast between its story—a group of workers in an auto industry company town, meet in an abandoned factory to plan a sit-down strike—and its poetic dialogue. For the Theatre Union, however, it seemed ideal. It was a moving and realistic study of workers, and it was highly topical, anticipating by only a brief time the wave of sit-down strikes which was to sweep the automobile industry.

It gradually became clear to the members of the Theatre Union's executive that *Marching Song* was a kind of last throw of the dice. Their creditors were dogging them. Some of the board members no longer bothered to attend meetings. Walker, at one point, came to the office and carried away some of the records and lists of supporters, claiming they were his own property. More and more of the decisions fell to the new general manager, Lem Ward. The play had a large cast, some Theatre Union veterans, and some new faces, such as Curt Conway from the Theatre of Action and Grover Burgess, crossing over from the Group Theatre. Rex Ingram, an outstanding black actor who had been seen as God in the film of *Green Pastures,* had one of the leads; previously he had had an important role in *Stevedore.* Although none received more than the Equity minimum, they added to the budget by their numbers. The Theatre Union would not abandon its policy of low-cost seats even though it was now on Broadway, and it fixed its top at $1.50. That meant there was an even smaller margin for error. The show *had* to be a hit.

Nervousness behind the scenes still plagued the group. They

hoped to open at the end of January, but the friction on the board made them announce that they would disband until the fall. They changed their minds and raised the curtain, at last, on February 17th.

In a reversal of roles, some Broadway critics took the play to task for not being revolutionary enough. Just as in the case of *Mother*, their reaction seemed to be one of disappointment. Richard Lockridge complained that the poetic speech in the mouths of the workers was fine but that it weakened the play's propaganda value. John Anderson said that it didn't reach the emotional pitch necessary to get its radical message across. Some reviewers charged that it was one-sided and unfair to bosses, but even they appeared to bend over backward to allow the Theatre Union to speak up for itself. The *Herald Tribune* ran a column pointing out that "the sadistic strike-breaking vigilantes, the torturing of labor leaders, and the black-listing of workers are not without corroboration in the news stories." Douglas Gilbert of the *World Telegram* turned over most of one of his columns to Peter Kalischer, who attacked his review and defended the play. Yet in the end, there was too much discussion and not enough whole-hearted praise.

When, after about six weeks, the cast was given the closing notice, they resolved to try to keep the play running. They petitioned Equity for permission to continue on a cooperative basis and this was granted. It meant, among other things, even tinier salaries for the cast. The Theatre Union withdrew from the production, and without their participation the weekly costs were pared to a minimal $1,600. The beleaguered company made its last gallant stand, the actors telling themselves that anything that came in over the $1,600 would be divided as profit.

At the end of not quite two weeks it was obvious that there wasn't going to be any profit. The curtain rang down for the last time on a Theatre Union production.

Members of the Shock Troupe of the WLT in scenes from FREE THAELMANN. In the right hand picture they are (left to right), front row: Jean Harper, Greta Karnot, Ann Gold; second row: Rhoda Rammelkamp, Harry Lessin, Perry Bruskin; third row: Curt Conway, (Unidentified). *Photo by Alfredo Valente.*

Members of the New Dance Group perform "Hunger," the first section of a suite called *On the Barricades,* in about 1934. Left to right: Edna Ocko, Rebecca Roland, Mildred Gold, Miriam Blecher (standing), Bea Siever, Fanya Geltman. *Photo by Alfredo Valente.*

The boys (Harry Lessin, Will Lee, Ben Berenberg, Curt Conway, Earl Robinson, David Kerman) arrive at the CCC camp, watched tolerantly by an army non-com (Jack Arnold) in THE YOUNG GO FIRST. *Photo by Alfredo Valente.*

Helen Henry, in the title role in the Theatre Union's MOTHER, tells of her son's death. The controversial caption screen appears above her. *Photo by Vandamm, courtesy New York Public Library Theatre Collection.*

 By the fall of 1935, when the theatre marquees displayed their autumnal colors and play scripts drifted along Shubert Alley like dead leaves, the Group Theatre was generally acknowledged to be "the finest acting institution in this if not in any other land," as Percy Hammond was to put it. Their new system of acting—or bizarre interpretations of it—was filtering through the theatrical world. Whatever objections might be found to the members' political or social beliefs, their courage and their technical superiority were nowhere denied. Young actors and playwrights hammered on their doors; letters by the dozen came to them imploring auditions—"I have many friends interested in my career," wrote one girl, "and that makes a neat sum of new subscribers." They inspired respect and admiration, but they couldn't seem to make any money.

They had closed *Waiting for Lefty* and *Till the Day I Die* after 136 performances, and recessed *Awake and Sing* through the heat of August. They reopened it in September, teamed with *Lefty*, and when they finally took the double bill on the road *Awake and Sing* had totalled a comfortable 209 performances on Broadway. Yet none of the three plays had really played to capacity houses. It had been the cheaper seats which had always been filled, and although the company had paid its expenses the backers had never seen much profit. A good deal, therefore, hinged on the choices for the coming season.

They began by turning down a potential money-maker. Maxwell Anderson offered them a new play, *Winterset,* based on the Sacco-Vanzetti case. It was read to the company and most of them opposed it. It lacked warmth and emotion, they felt, and it spoke of its revolutionary subject in language too coolly poetic. Years later, when Clurman said that in spite of his own lack of enthusiasm for it they should have done it, the actors maintained heatedly that they had been right.

They chose, at last, to begin the season with *Weep for the Virgins,* by a newcomer, Nellise Child. This was a play about a family working as fish packers in a San Diego cannery. It centered mainly around the mother, a blowsy ex-burlesque queen, and her three ambitious but doomed daughters. It had its defects but it seemed to the directors that it was time they encouraged new writing talent, and the actors found it amusing and interesting. It was to be followed by another Odets play, *Paradise Lost.*

Odets was tasting the doubtfully-flavored fruit of success usually served up to writers. If he was praised by Broadway as a playwright, he was at the same time accused of being too deeply enmeshed in Marxism; if he was hailed by the workers' theatres as a giant for *Lefty,* he was also admonished for his lack of Marxist perception in *Awake and Sing.* Although he had lived from hand to mouth for so many years, he was accused of stinginess by those who thought he was now a millionaire. The truth was that he had not made much money out of his plays and that he had put some of it back into their production. If, at a party, he sat in a corner and made notes, he was said to be posing; if he seemed to enjoy himself, he was said to have become a playboy. And when he began considering the offers that came in from Hollywood, everyone observed with satisfaction that he was about to sell out to the enemy.

He was not quite thirty, a tall, good-looking man with a pointed nose, curly hair, and a sensuous mouth. He was mad for music, and a large part of his new earnings went on progressively better phonographs and new records. He was ambitious, too, and had difficulty reconciling his desire for recognition with his personal ideals, which were inextricably interwoven with those of the Group Theatre.

He was as suited to the Group as a playwright as they were to him as an acting company, more especially as he had worked and studied with them as an actor himself. Their strength lay in their ability to mold rich characters, full of idiosyncrasy, hinting at layers far beneath what was seen on stage, and on their masterly skill at interplay. Odets' work rested on the same base. As individuals, the Group members were extremely versatile, and yet one could neither imagine them romping through a high-speed farce nor performing a detective mystery. No more could Odets write a play that rested solely upon a strong, intricate plot or upon witty, bantering dialogue. It was often said of him that his plays resembled those of Chekhov. Harold Clurman's view was otherwise. "Odets knew very little of Chekhov's work at this time," he wrote, "but quite a lot about Lawson's *Success Story*, in which he had served as Luther Adler's understudy. It was Lawson's play which brought Odets an awareness of a new kind of theatre dialogue. It was a compound of lofty moral feeling, anger, and the feverish argot of the big city."[65] Whatever his inspiration, Odets seemed to catch tormented and uneasy people, snared in a conflict identical with his own, and to isolate some moment of crisis in the stream of their lives. If not precisely Chekhovian, it was as one critic put it, a preference for "life's strange irregular rhythm over the charted beat of theatrical narrative and plot." He spoke primarily for the middle class in that decade, crushed by the Depression, laden with guilt, and torn by America's own ambiguity of purpose—idealism or wealth. Even in *Waiting for Lefty*, it is significant that of the five exemplary characters portrayed in flashback, three are just such people: an actor, a chemist, a doctor, all faced even more by moral dilemmas than economic ones. Most of the Group Theatre people were the same. One wishes they had produced *The Cherry Orchard* or *Uncle Vanya*, but it seems likely that if they had, they would have performed them as if they had been written by Odets.

Paradise Lost dealt with the collapse of a family, the Gordons, the father swindled by his business partner, the three children condemned to tragic fates. There were motifs which had appeared and were to appear in other Odets plays, clashes between children and their parents over middle-class values, the struggle between music and poverty (this was to be the theme of a later play, *Golden Boy*), a strong-minded, practical mother, a harassed, betrayed father. Harold Clurman was the director, and not only was he in fine form but all financial pressure was off since Metro-Goldwyn-Mayer had turned up with ample funds for the movie rights.

Weep for the Virgins was less fortunate. Clurman later described it as "characterized by neglect." Strasberg refused to direct it and it thus went by default to Cheryl Crawford—not a good way for a director to be chosen, and in any case her confidence in her ability had not been enhanced by either of her former assignments, *Big Night,* or *Till the Day I Die.* When it opened, at the end of November 1935, it was received almost with contempt. Many people could not help wondering why the Group had chosen to do it. It ran for a week. On the heels of its closing, *Paradise Lost* opened.

It turned out not to be completely satisfying to anyone. Clurman was later to sigh that for most reviewers it was neither more radical than *Waiting for Lefty* nor more neatly constructed than *Awake and Sing.* Odets didn't help matters by writing to the press to point out some similarities between himself and Chekhov; critics generally prefer to find these things out for themselves. Even those who liked it—and there were quite a few—did so, they said, in spite of its many faults, which worked out to be not very helpful in attracting audiences. The Group ran a determined publicity campaign affirming their belief that it was "a great and important play," and by hook and crook kept it going for nine weeks. Nevertheless, it could not really be considered a success.

Financially, the company was in trouble. They had used up their bank account and their backers' money, including Odets's contributions. The actors had all taken cuts and were back to the days of scrimping and saving. They needed another vehicle, and one for which the production costs could be easily raised. At this point, Milton Shubert brought them a play he had seen performed at the Hedgerow Theatre. It was a dramatization of Theodore Dreiser's widely-read novel, *An American Tragedy,* which had been based on the true case of a youth who had seduced a working girl and then drowned her. The book had been poorly dramatized and badly performed in 1926, but the new version had been done by the eminent expressionist director, Erwin Piscator, then a refugee from his native Germany, in collaboration with Lina Goldschmidt. The Group agreed to make it their next production.

Piscator had given the play some of the stylized, exhortatory quality for which he had been famous in Europe. It was episodic, it rested on the position that the murder had been the result of economic pressures caused by the class struggle, and its points were explained by a narrator, the Speaker, who served much the same function as Brecht's screened captions. This character proved to be one of the stumbling blocks in the play. Lee Strasberg, who directed, did his best to overcome the didactic effect. In rehearsal, he said, "The [Speaker's] speech must not be propagandistic but affable." But when the play was presented, on March 13, 1936, it was obvious that not even the usual spectacular excellence of the Group's playing could sugar-coat the pill. Few could accept the premise that the laws of economics had caused the girl's death. "Any casual reader of crime news could name a dozen cases which would better support the thesis here so dogmatically advanced," scoffed Richard Lockridge. John Anderson suggested that if this story could be turned into a Marxist parable, *Dracula* might be an even apter subject.

The final word on the production came from the Group's highly esteemed property man, Moe Jacobs, who felt that its real trouble lay in the fact that it had no props, not even a chair. "And listen," he added, "at last we got here a play with no birds or goldfish, thank God, so when you got a play that's a play, if you don't figure out a place in it to use beer, you're crazy!"

The Case of Clyde Griffiths hung on for only 19 performances. It was a measure of the Group's indomitability that Clurman, assessing the three failures in a row, could find a bright side. "Only in a theatre with a conscious approach in matters of artistic and cultural growth, can failure become a step toward further advancement," he wrote.

> In general, what stays with me most in relation to our last season is our need to keep up the spirit of constructive self-criticism, to bring up ever new points of attack, new objectives. . . . We should never lose a sense of our value, but we must also never lose sight of the fact that our value diminishes the moment we become easy with ourselves in relation to craftsmanship. . . . The Group must always be inspired by inspiring itself—urging itself to greater efforts. . . . We

used to say that only "good people" could bring forth good theatre; we must now reverse this to say we are "good people" only in so far as we bring forth good theatre. Our "morality" must consist in the most complete professionalism.[66]

Nothing could have been more characteristic of Clurman. If Strasberg was the Group's savant and Crawford its realist, Clurman was its conscience. He had always held before them the notion that art was a Grail to be achieved only by people of the highest principles, that a good actor was also a good person. "It took some of us a long time to find out that this wasn't so," one of the actors later said ruefully. Many of the company—perhaps most of them—were in complete accord with Clurman. It explains the zeal with which so many of them devoted themselves to radical causes; they felt a profound moral obligation to be "good people" by reforming what they thought was wrong in America. It was that same spirit which motivated the hundreds of companies in and around the workers' theatres. It explains, too, the vehement sense of loyalty which helped to hold them together so long. When someone wanted to leave the Group, it always took on the nature of a moral struggle. After *Paradise Lost,* J. Edward Bromberg broke the news that he had secretly signed a contract with a movie company. Clurman, in a fury, asked why he hadn't discussed the matter with the whole Group. "I was afraid to," said Bromberg, "because I knew they'd talk me out of it." Before the close of that play Odets finally accepted a Hollywood offer, and when he left some of the Group members felt that he was little better than a traitor to his own ideals and theirs.

This emphasis on Clurman's aesthetic evangelism should not be taken to mean that his colleagues, Strasberg and Crawford, had any less fervor. They tended, however, to give more attention to other aspects of the Group's work, Crawford to the practical affairs which reinforced the creative bond, Strasberg in pursuit of erudition and expertise. Morris Carnovsky, in a series of imaginary dialogues called "Counterfeit Presentments," designed for a short-lived magazine, *The Flying Grouse,* which Luther Adler got out as a Group Theatre house organ, wrote a pungent caricature of Strasberg, and of Julie Garfield, whose confusion with words was notorious:

(The scene is Lee's apartment. The radio plays the Missa Solemnis. *The victrola plays a Balinese dance. Lee is reading simultaneously* The Cadaver of Gwendolyn Gwyn *and* Die Entwicklung des Basso-buffo im Weltpolitik der 16-jahrhunderd. *Julie bursts in.)*

JULIE: Give me some advice, Lee. I have developed a new atrophacy in my diction. With me, this is tantamount.

LEE: *(after thinking about the Talmud a little):* Say, what do you think, I was reading just the other day, a very interesting treatise—of Yucatan—and of course as usual the priestly cult finds its counterpart in a popular one, and sooner or later a new theatre—

JULIE: Gee, thanks, Lee. I'd gladly listen to you all day for you know my ambition. It is to play a cultural man . . . to say to the dame, "Madam, softly downs the couchy moon. Pray, dismiss Parkerhouse your butler and lay with me before I knock you down."

LEE: Take a piece of corn beef and hack on my books.

JULIE: Gee, thanks, Lee. Now Shakespeare—there's a man!

LEE: You think you've said something? You haven't said anything. The great thing in Shakespeare is not to know what you're saying but to know what you're not saying. You must not only read between the lines, you must read between the words. And you must not only read between the words, you must read between the punctuation marks. And it would be still better if there were no words on the page, then you would begin to get the true greatness . . .

(He suddenly flies into a rage, and calms down at the thought of Meyerhold and the Kabuki.)

Take a piece of salami and the shirt off my back.

JULIE: Gee, thanks, Lee.

In another of his "Counterfeit Presentments" Carnovsky satirized some aspects of the Group's endless absorption in acting problems. This one involves Sanford Meisner and Herbert Ratner, who was generally called "Herbie the Actor," following an unfortunate incident during the summer at Green Mansions when he identified himself that way. The piece begins with Ratner bounding backstage, singing merrily, on his way to the dressing-rooms. Meisner stops him.

SANDY: You came in singing. Why were you singing?
HERBIE: *(nostalgically):* I was happy.
SANDY: Why?
HERBIE: I was feeling good.
SANDY: Why were you feeling good? What would you say was your action?
HERBIE: *(miserable and confused):* To be happy.
SANDY: My God! After five years in the Group he gives me an action—to be happy! . . . What did you come here to the theatre to do?
HERBIE: To—to change my clothes.
SANDY: Aha! Why are you ashamed to admit it? Action: to change clothes.

The Group's attitude towards, and use of, the Stanislavsky method had undergone profound transformations since the early days. In 1934, Clurman and Stella Adler went to the Soviet Union to inspect at first hand the work of the leaders of the Russian stage. From there, they went to Paris, where they found that Stanislavsky was staying, having been sent abroad on a holiday for his health by the Soviet government. When Clurman returned to the United States, Adler remained behind for some weeks of detailed talks with the master. When she rejoined the Group, which was then rehearsing *Gold Eagle Guy* in a summer colony in the Catskills, she brought with her some important revisions which helped to alter the approach to acting of everyone in the Group.

The main change was a movement away from the use of affective memory, which it will be remembered was that system by which an actor attempted to draw upon his store of emotional memories in order to reproduce an emotion on the stage. While some of the older, more experienced actors had been able to use affective memory by keeping it in proportion with other aspects of the method, many of the younger ones had been swamped by it and found that they were playing an emotion rather than a role.

According to Tony Kraber, "Half the time the audience couldn't hear what was going on on stage. The actors were fishing so for emotion that sometimes what came out was unintelligible." Phoebe Brand puts it, that "Almost nobody in the theatre had been using real emotion before us, just indicating it, or suggesting it, and when we began to really laugh and cry and have a ball as we did in *House of Connelly* people were just amazed." But there had been increasing discomfort among the Group members with this path. "The attempt to reproduce the same emotion night after night," says Carnovsky, "led to something stultifying. It was like rubbing the same spot over and over—it just made for irritation. And it led to a lack of self-confidence, too, because your own sense of truth told you that the emotion you were striving for in the sixteenth performance was a strained and imitated thing based on the first successful accomplishment." The answer, as Stella Adler now pointed out, lay in the circumstances of the play, on the actions by which an actor justified what he was doing and out of which emotions grew.

What they were all after was truth, and what they were discovering was that it cannot be put on the stage. The theatrical artist must instead create a simulacrum so consistent, so compelling, and so grounded in real life that it will be accepted by the audience as if it were the truth. What the Group people now began to do, says Brand, was "to try to find the truth of a *given circumstance.* The realer we could make the environment and the circumstances, the more we would be able to live in that environment and those circumstances and respond to them in a real way. We would try to find the truth of a situation and walk into it, and then the emotion would follow naturally. In other words, emotion follows action."

The transition was neither easy nor instantaneous. It produced its own stresses; for example, there was a growing dissatisfaction on the part of some actors with Strasberg's direction since he tended to emphasize the reproduction of real emotion. It in no way diminished the respect they felt for him, but it did make it harder to work with him. In any case, it would be a mistake to think of the Group's use of the Stanislavsky method as uniform or homogeneous. Everyone in the company, including the directors, was constantly studying, searching for personal applications to his own work of the spectrum of technique that was being developed as much by the Group Theatre itself as it had been in the past by the Moscow Art Theatre. Elia Kazan gives some insight into directorial approaches by pointing out, "There is no *wrong* in art. The search for an authoritarian, ritualistic, set thing has always existed but it is only uncertainty that's certain. Nobody in the Group worked the same way. Harold's best time is in the first week of rehearsals when he lays down conceptual ideas about the play; in that he's brilliant. Lee's got a strong emotional tie with the core of the play, makes you break your neck for him trying to live up to his standard. Bobbie Lewis is very witty, very precise with business. I believed in the eloquence of a picture, or a movement —psychological movement." The thread which connected all of them was, as Lewis put it in a brilliant series of lectures given in 1957, "[The] truth that is really experienced, but artistically controlled. . . . Imagination *is* the reality of the artist! . . . In art, truth should be the search for truth."[67]

It was this search for truth, in a larger sense, which made the Group so concerned with the reflection of real social problems in their plays. It also carried over into their activities away from their own theatre. Some, like Art Smith, wrote their own plays for off-Broadway companies. Smith's *The Tide Rises*, a short work about the San Francisco General Strike in 1934, was called by John Gassner, "one of the clearest and most mature expositions of class conflict that has yet appeared." Some, like Kazan, directed other groups. Some taught or conducted studios, Meisner at the Neighborhood Playhouse, Lewis at Sarah Lawrence College. Lewis, in addition, wrote a series of columns on acting for *New Theatre* magazine, called "Five Finger Exercises," which he designed to be useful in "the training of the senses, concentration, the experience that underlies the lines . . . emotion, relation to objects on the stage, 'talking' and listening, connection with the other actors, characterization, imagination, etc.," which gives some idea of the extensive scope of technique covered by the Group's investigations. Some lectured or spoke at public meetings, not only to urge further support for the Group but to stimulate a wider discussion of their method, which was affecting more and more actors, directors, and playwrights. In the fall of 1935, the Group conducted a course at the New School for Social Research of six symposia on the modern theatre which included tickets for six plays, among them the Guild's *Taming of the Shrew,* the Theatre Union's *Mother,* and an unannounced Group production. The classes were led by Strasberg, Clurman, and Crawford, with the addition of a mixed bag including Paul Green, Theresa Helburn, Clifford Odets, John Mason Brown, Herman Shumlin, Alexander Kirkland, Leslie Howard, and John Howard Lawson. The line of demarcation was drawn in one of the first courses, when John Mason Brown said that there were two kinds of theatre, the theatre of entertainment and that of "point of view," to which Odets replied that all artists either consciously or unconsciously express in their work some point of view about the world and society.

Group actors were busy, too, as union members in their profession. A great many of them were active in an insurrectionary movement, Actors' Forum, which had grown up in Equity in defiance of its long-time leadership. It advocated reforms within the union, such as monthly meetings and the establishment of a board to defend actors against unfair wages cuts, and within the industry, such as better rehearsal pay, the adjustment of the proportion of senior to junior members in a show, and unemployment insurance and old age pensions for actors. In spite of a clamor by some of the stodgier members that these young trouble-makers would only make things too hard for producers and would thus reduce the number of shows that could be done, many of the points pressed for eventually came quietly into effect for the benefit of all Equity members.

The same kind of insurgency, but on a more intimate level, was taking place within the Group itself. In the early days of its formation, there had been little question that the chief responsibility for policy and decisions lay with the three directors who had founded it. But by its very nature, the organization demanded more from its actors than just acting. The pride they took in it meant an increasing participation in every phase of its work. It had always been run democratically, to the degree that matters had been discussed openly and criticism of the directors or plays had been voiced, but no one denied that the leaders should take full responsibility for leading. The real issue lay in the fact that for its members, it was not The Group but Our Group. It was not a mere commercial venture but a kind of sacred brotherhood, in which the word "dedication" was more often heard than "profit." It was inevitable that the members should begin to campaign for a greater voice in the management of what concerned them all. At first, the directors resisted what seemed an encroachment on their prerogatives. But the simple economic fact was that the company was not held together by any security that was offered them but by their own enthusiasm and will to be part of it. Near the beginning of their third year an Actors' Committee was voted into being which was to serve in an advisory capacity with the directors.

Over the next three or four years, and particularly as their participation in political activities such as the workers' theatres grew, the committee became more vociferous. It cannot be said that they actually thought of the directors as bosses, but they sometimes behaved as though they did. Disputes sometimes developed over issues such as the choice of plays which seemed too mild or even downright conservative, or over the management of business matters. At the same time, by no means imperceptible cracks had appeared in the directorial façade. Aside from disagreements over policies or scripts, they began to draw apart on such questions as how much control the actors should exert, how much responsibility they themselves should assume and how it should be shared, and even more touchy matters of aesthetics and directorial ability. Some of this had come to a head when, in Clurman's words, after *Gold Eagle Guy* Strasberg "retired into a state of impassivity" from which he only emerged to direct the ill-fated *Case of Clyde Griffiths.*

After the closing of that play, things looked very bleak. Funds were as low as morale, and the company made a spring road tour with *Awake and Sing* which, if it brought them credit, lost them money. Several members—J. Edward Bromberg, Walter Coy, and Alexander Kirkland—had been forced by the pressure of circumstances to leave for other jobs. Odets had settled in Hollywood where he was working on a film, *The General Dies at Dawn,* writing a play called *Silent Partner* based on a strike, and wooing Luise Rainer, whom he described rather coolly to Clurman as "the best actress out here." Clurman went on a tour of his own in search of playwrights, visiting a promising young writer named Robert Ardrey, in Chicago, going to the Coast to line up Odets's play, and seeing Paul Green in North Carolina. Around the time of the

Theatre Union's *Mother,* some of the Group members had met and become friendly with Kurt Weill, and Stella Adler had suggested that he do a musical play for them. He had said he'd like to try an American equivalent to the European anti-war play, *The Good Soldier Schweik,* if a playwright could be found. Clurman sounded out Green, who had soldiered in World War I and who proved eager for the project.

The Group now had two possible productions in the offing. Furthermore, Clurman came up with a plan to reorganize the company, centralizing its leadership with himself as managing director, forming a new Actors' Committee composed of Stella Adler, Roman Bohnen, Morris Carnovsky, and Elia Kazan, and giving the actors a little more say in affairs. The Group pulled itself together again and took heart. Arrangements were made with an adult summer camp, Pine Brook, in Connecticut, similar to those with Green Mansions some years before, by which the company would perform three times a week in exchange for board and lodging and would still have enough free time in which to rehearse and study.

The summer turned out to be both busy and frustrating. There were twelve apprentices as well as nearly thirty regular members, plus Odets, Green, and Weill, several instructors, and some wives and friends, so that they threatened to outnumber the campers. Everyone worked hard at obligatory classes: dancing, under Felicia Sorel and Gluck Sandor; acting technique with Strasberg; analytical studies in approaches to roles, under Stella Adler; speech and language in poetic drama, given by Morris Carnovsky; and singing for the theatre, led by Kurt Weill. It was all very exciting and companionable. But they were not so lucky with plays. Odets's *Silent Partner* had great weaknesses and needed a good deal more work. John Howard Lawson's play, *Marching Song,* for which they had been waiting with high expectations, arrived early on and was rejected. And Paul Green's script, *Johnny Johnson,* was not delivered until near the end of the summer. It had great charm, humor, and style, and everyone liked it, but only a week or so remained of the free time guaranteed by working for the camp. When they got back to New York, instead of being ready to start the season, as they had expected, they were a long way from opening.

Johnny Johnson was an expensive production with a large cast, and backing was hard to find. Some of the actors had been offered good parts elsewhere and were tempted to leave. Clurman put the matter up to the whole company. Did they want to continue with the show or not? They voted overwhelmingly in favor of sticking together and going on.

Strasberg took up the direction of the production, while Clurman and Crawford flew about raising money. A theatre then had to be found, and it was at this point that a perhaps unavoidable mistake was made which turned out to have calamitous consequences. Only one house was available, the Forty-fourth Street Theatre, and rather than postpone the play indefinitely, they took it. It was a noble barn of a place with an immense stage, and for that stage Donald Oenslager, who was noted for the grand scale on which he worked, designed equally vast sets. Originally the play had been conceived of on an intimate scale and in rehearsals it had been kept that way. When it was moved into the Forty-fourth Street for dress rehearsals and previews, it was suddenly dwarfed and the light-handed informality of the performance lost its effectiveness. During the first preview, people drifted out of the theatre in shoals, something that had never before happened to the Group.

The company toiled heroically, rehearsing afternoons, giving previews, at each of which the show improved, and then staying up until all hours of the night polishing, cutting, and revising, and thus wearing themselves out to the point where they hardly knew what they were doing. Two of the largest sets were abandoned. Some of the musical numbers were deleted. At last, on November 16th, the curtain officially rose.

Almost everyone who saw *Johnny Johnson* was charmed by it. As an argument against war it was ironic where it should have been scathing, but it had a subtlety and wit which were thoroughly engaging. It tells the story of a gangling young man from a small town, played with gentle humor by Russell Collins, who goes off to fight in the "war to end all wars" and finds that the enemy is his own counterpart. Using laughing gas, he induces the High Command to call a halt to the fighting, but they recover, start the war again, and send him to an insane asylum where he organizes a debating society which parodies the speeches of the world's statesmen. At the end, he sells toys on a street corner as everyone prepares for another war. Its music was haunting and some of it was Kurt Weill at the top of his form. The Group's work, too, was impeccable, especially in the contrast between the broad caricature of the debating society or an interview with a lunatic psychiatrist, and the touching but bitter simplicity of such scenes as that in which the big guns rise to sing a lullaby over sleeping soldiers, or Johnny's last, wistful song as the only sane man in a mad world. Audiences enjoyed it so much that people returned several times to see it. Critics praised it, Mantle putting it on his Best Ten list, Watts comparing it with Chaplin's *Shoulder Arms*, Douglas Gilbert of the *World-Telegram* calling it, "diverting and occasionally poignant," and even George Jean Nathan growling sourly that it was "feather in the cap of an acting organization that . . . doesn't seem to know much about acting." And yet, the truth was that there was too much to find fault with. In a world that was really preparing for war, in which fascism had conquered Ethiopia and was practicing with its dive bombers in Spain, the play seemed merely muddled and well-intentioned. In a theatre suited to its scale, it would have come across with much greater bite; on that huge stage it seemed weak. Almost every critic qualified his review in some way so that there were few notices that could be quoted to bring in the crowds. And the play's running expenses were fearfully high. Sacrifice as they would, the Group could only keep it going for 68 performances.

By this time, the friction between Clurman and Strasberg had produced a good deal of heat. Strasberg felt the new managing director was dithering instead of showing strong organizational leadership. Clurman found Strasberg ill-tempered and resistant to criticism. In part, the disagreement may have rested on their aesthetic divergence as stage directors, but it went much deeper to a clash of wills and temperaments which was becoming irreconcilable. In many matters, Cheryl Crawford tended to side with Strasberg, which made Clurman's managerial task more difficult.

The rest of the Group, fully aware that the organization was threatened, wanted only to save it. The Actor's Committee, after much deliberation, produced an analysis of the situation including an incisive examination of the three directors which, after paying tribute to their inspiration, hard work, and leadership, concluded that Strasberg should have no responsibilities other than artistic ones, Clurman should be given a firm plan of action since he was a poor organizer, and Crawford should be allowed more leeway in the creation of scripts—she had worked closely with Weill and Green on *Johnny Johnson*—and be given a rest from business management. The report ended by urging that the actors somehow be guaranteed a regular income, that somehow a program of work be arranged for the company, and that somehow the Group should have its own theatre. Everyone including the directors agreed with and accepted the analysis. The trouble was all those "somehows."

They had already begun rehearsing *Silent Partner* although the script was by no means satisfactory and Odets, busy in Hollywood with another movie and newly married to Lusie Rainer, was unable or unwilling to work on it. Both Strasberg and Crawford felt it was in no condition to be taken any further, and eventually Clurman concurred. All three, somewhat chastened by the actors' white paper, offered to resign. The Group voted to reconstitute itself, forming a committee composed of the directors and some of the actors. Its task would be to find ways of implementing the proposals for continuing, and somehow getting around the bothersome somehows.

Meanwhile, people had to eat. They couldn't spend their time debating and planning; they were actors, and there were plenty of producers ready to snap them up. Early in 1937 Clurman announced that they were postponing work on *Silent Partner* with no other play in view, but that the office would remain open and that they hoped to get together again in the summer. This was taken by everyone to mean, "Send no flowers."

The office was promptly deluged with letters and phone calls from people outraged and horrified at the Group's death. Some of them said it was the company's *duty* to go on and that even a temporary layoff was a loss to the theatre. Clurman replied with a letter to the *Times,* saying, like Mark Twain, that the report of their demise had been greatly exaggerated and that the Group would, indeed, continue. They needed, said he, a subsidy to keep the actors together and find plays and a permanent home to be used as a playhouse and studio. "The actors and directors of the

Group Theatre," he concluded, "look forward to a future of the most creative activity."

Notwithstanding these brave words, it looked as though everything was finished. The Group members were swept apart. Julie Garfield, Tony Kraber, Paula Miller and Lee Cobb went into the Arthur Kober play, *Having Wonderful Time,* from which Garfield was to emerge a star. Others found parts in other shows. Many took the Hollywood trail. Stella Adler had gone there petulantly, even before the final meetings, to change her name to Ardler and appear in a film in which someone hit her in the face with a custard pie. Now Clurman followed her west, and over a short period so did others, including Phoebe Brand, Ruth Nelson, Morris Carnovsky, Elia Kazan, Roman Bohnen, and Luther Adler.

Crawford and Strasberg remained in New York. And in April, Clurman, still nominal managing director of the Group, received letters from both resigning for good. Strasberg's note added caustically that the actors, by insisting on having their way, had destroyed the company's leaders. On the 13th of the month Crawford announced that she was forming a new, independent cooperative venture and that Strasberg would probably direct some of its plays.

There now seemed little doubt to most people that the Group was not only dead but disintegrated. It would, in fact, arise from its own ashes, but it would never be the same phoenix.

 **1935-1940**

Early in the summer of 1935, a new producing company began preparing for the coming season. It was to be one of the most exciting yet to appear, and one of the most ambitious, for it would include extravagantly experimental work and old-fashioned conservative theatre, presentations of the classics and of brand-new plays; it would be as sharply criticized as the workers' theatre for its social bias; it would resemble in some ways the Guild, the Group, and the Theatre Union, and would vie with the best and worst of both the workers' theatre and the commerical theatre; it would give black playwrights and performers their first serious chance at full-length productions on a major scale, and it would introduce a stunning new theatrical form to the American stage. It would finally solve the knotty problems of audience and budget, and it could do all this because its sole angel was the United States government.

The formation of the Federal Theatre Project was the the kind of bold move only the Roosevelt administration was capable of, especially daring since it was linked with similar projects for art, music, and literature. They were all part of the program for restoring not only the economy but the morale of America, which expressed itself in the notion that men would rather have work than charity. The Work Relief Act of 1935 appropriated more than $5 billion dollars which was to be spent on highways, rural rehabilitation and electrification, the Civilian Conservation Corps, reforestation, flood and erosion control, water works, sewage plants and power plants, housing, and a variety of other important public works on every level right down to the municipal one. It was as vast as it was unprecedented, and perhaps nothing but so drastic a plan could have revived the country. What was most visionary was that room was found in it for the arts, with incalculably beneficial results to America's cultural life.

In April, after the passage of the Work Relief Act, its administration—and the spending of all those billions of dollars—was put into the hands of Harry Hopkins, one of the ablest of FDR's New Dealers. A provision of $300 million had been made for white collar projects and one of these was envisioned as a way of putting theatrical people to work. The theatre, never one of the safest ways of making a living, had been slow to recover from the Depression. Equity estimated that there were about eight thousand unemployed actors and more than half that many jobless members of Chorus Equity in New York alone. Even those who had jobs had no security. The average play was about as long-lived as a martini at an advertising convention. Until Equity, goaded by the Actors' Forum, took up the cudgels, managers had a bad habit of declaring unexplained losses and cutting actors' salaries without warning. Even actors in demand might work for only a few months a year, and part of that time was spent rehearsing on lower pay—in the case of many black actors, on no pay at all. The actors' own Stage Relief Fund helped some indigent performers, but its money was limited. Hungry actors could get a free meal at the Actors' Dinner Club where those who could afford it paid a dollar while those who couldn't paid nothing, but black actors were not admitted. The Club's secretary said, "I wouldn't go into Schrafft's . . . and sit next to a colored person. . . . We don't discriminate against them, but we don't want them here." Because of the irregularity of their work actors had trouble qualifying for unemployment insurance or relief. And in any case money was secondary; as the history of so many groups shows, actors wanted to act more than they wanted to eat and there just weren't that many shows.

To form the Federal Theatre Project, Hopkins called an old friend to Washington, Hallie Flanagan, who had been his fellow student at Grinnell College, Iowa. Flanagan, a small attractive deceptively soft-spoken woman, at first seemed an unlikely choice. She had worked in the theatre all her life, as a student and then production assistant to George Pierce Baker, and then as the director of experimental theatres at Grinnell and Vassar College, but she had no big-time professional experience. However, her trim exterior concealed a charge like that of a high-tension cable. She took on the immense task of setting up the complex machinery of the project and administering it with the assurance of a David. It was significant that her regional directors were mainly people who had been active in the Little Theatres or Community Theatres, for instance, Jasper Deeter for Pennsylvania, Professor Frederick Koch of the North Carolina Playmakers for the South, Frederic McConnell of the Cleveland Playhouse for Ohio, and Gilmore Brown of the Pasadena Playhouse for the West. Rosamund Gilder, associate editor of *Theatre Arts Monthly,* headed the Bureau for Research and Publicity. And for the most important of the branches, New York, Elmer Rice was selected, with Philip Barber as his assistant. Only a few months earlier Rice had publicly said good-bye to Broadway in a letter to the newspapers in which he declared that the profit system in the theatre "stifles the creative impulse and dams the free flow of human vitality." He turned eagerly to what was planned as a theatre which intended to spend money, not make it.

The predecessor of the Works Progress Administration had been the Public Works Administration which, in New York, had run a tiny entertainment program that sent ill-equipped companies to public schools. Its head had been a former military man, Colonel Earle Boothe, whose favorite play for PWA performances was *Meet the Enemy,* a jingoistic drama written by himself. More to set people's minds at rest than because he doubted her integrity, Herb Kline wrote to Hallie Flanagan asking for details of the new project and reassurance that it wouldn't follow Colonel Boothe's pattern. Her reply gave a view of what the Federal Theatre might become:

> [W]hile our immediate aim . . . is to put to work thousands of theatre people, our more far reaching purpose is to organize and support theatrical enterprises so excellent in nature, so low in cost, and so vital to the communities involved that

they will be able to continue after Federal support is withdrawn. . . .

We need the support of people who share our belief that the theatre horizon is not contracting, but widening to include the Santa Fe Desert, the Rocky Mountains, and the valley of the Mississippi . . . widening to include consciousness of the social scene as well as the social register; widening, in short, to include the impossible—that same impossible which has led our contemporaries to soar to the stars, whisper through space, and fling miles of steel and glass into the air.[69]

The language might be thought a little high-flown, but the reality was to come very close to matching it. Within a year after Flanagan took the reins, the Federal Theatre had two hundred producing groups across the country and employed more than twelve thousand people. It was performing before audiences of thousands, for many of whom this was the first experience of the theatre, and its stages ranged from public parks, armories, or auditoriums, to professional houses. Its program included Pulitzer Prize winning plays like *The Old Maid,* old-fashioned long running hits like *Lightnin',* well-known classics, children's plays, plays in foreign languages, and unusual dramas like T.S. Eliot's poetic *Murder in the Cathedral,* which the Theatre Guild had rejected and on which no ordinary producer would take a chance. It was doing all that Flanagan and her aides had hoped for, presenting low-cost and in most cases admirable shows from coast to coast. It had won wide critical approval and had made itself a vital part of the cultural life of many communities. It had widened the field of theatre to embrace "the social scene as well as the social register." It was, indeed, so satisfactorily accomplishing the impossible that it began to unsettle both commercial producers and all those watchdogs in authority who feared that open windows, instead of letting in fresh air, would admit criminals. In Chicago, a production called *Model Tenements,* by Meyer Levin was halted by the mayor because it seemed too radical. Anderson's *Valley Forge* was banned in a Massachusetts town because it treated Washington disrespectfully. *Turpentine,* by J.A. Smith and Peter Morell, a serious play about labor camps done by the Negro

Theatre, was bitterly attacked by some southern papers and southern legislators for being "provocative." In New York, several producers claimed that Federal Theatre productions, because of their low cost of admission—when they performed in professional theatres the Treasury Department allowed them to charge up to fifty cents, or in rare cases a dollar—were unfairly competing with Broadway. Even Lawrence Langner, while approving of the project in general, held that it should limit itself to the classics, to revivals, and to noncompetitive experimental plays. The real cause for objection, never openly stated, was that the quality of work was so high that it drew crowds; obviously, no one would have complained if it had been second-rate.

But the loudest outcries came over the project's most striking and most socially barbed creation, the Living Newspaper.

The Living Newspaper began when Rice and Flanagan were discussing how large numbers of actors could be employed in relatively quick and inexpensive productions. She proposed using them in dramatizations of the news which would rely on lights, music, and stage movement and which could be put together swiftly, almost like a daily paper. Rice liked the idea and promptly put a journalist in charge of it, Morris Watson, president of the Newspaper Guild. Watson set up his office like a city desk and started his people preparing a script. For the first New York production a subject was chosen which was making headlines, the Italian invasion of Ethiopia. An additional, if minor reason for this decision was the fact that the Federal Theatre had on its rolls a troupe of native African dancers who had been stranded in the United States and had been among the first batches of theatre workers sent to the project by the relief office.

Dramatizations of news stories were by no means original with the Federal Theatre. They had been done in political cabarets in Europe for decades and had been used by the workers' theatres in the United States, most effectively by the Workers' Laboratory Theatre in sketches like *Free Thaelmann* and *Newsboy*. The title "Living Newspaper" had been invented by the Soviet Blue Blouses, mobile theatrical troupes that had been organized in the late 1920s by journalists who aimed their work at the semi-literate peasants and workmen in the provinces. The form, wherever it was used, had employed mime and dance, dramatic sequences, quotations and speeches, posters and charts to make its points. It had been essentially fluid and swift-paced, depending on movement and lighting for its dynamic effect. The Federal Theatre's Living Newspaper took the form a step further to produce full-length theatrical spectacles, using dramatized scenes or rhythmic mass movement interspersed with direct speeches and quotations from public figures, expository charts, graphs, film clips, and magnified teletype to create an electrifying montage. They relied on complex light plots rather than settings, but when they did have sets they used them not so much as background as levels on and around which to choreograph movement.

The material used in the Living Newspapers was researched by a staff of newsmen. Some of the scripts were collaborated on by a team of sixteen writers headed by Arthur Arent, who later wrote one or two by himself. The shape of the shows was hammered out by experience in a kind of triumph of the collective effort. They were supervised by Morris Watson, who knew nothing at all about the theatre but a good deal about how a newspaper was put together, and their directors and producers added to the development of the form as they went along—Joseph Losey and Gordon Graham doing *Triple A Plowed Under* and *Injunction Granted,* Lem Ward working on *One-third of a Nation,* Brett Warren and Edward Vail on *Power.* Inevitably, as is the case with even the most balanced news feature story, some editorializing crept in, although the staff did its best to keep its viewpoint unbiased and to base its scripts on publicly reported facts and direct quotations. They were, however, dealing with explosive issues. In *Triple A Plowed Under,* which had to do with the Agricultural Adjustment Act, the desperate plight of farmers and farm laborers was revealed; in *One-third of a Nation,* which took its title from an address by Roosevelt in which he said, "I see one-third of a nation ill-housed, ill-clad, ill-nourished," the slums and their landlords were exposed; *Injunction Granted* told of the struggles of the American labor movement. It was inevitable that some toes would be stepped on, and the Living Newspaper became an early target for conservatives of every shade.

The Ethiopian war offered an especially ticklish situation since the United States was keeping up an attitude of neutrality. Trouble began for the first Living Newspaper when it was planned to have speeches by Emperor Haile Selassie, Mussolini, and President Roosevelt delivered by actors taking those parts. Morris Watson asked Washington for permission to use a transcript of one of the president's broadcasts. He was told by Jacob Baker, assistant administrator of the WPA, that because of the sensitive international situation, the Living Newspaper was not to use any impersonations of the heads of governments or members of a ministerial cabinet unless approved in advance by the State Department. And since it would be impractical to get such approval in time, it would be safer not to bother in the first place.

Elmer Rice had been battling from the start for the integrity and independence of the New York project whenever he thought it threatened, and had been especially caustic about red tape, which he said "prevented the creation of a flexible theatre." He now went to bat for the Living Newspaper, which was particularly close to his heart. Baker modified his stand sufficiently to say that speeches could be quoted by others onstage, but that the appearance of figures representing chiefs or ministers of a foreign power could not be allowed. He also wanted some important changes made in the script. Rice felt this was nothing less than censorship and, as he explained, this was born out by the fact that the changes were only insisted on after he had outlined to Baker some future productions which had as their subjects unemployment and discrimination against blacks. According to Rice, Baker knew in advance that he would quit rather than agree to curbs, and was actually hoping for it, for when Rice offered to resign Baker pulled a prepared letter of acceptance from his pocket and handed it over. Philip Barber became regional director for New York in Rice's place and brought in Walter Hart as his assistant. *Ethiopia*, unfinished as it was, was given a single uncensored showing for the press and then packed away.

As a result, many theatre people particularly, as might be expected, on the Left, expressed concern about the fate not only of the Living Newspaper but the whole project. John Howard Lawson, in a piece in *New Theatre*, tied in the suppression—for that in effect is what it was—of *Ethiopia* with a wave of censorship of commercial plays and films all over the country, most notably the arbitrary closing of *Tobacco Road* in Chicago as lewd and the banning of *The Children's Hour* in Boston as immoral. Censorship of the Living Newspaper, Lawson warned, was federal censorship of the arts, and added, that "It means using public funds for the suppression of public opinion; it means an attempt to harness culture in the service of reactionary politicians." That may have seemed far-fetched at the time, for in the course of its relatively brief life the Federal Theatre was able to speak fairly openly in a variety of ways on a number of important subjects; and actually Rice's battle went far towards keeping the project relatively free from interference. In the end, however, Lawson's foreboding turned out to be warranted. Like the entire Works Project Administration, the project was fair game for politicians who saw it only as another subtle maneuver by That Man in the White House to get votes and win public favor. The word "boondoggler" was invented by hostile congressmen to describe the average WPA worker who, it was held, was nothing but an idler who took the government's money for leaning on a shovel. Still, no one could shut his eyes to the fact that dams and buildings were actually rising and roads were spreading. So a good deal of enmity focused on the arts projects, for who could claim that people doing shows or painting pictures or playing music were really working? They were, fumed many politicians, only furthering their own careers at the public's expense, and in any case most of the plays done by the Federal Theatre were clearly Red propaganda. How well equipped some congressmen were to judge the matter may be seen from the words of Representative Joe Starnes of Alabama, a member of the House Un-American Activities Committee which cross-examined Hallie Flanagan in 1938. Starnes read a section from that article in which Flanagan had reported on the first meeting of the Workers Drama League in 1931, and which had ended by saying that they were invested "with a certain Marlowesque madness." "You are quoting from this Marlowe," Starnes glowered. "Is he a Communist?"

The proportion of social-conscious to non-political drama on the project was actually about the same as on Broadway: small. The difference was that since the government was picking up the bill, the opposition tended to take more notice of anything even mildly leftish. A good example was the Children's Theatre. It did hundreds of performances of innocuous plays in schools, parks, and playgrounds; it drew wide praise for a glittering, long-running production of *The Emperor's New Clothes* by Charlotte Chorpenning. But when it presented a fantasy called *The Revolt of the Beavers*, by Oscar Saul and Lou Lantz, in which the inhabitants of Beaverland kick out their wicked king in the best approved fairytale style so that they can play games, eat ice cream, and stay nine years old, a perfect scream of wrath went up that it was a Communist allegory. Jack Renick, the director of the Children's Theatre, sighed that if only they had given it a less provocative title, the play would have attracted no adverse attention. "We should have called it *Rumpelstiltzkin*," he said. As it was, thousands of children saw it and loved it without a single known case of subversion.

Among its more than ninety productions in New York City alone, the Federal Theatre did, in fact, find room for some important social plays. Lawson's *Processional* was revived in a slightly rewritten version with great effect. That staple of dozens of workers' theatre groups, Alfred Kreymbourg's poem "America, America," was shown briefly. A moving production of Friedrich Wolf's anti-Nazi play, *Professor Mamlock*, ran for nearly a year. George Sklar's *Life and Death of an American*, which the Theatre Union had refused, was called by Piscator the most superb stage production he had seen in America. Virgil Geddes's *Native Ground*, and *Battle Hymn* by Michael Gold and Michael Blankfort, were much lauded. The Living Newspapers all fell into the category of social-conscious drama, but so prodigious was their impact that hardly any reviewer remembered to call them propaganda. *The Cradle Will Rock*, Marc Blitzstein's play with music, one of the most brilliant pieces of political theatre ever done in this country, came out of the project, although, as it happened, it was never done under its sponsorship. *Chalk Dust*, by Harold Clarke and Maxwell Nurnberg, called attention to the evils in the public school system; it was very well received and in addition to its two-month run in New York flourished in ten other cities. One of the most outstanding of the Federal Theatre's productions, as well as one of its most blinding headaches, was *It Can't Happen Here*, dramatized by Sinclair Lewis and John Moffitt from the former's novel, a cautionary tale of how fascism might come to America. The movies had been frightened of it, but a number of Broadway offers had been made. Lewis, in the end, decided to let the Federal Theatre have it because of his "tremendous admiration for its work and, secondly, because I know I can depend on the Federal Theatre for a non-partisan point of view." Flanagan and her aides decided that the story of how a demogogic politician builds a strong-arm machine and silences all opposition to make himself the Hitler of the United States deserved the most important treatment. They resolved to open it simultaneously in a number of cities. Lewis and Moffitt set to work on the script and very shortly were at daggers' points over it. Sitting in separate rooms in the same hotel, they sent word to each other by way of Hallie Flanagan, who acted as a go-between and nursed the play through to completion. The non-partisanship Lewis had hoped for was guaranteed by a ruling that no references to a foreign power, system, or personality could be made. The play was to be kept a strictly American parable. As rehearsals got under way, a hot advance controversy began in the national press, that it was nothing but propaganda, that it was *not* propaganda, that it would antagonize Hitler, that it was a patriotic necessity, and so on. Feeling ran high against it in Louisiana where many people felt it was a slur on the late governor, Huey Long. In Missouri, the authorities wanted to modify the message of the script. Flanagan cancelled productions in both states. To everyone's astonishment, the play actually made its scheduled opening on October 27, 1936, in seventeen theatres across the country, including a second version in New York in Yiddish and one with a black cast in Seattle. Almost all the reviews were extremely favorable and pointed out the play's political importance—if anything, some critics felt it could have been a good deal harsher in its strictures on fascism. By the time it had finished all its runs including repertory and tours, it had done the equivalent of 260 weeks of performance. Hallie Flanagan's later assessment of it summed up the general feeling of most of those associated with the project. "In producing that play the first government-sponsored theatre of the United States was doing what it could to keep alive 'the free, inquiring, critical spirit' which is the center and core of a democracy."[70]

Another vital field in which the Federal Theatre proved its leadership was that of the black theatre. Aside from the Harlem Suitcase Theatre and the Rose McClendon Players' Theatre Workshop, both in New York, and the Karamu Theatre in Cleveland, black actors and playwrights who wanted to do serious works about their own people had almost no outlet since the chances of such plays getting a Broadway viewing were bound to be slim. Even in the black communities there was some opposition to political drama. When the Karamu Theatre, which had been a fixture in Cleveland since 1920, announced that it was going to do *Stevedore*, in 1935, it not only ran into police threats of closing, but the local black newspaper and several ministers spoke against the play as being likely to arouse bad feeling. It was done anyway, and sold out the fourteen days of its scheduled run. The Harlem Suitcase Theatre and the Rose McClendon Players concentrated on original plays by black playwrights, but could hardly afford any but the cheapest and simplest productions. The Suitcase Theatre, performing in a fraternal hall in Harlem, gave the work of Langston Hughes an airing; his *Don't You Want to be Free?* shown on weekends went to 135 performances, the longest run a play had had in Harlem. The Rose McClendon Players gave a start to Abram Hill and Warren Coleman, among others. The Federal Theatre, however, became the pivot on which the condition of black theatre turned for the better. Negro companies were set up in New York, Chicago, Seattle, Birmingham, Los Angeles, Philadelphia, Hartford, and other cities, and their repertory embraced fifty-five plays, most of them new ones. Classics—if so staid a word can be applied to so youthful a department as plays about American blacks—included *In Abraham's Bosom*, *Porgy*, and *Stevedore*. Three of O'Neill's plays were done, although *All God's Chillun Got Wings* was not one of them, possibly because it was not quite as relevant to the lives of blacks as may once have been believed. Paul Green was very popular, with almost everything he had ever written finding its way to the stage. Black playwrights were especially encouraged, among them Ted Ward, Theodore Browne, and Frank Wilson, and from them came a stream of hard-hitting dramas which were given excellent professional productions and were seen by large audiences of blacks and whites. The New York Negro Theatre became a particular favorite with playgoers for the imaginative flair of its staging and the ebullience and virility of its performers. It showed a nice balance in its choice of plays, ranging from a powerful *Macbeth* to the riotous *Swing Mikado*, nor did it dodge real social issues, from Frank Wilson's *Walk Together Chillun*, a plea for black labor unity, to William Du Bois's *Haiti*, which described the historic rising under Toussaint l'Ouverture and which was one of the hits of the season of 1937–38.

The Federal Theatre proved a boon, too, to the dance. Those small bedraggled groups which had had to work so hard for recognition around the fringes of the workers' theatres had grown to the point where they were pressing hard on the heels of the leaders of the dance world. They were bridging the gap between ballet and modern dancing by introducing social themes and the use of narration, poetry, or jazz into their programs. Even the primmest dance critics, people like John Martin and Lincoln Kerstein, were coming to accept the revolutionary innovations they had introduced into their forms, and the time was not far off when the most successful Broadway musicals would draw not only on those forms but the dancers themselves. They had come a long way from the burlap and safety pins of their beginnings. In 1936, the New Dance Group had become sufficiently established to conduct a highly popular school in which the major techniques of modern dance were taught, with advance work being supervised by Edith Orcutt of the Humphrey–Weidman Concert Group, Jane Dudley of Martha Graham's group, and Nancy McKnight of Hanya Holm's School. José Limon taught the men's classes. The following year the three main groups, the New Dance League whose executive secretary was Louise Redfield, the Dance Guild headed by Blanche Evan, and the Dancers Association led by Helen Tamiris, merged to make one national professional organization, the goal of which was mainly to campaign for a modicum of economic security for dancers. A year before that, the joint efforts of the three groups had won a Dance Project which was affiliated with the Federal Theatre. It had as choreographers Tamiris, Gluck Sandor, Felicia Sorel, and Don Oscar Becque, with Charles Weidman and Doris Humphrey as advisers. Its twenty-four new productions included an elegant version of *Candide* by Weidman, and Tamiris's ballet *How Long Brethren?* supported by a Negro choral ensemble and including dances based on Lawrence Gellert's *Songs of Protest*. Some of the dancers also crossed over to do choreography for plays, as Tamiris did for *One-third of a Nation* and *Trojan Incident*.

In short, the Federal Theatre contained almost all the areas of the experimental and social theatre, and managed to solve nearly all the problems connected with them which had stymied all the independent groups that preceded it. About all that was left out was straightforward agit-prop, which had been abandoned by most of the workers' theatres anyway, and plays with a direct Marxist orientation which came right out and preached revolution, and, there were very few of these left in the workers' theatres repertory and none which could touch the quality of, say, *Waiting for Lefty.* One or other of the project's many companies sooner or later would do a play dealing with war, labor relations, social satire, fascism, racial discrimination, or any of the other issues which exercised the Left, and what was more could give them full professional productions with topnotch music, sets, lighting, costumes, and choreography. The price of seats could be kept lower than the Theatre Union's top, and plays would still reach the widest possible audience. There was room to bring to that audience not only up-to-date plays with a social slant, but Ibsen, Shakespeare, and even Shaw—the usually intransigent old man had given his plays to the Federal Theatre for a fifty-dollar a week rental as long as they stuck to their low cost tickets—and to present them in German, Spanish, and Yiddish in the bargain. The Federal Theatre's competition with Broadway is debatable, but there is no question that it affected the workers' theatres. The Theatre Union's failure rested in part on this competition; the project could offer Paul Green's *Hymn to the Rising Sun* or George Sklar's *Life and Death of an American* in full dress and at half the price of admission, and absorb any loss without blinking. It was no wonder that before long the best of the workers' theatre groups melted away into the Federal Theatre. They brought with them their determination to do social-conscious works if they could and to reach the mass of the non-theatre-going public. They did not altogether abandon their activities and continued to perform off the project to some extent, but it was inevitable that their movement should be weakened.

The Theatre of Action was one of the first to join, and indeed, the only one to transfer almost intact to the project.

When *The Young Go First* closed, they had more or less marked time for the rest of the summer and had done mobile work through the fall and winter to keep themselves going. One of the casualties was the Evening Troupe. There were stormy meetings, and a long report was written assessing their work, but it was perfectly clear the company could no longer sustain so many people. "It went to a vote," says Florence Kamlot, "and everyone who was in the Evening Troupe voted themselves out of the theatre. It had to be done. There were lots of tears that night because for many people it was cutting themselves off from an important part of their lives." A few steady workers remained clustered around the nucleus of the Shock Troupe, and so did some of the people who had been brought in for *The Young Go First*. One of these, Joan Madison, left to take the part of Pearl in the Group Theatre's *Paradise Lost*. "I remember how overjoyed everybody in the Theatre of Action was at my good fortune," she says. "That was the manifestation of their spirit—there wasn't a trace of envy." A little later one Shock Trouper, Curt Conway, was given some roles in *Johnny Johnson*. Several people, like Harry Lessin, moved out of the house on East 27th Street but continued to work with the troupe. The company resolved that the debts run up by *The Young Go First* must be paid. "They were nice people, the people who had loaned us money," Will Lee says. "It took us a long time, but we managed to pay off three-quarters of those debts. We had a sense of responsibility for what we were doing."

They tried to get *Bury the Dead* and failed. "Our history might have been different," a former member says wistfully. "We were the right group and that was the right play." Early in 1936, they chose a one-act play by Michael Blankfort, *The Crime*, based on a real strike of meat-packers which was unintentionally betrayed by weak and timorous leadership. At about the same time, they began making overtures to get themselves accepted into the Federal Theatre. Their work as a group was known to Hallie Flanagan, as well as to Philip Barber and Walter Hart, both of whom had taught at the Theatre Collective. The troupe began the procedure of qualifying for relief—not a difficult thing to do since they hadn't enough money among them to buy a three-course dinner—and meanwhile they went ahead with rehearsals of *The Crime*.

Once again, Elia Kazan, then in *Paradise Lost*, agreed to direct, with Al Saxe as his teammate. The play had a big cast and a number of outsiders were brought in. They presented it at the Civic Repertory Theatre on March 1st and for two more Sundays thereafter as a New Theatre League benefit. As a curtain raiser, they did a brief piece by Paul Peters, *The Little Green Bundle. The Crime* pleased few people. John Gassner, the perceptive and sympathetic critic of *New Theatre* magazine, summed things up when he credited the Theatre of Action with an expert performance but added that the play "did not arouse any excessive interest or excitement on the part of this reviewer." The only really outstanding thing about the production was that it set a record of some kind in that no fewer than four of the people concerned with it later made major reputations as directors in films, television, and on the stage: Elia Kazan, Norman Lloyd, Nick Ray, and Martin Ritt.

By the end of March, the Theatre of Action was taken into the Federal Theatre as the One-Act Experimental Theatre. Not everybody went along. Stephen Karnot had made separate arrangements and was given the post of manager of the dozen or so groups in the Manhattan project. Harold Jacobson went with him as general stage manager. He and Berenberg were to perform together as a team only once more, at a nostalgic one-night revival nine years later. Charles Friedman had already left to return to the Theatre Union. But most of the Shock Troupe stuck together, and some continued for a short time to live on in the 27th Street house.

Their first, and as it turned out, only, program was presented on May 13, 1936. It consisted of three one-acters, beginning with Molière's *The Miser*, which Saxe had done with the Theatre of Action some years before and which he saw as sharp social commentary. He now staged it with the assistance of Peter Hyun, with Will Lee in the title role. This was followed by a strange, verbose harangue against militarism called *Snickering Horses*, by Em Jo Basshe. It had originally been a scene from his longer play, *Thunderclock*, and had been done two years before as part of an anti-war demonstration in Hollywood. It was directed by Maurice Clark. Lastly, there was Shaw's *The Great Catherine*, co-directed by Saxe and Brett Warren. In addition to the Shock Troupe members, all three plays included actors who had appeared at one time or another with the Theatre of Action, the Theatre Union, or the Group Theatre. There were so many of them that they quite outnumbered the Shock Troupers.

After this program, the One-Act Experimental Theatre disbanded. The Theatre of Action people dispersed through the New

York project, their names turning up frequently in connection with various productions: Nick Ray as one of the stage managers for the Living Newspaper, Will Lee in several of their shows, Greta Karnot and Harry Lessin in roles in *Professor Mamlock*, Alfred Saxe as assistant director of *One-third of a Nation* and Rhoda Rammelkamp as its costume designer.

With equal frequency, the names of members of the Theatre Collective appeared on Federal Theatre programs. The Theatre Collective had maintained its headquarters in the tall old house fronting Washington Square, but had long since given up its ambition to do full-length productions in favor of mobility. Late in 1935, it developed a repertory of three plays, one of them a comedy sketch from *Parade*, which it took to union halls and fraternal organizations. Until the spring of 1936, it continued its laboratory and studio work, running excellent acting, dancing, and directing classes under professional leadership. In March, at about the same time the Theatre of Action was presenting *The Crime*, the Collective took over the dusty Provincetown Playhouse for a nine-day run of three one-acters, Philip Stevenson's *You Can't Change Human Nature*, in which some of the issues of the American Revolution were satirically paralleled with those of 1936, a new version by M. Jagendorf of Lope da Vega's farce, *The Pastry Baker*, and Albert Maltz's prize-winning play about the use of national guardsmen in a strike, *Private Hicks*. The program was well attended, and it was hoped it would lead to a season of summer work and a new repertory in the fall. But the Federal Theatre beckoned irresistibly to theatre people who wanted to work and be paid for it. Both Brett Warren and Maurice Clark, the most active of the Collective's stage directors, went to the project. Among other plays, Warren did the Living Newspaper's *Power*, and Clark the hit production of *Haiti*. Some of the executive board followed, as did some of the actors. The Collective limped along for another few months but by summer it was obvious that it could no longer be kept going.

There were still plenty of busy groups in the New Theatre League, but they, too, soon felt the effect of the Federal Theatre's competition, and the more the project gained in popularity the more it seemed to be taking over the goal of the League of reaching large masses of people with plays on important social themes.

At the end of 1936, the weakness could be seen most clearly in *New Theatre* magazine, which began to falter. Because it had stubbornly refused to raise its price or to charge high rates for advertising, it had with clockwork regularity gone into debt and had to appeal to its readers to send in donations. Bad luck plagued the board as well. Two burglaries in a month, three New Theatre evenings which lost money, and a printer's bill sixty days in arrears, at one point piled up a debt of $5,000, and even though they eventually paid it off, by the time they did so they had run up other bills so that they never really broke the circle. In November, the managing board met to survey the past two years of the magazine's life. John Howard Lawson, then acting as a consultant on the board, proposed that they close down for a month to give themselves a chance to recuperate. Herb Kline opposed the plan. He had been with the magazine since its fourth issue, in April 1934, first as managing editor, then as editor-in-chief, and he felt he knew its audience and its special circumstances. He insisted that if the magazine skipped even one issue it would be fatal. "I told them it wouldn't last another three months," he says. The board nevertheless decided that a holiday was essential. This helped make up Kline's mind. He resigned, and declared that he was going to Spain to join the International Brigade, which consisted of foreign volunteers who fought on the side of the government. He never fought. Instead he found himself regarded as an authority on films because of his association with the magazine, and ended up making a movie called *Heart of Spain*, which did so well that he remained in films from then on.

New Theatre suspended publication until March, 1937. When it reappeared, it was called *New Theatre and Film*, and it announced that it was now to be aimed at the workers in the film, theatre, and dance fields rather than at their audiences. Its format was more sober, and while it was easier to read it lacked the whirling energy which had formerly characterized it; it looked middle-aged. It appeared once more in April, and then vanished for good.

The New Theatre League, however, was by no means defunct. It kept an office on West 46th Street which remained the organizational center for some two dozen active theatre groups, it provided a bureau for the distribution of scripts, published a small but interesting quarterly journal, *Theatre Workshop*, which contained articles on the craft of the theatre, film, and dance—filling precisely the spot *New Theatre and Film* had hoped to occupy, but on a more modest level. It also maintained an artists' service bureau which supplied performers for bookings, and it ran a school of acting under the direction of John Bonn. In November, 1938, it once again found a public voice, publishing a pocket-sized magazine, *New Theatre News*, the first issue of which contained a letter from Frank Gilmore, who as Equity's perennial president had so determinedly opposed the reformist campaigns of the Actors' Forum. "Everybody associated with the theatre and the trade unions," said he, "has been following your work with keen interest. Your prize plays for 1935, 1936, and 1937 are notable . . . the theatre is the best medium through which new ideas of worthwhile character can be first presented to the public. . . . Assuring you of my sincere regard for the New Theatre League, I am, etc." It was as if Cinzano had sent a bouquet to Alcoholics Anonymous.

The labor unions had, of course, been following the League's work with interest, for it had always endeavored to develop their theatre groups. As a result of legislation encouraging collective bargaining between management and labor, the unions were not only gaining strength but great masses of hitherto unorganized workers in industries had, by 1935, begun to band together. Eight of the new unions, led by John Lewis's United Mine Workers, formed the Congress of Industrial Organizations (CIO) and set about the task of organizing in two of the largest fields, steel and automobiles. In both, they met with savage opposition. The auto industry tried to crack sit-down strikes with squads of professional strike-breakers, and used spies and company police freely to weaken the unions. In the so-called Little Steel companies, the clashes were bloodiest. The worst was probably that in Chicago, in 1937, when a strike at the Republic plant climaxed with the police opening fire without provocation on an open-air meeting; ten people were killed and ninety more wounded. Nevertheless, the CIO gained strength and within four years had reached almost all its objectives. During that time, the workers' theatres had not only continued performing for unions but had encouraged the formation of groups made up of union members, at first preparing their own crude material based on local problems, then running through the New Theatre League's repertory and, in the case of more ambitious troupes, doing longer plays such as *Black Pit.* By 1937, there were dozens of these union companies, particularly in industrial centers like Pittsburgh, Cleveland, and Detroit, under the wings of CIO unions such as the United Auto Workers. Two of the most active were the Amalgamated Clothing Workers of America, which had choruses, dance groups, and drama units, and the International Ladies Garment Workers Union, which opened its own theatre, Labor Stage, on West 39th Street in New York. The latter began with John Wexley's play, *Steel,* which had originally been given a short Broadway run in 1931. Revised and brought up to date with an eye on the new CIO, it was done at Labor Stage on weekends, since the garment industry was in its spring rush and the players couldn't cope with their regular jobs as well as nightly performances. The ILGWU also conducted a play contest with prizes totalling $3,000 for full-length original plays dealing with social conflicts, but with the proviso that they must "avoid sectarian criticism of any part of the labor movement," a move designed to promote unity between AFL and CIO members. No really noteworthy plays turned up in spite of the amounts of the prizes, but what did appear, in November, 1937, was a revue, *Pins and Needles.* With music and lyrics by Harold Rome, it contained sketches by Arthur Arent, David Gregory, and Emanuel Eisenberg, and some special numbers by Marc Blitzstein. Gluck Sandor, who had been one of the Group Theatre's instructors, did the dance direction, and Benjamin Zemach the choreography. Charles Friedman, at a loose end since the dissolution of the Theatre Union, directed the show. Echoing *Parade,* it was full of political satire, but it also contained some memorable tunes and some of the wittiest numbers Broadway had seen or heard. It was an instant, irrepressible triumph. Its freshness and impudence won over everyone who saw it, and it ran for nearly three years in New York alone, forcing many members of its cast to become members of Equity as well as of their own union and in some cases inducing them to change professions permanently. The ILGWU found nothing of importance with which to follow it. *Pins and Needles* was the melodious swan-song of the labor union theatre in the United States.

In the autumn of 1938, Ben Irwin, national secretary of the New Theatre League, and John Bonn set out in a rattletrap old car piled high with scripts and pamphlets, and in two weeks visited sixteen of the League's affiliates in New York, Michigan, Ohio, Illinois, Pennsylvania, and Canada. They had a budget of $50, but so hospitably were they received that they came back with more than half of it. On the surface, their report seemed to indicate that there was a good deal of activity, but a closer look at the details showed that many of the groups were disorganized or exhausted. Their repertories were limited and little fresh material was being produced, either independently or by the League's headquarters. Only one new play of any quality had appeared, *Plant in the Sun,* by a social worker, Ben Bengal. It dealt with a sit-in strike involving a group of tough New York youngsters and had been given half a dozen Sunday showings at the little Nora Bayes Theatre by members of the late Theatre of Action, directed by Art Smith, who also acted in it. It was being gratefully seized upon by all the other groups as a welcome alternative to *Waiting for Lefty,* which had been performed beyond endurance. Nevertheless, Irwin looked on the bright side. The twenty-five affiliates of the League had, he said, "trained actors and well-equipped theatres or studios of their own, and play to an average of five thousand people with each production. . . . The New Theatre League pledges to have fifty such theatres within a year."

After three issues, the printed *New Theatre News* became a mimeographed bulletin, as if coming full circle back to *Workers Theatre.* By November, 1939, a year after Irwin's optimistic vow, the League was hobbling along under an accumulated deficit of several thousand dollars. The school was its liveliest limb, giving acting instruction to 125 people, turning away an overflow for lack of room, and amply paying for itself. John Bonn had gone to Cleveland to start a school of acting there for the League, and his place had been taken at first by Michael Gordon, then by Lem Ward. There was still a good deal of activity by the drama units of various labor unions, but the independent groups, which were all that was left of the workers' theatres, were dwindling. Things were at so low an ebb that the League had to publish a Dishonor Roll of nine companies which had failed to pay royalties for plays, and it even threatened to take legal action against any others which didn't pay within two weeks of production.

In June, 1940, the League held a national convention with the

Philadelphia New Theatre as host. "We are here to stay, here as an integral part of our national cultural life," they said, firmly, in announcing the convention. Afterwards, they reported that a hundred delegates from twenty-seven groups had registered, "a true cross section of the forces that are creating the basis for the theatre of the future: the American People's Theatre." The break-down of attendance showed, however, that they were deceiving themselves. There were actually only eighteen real theatre companies in the League, and not all of them may have been as active as was hoped. Most of them were in or around New York. Only nineteen official delegates showed up; the rest were observers. That issue of *New Theatre News* containing the convention report was the last to appear. The few groups which were left worked on until the loud rumor of war drowned their voices.*

The "People's Theatre" which it had been the League's ambition to create had really come into being with the Federal Theatre Project. At its zenith, it was the second largest and busiest nationally sponsored theatre in the world—that of the Soviet Union was its only superior—showing plays, circuses, puppets, vaudeville, and dance to an audience of nearly 400,000 people a week. Its average ticket price was fifteen cents, with nearly 87% of admissions free, and yet it had brought in more than two million dollars in gross receipts in three years. It was employing over eleven thousand people, in 150 companies in twenty-nine states, and in addition servicing some 390 centers with drama coaches. It might have become the wonder and envy of the world, but the vision was too dazzling for myopic political eyes.

The Federal Theatre was from the start under attack on two levels. Although its social or left-wing productions were only a fraction of its work, they were used as a pretext for labelling it a Communist hotbed. And, since it was tied in with Roosevelt's relief measures, it was constantly threatened as that program itself was chipped away under pressure from political opponents. The

*Curiously enough, one of the many theatre and dance companies affiliated with the League has survived to the present—the New Dance Group. With astonishing juvenescence it has remained as buoyantly vigorous as its founders. It now operates from its own building on West 47 Street, with Jane Dudley as Honorary Director, Sophie Maslow as president, and William Bales as a member of the board. Over the past three decades it has had associated with it such outstanding dancers as Pearl Primus, Donald McKayle, Ronnie Aul, Eve Gentry, and Jaime Rogers.

presidential election of 1936, with its Roosevelt landslide, gave the relief program new life, but as the country slowly pulled itself out of the Depression the administration had to sacrifice some of its more liberal projects, and appropriations for the arts were among the first to go.

The Act of Congress under which the Federal Theatre was set up was to expire on June 30, 1937. Long before that date the theatrical unions began objecting to personnel cuts on behalf of their members, and audiences joined with the casts of shows in sit-ins in theatres after the performances. Late in May, there was a one-day work stoppage of WPA workers. Nevertheless, on June 10 the orders came to cut the New York project by thirty percent. Furthermore, the opening of any new play or musical performance before July first was forbidden. One of the productions threatened was Marc Blitzstein's opera, *The Cradle Will Rock*. Whispers had gone round in Washington that it was dangerously controversial, and in any case its opening coincided with the threatened cuts and was scheduled before the deadline. Although it had an advance sale of fourteen thousand seats it was banned from opening. The story of how Orson Welles and John Houseman found a theatre and raised their curtain is dramatically told by Houseman in his biography, *Runthrough*. This case of what looked like a combination of censorship and financial attrition of the project marked the beginning of a period of nervousness, cowardice, and finally collapse.

In the next twelve months, there were many demonstrations against cut-backs by the project workers. Producers and directors resigned, often in protest against excessive red tape. A typical problem, for instance, arose in the winter season of 1936–37, when telephone operators refused to give the numbers of Federal Theatre box offices to callers because the information was classified "confidential." When William Farnsworth quit as New York director, seven Broadway producers were approached, and one after the other refused the post because they feared political interference. There were charges that the FBI maintained surveillance of personnel, and in at least one instance the director of a department was fired as a Communist because some of her subordinates had collected money for the Spanish loyalist cause, even though this was done without her knowledge.

In July, 1938, Hallie Flanagan was infuriated to read the charge, in a New York paper, that the Federal Theatre was dominated by Communists and that no one who was not a member of the Workers' Alliance could be hired. She sent out a public statement of refutation and was told by her superiors that she must not answer such charges since only the WPA Information Service was allowed to act as a liaison with the press. Further attacks came later that year from the House UnAmerican Activities Committee, then headed by Representative Martin Dies, and although Flanagan and several other Federal Theatre officials wrote indignantly asking to be heard by the committee, their letters went unanswered. Representative J. Parnell Thomas, a Republican member of the committee, stated publicly, "Practically every play . . . is sheer propaganda for Communism or the New Deal," thus showing which way the political wind blew, and Dies himself charged that the Communists wanted the government to pay for Stalin's propaganda. At last, in December, 1938, Flanagan was given her chance to appear before the committee, where such matters as her article in *Theatre Arts Monthly* on the first meeting of the Workers Drama League and the fact that she had spoken with approval of the Russian theatre were solemnly adduced as evidences of her excessively radical leanings. Misquotations and wrongly attributed statements were read to her as her own, and scenes which had been cut out of plays were submitted, proving that the committee members had never so much as seen one of the productions they were objecting to. Flanagan's defense exposed the flimsiness of the committee's charges, and at last, when it was proved that an earlier witness who had admitted to being a Communist had never actually had anything to do with the Federal Theatre, the hearings were cut short and she was not allowed to complete her testimony.

In 1939, appropriations committees in both the House and the Senate debated further funds to the Federal Theatre. Representative Clifton Woodrum announced that he was going to put the government out of show business if it was the last thing he did, adding that "every theatre critic of note has expressed his disapproval of projects of this type." The next day he got a telegram denying the charge and signed by every major New York critic. Senator Robert Reynolds decried plays which were "spewed forth from the gutters of the Kremlin," giving as examples *Love 'em and*

Leave 'em and *Up in Mable's Room.* In the House debate, attention was called to the "salacious tripe" that the project performed: Molière's *School for Wives* and Sheridan's *School for Scandal.* "What apparently turned the tide," said *Equity Magazine,* "was the discovery that artists on the New York WPA Arts Project had a two-volume collection of nude artists' models from which they could order." Under the impression, perhaps, that this evil influence might creep across the footlights, the House Committee voted in favor of cutting the theatre's appropriations. The senate Committee, however, approved the funds. But then, a joint House and Senate committee reported back a compromise bill which struck the Federal Theatre out. It was passed, and on the last day of June the project ended. At the moment of its demise, it was, ironically, having some of its greatest successes. Yasha Frank's *Pinocchio* was still filling houses after six months and had been chosen as the first children's play to be shown on television. *Sing for Your Supper,* a topical revue on the lines of *Pins and Needles* which had been assailed by some congressmen as subversive, was packing in audiences. One of its high points was a song written by Earl Robinson with lyrics by John LaTouche, "Ballad of Uncle Sam," which had people cheering at every performance and ironically was to be chosen the following year as the theme song of the Republican National Convention. Half a dozen plays, including an immensely popular black version of Shaw's *Androcles and the Lion,* had been selected to open at the World's Fair. Perhaps not since the killing of the goose that laid the golden eggs had so profitable an enterprise been so witlessly terminated.

 Properly speaking, the story ends there. All that remains is, as in an Elizabethan tragedy, to kill off the rest of the main characters.

It is curious that both the Theatre Guild and the Group Theatre found it necessary around the same time to disavow any left-wing tendencies. In 1936, after *The Case of Clyde Griffiths,* a letter was sent out over Cheryl Crawford's signature saying that the Group's social convictions were not necessarily those of the dramatists whose work they had done. There was some chuckling over this, and John Mason Brown pointed out that as a man is known by the company he keeps, a theatre is known by the playwrights it performs. The Group's leadership had often enough stated in programs and open letters that it wanted to do plays of some social pertinence. Brown remarked, in passing, that you could carry caution too far; the programs of the Federal Theatre's black production of *Macbeth* had displayed a notice saying that the viewpoint of the author was not necessarily that of the WPA or any other agency of the government. The Guild, a year later, apologized in its Bulletin for the strong social consciousness of some of its recent plays, explaining pathetically that many authors were concerned with the crucial things that were happening around them and that it was, consequently, hard to find good plays of contemporary life which didn't have some awareness of these facts. In the preceding year they had done two very tame anti-war plays, *If This Be Treason* and *Idiot's Delight,* driving Brooks Atkinson to say, of the latter, "Liberalism, we are beginning to find out, is a weak force in a world that quivers with fear and suspicion," and comparing the play unfavorably with the unequivocal stand of *Bury the Dead*. The country was racked with industrial strife, attempts to censor the arts were increasing and the irresponsible charges and scare-mongering of the House Committee on UnAmerican Activities led by Representative Martin Dies were beginning to disturb even the most complacent citizens. Fascism was gathering power in Europe, and the portents of the coming war were by then very real. Nevertheless, from 1937 on, both the Guild and the Group were to avoid plays with any but the most shufflingly liberal viewpoint.

The Group made its reappearance on Broadway in the fall of 1937. Emanuel Eisenberg, then its press agent, was writing publicity releases similar to those Helen Deutsch, who had nursed it through many previous years, had written, pointing out that every time the experts had declared the Group dead it had managed to confound them by bursting nimbly out of the coffin. Its organization was a little different this time. Instead of its original managerial board it was headed by Harold Clurman, with a council of three actors, Luther Adler, Roman Bohnen, and Elia Kazan. Its first play was a new one by Odets, *Golden Boy*, the story of an Italian-American youth whose promise as a violinist is destroyed, like his hands, by his prowess as a prize-fighter. There were reminders of *Gold Eagle Guy* and *Success Story* in its account of how ambition for wealth and fame can distort the best of men. If it was, as a few people suggested, symbolic of the vices of capitalism, it was so only cloudily. What came through most strongly was a powerful, compassionate tale with the Group performing at its peak. Stunning examples of their ability to tackle anything were Morris Carnovsky, once again playing what Clurman called "an Odets father" but this time a thoroughly credible Italian one, and Elia Kazan as possibly the most chilling gangster ever seen on the stage. But it was Luther Adler who provided the greatest surprise. It was unlikely that he had ever struck a blow at anyone in his life, but he gave a compellingly realistic portrayal of the sensitive boy turned boxer. To help him with this transformation, he had Martin Ritt, who had been hired for the show because he could punch a bag and that rhythmic sound was needed offstage. Ritt had come to acting, improbably enough, from professional athletics, and he took Adler to the Pioneer Athletic Club to get him into shape and to give him the right background. "When we first walked in there," Ritt recalls, "the stench was so incredible that he almost fainted. He had never been around jock straps and sweat shirts before." The Group had taken on some other new people for the play, among them Howard da Silva, Lee Cobb, Bert Conway, Harry Bratsberg, Leif Ericsson, and Karl Malden, but its most talked-of addition was the movie star, Frances Farmer, who had the feminine lead. She was able enough as an actor, but there were not lacking people who muttered that she was not exactly Group Theatre material, being better known for her beauty than for outstanding talent on the stage.

Golden Boy proved to be the Group's biggest money-maker. It reestablished them in the top rank of the theatre, allowed them to expand, and, over the next two years, helped them produce nine plays, three of which introduced new playwrights of real merit. Unfortunately, although some of their subsequent productions did well and all displayed the Group's artistic prowess, none equalled *Golden Boy* in financial returns that would have put the company firmly on its feet. Personal ambition, restlessness, a sense that the organization was too confining for some of the members began heaving beneath the surface and driving them apart.

Casey Jones, which concerned an engine driver who refuses to accept age and retirement and goes off to find a new life, was by Robert Ardrey, whom Clurman had met in Chicago the year before. It was also Elia Kazan's first chance to direct a Broadway production completely on his own. Since most of the Group were busy in *Golden Boy,* Charles Bickford and Van Heflin were brought in for the leading roles. Kazan did his best, but his inexperience hampered him and he found himself unable to manage Bickford, whose understanding of the Group's acting methods was less than thorough. The most arresting part of the show was its scenery, designed by Mordecai Gorelik, particularly a stylized locomotive which gave the illusion of tearing along at full speed before the audience's eyes. Not even that, however, could save the play.

After 248 performances of *Golden Boy,* the Group took it to London where it was received with jubilation and the company's performance hailed as acting on a level higher than anything achieved in England. The following year the Group sent a second company over to repeat the triumph of the first. They were seeking to expand their acting troupe and continued to bring in fresh blood whenever they could; both first and second companies included former Theatre of Action people, Curt Conway, Will Lee, and Lou Polan, who had come in by way of the Group's studio.

The fall season of 1938 found them busier than ever. A new play by Odets, *Rocket to the Moon,* which had the curious distinction of being the first serious play about a dentist to reach Broadway, opened, and was followed by *The Gentle People,* Irwin Shaw's first long play. Franchot Tone was persuaded to return to the Group from Hollywood, for the latter, with Sylvia Sidney as his leading lady. In the former, Morris Carnovsky had the lead and a promising youngster, Eleanor Lynn, was chosen to play opposite him. There was a certain amount of bitterness generated by these choices. For three important plays, the feminine leads had been chosen outside the Group, and two of them were movie names. It was felt that the leadership was star-gazing, and this in an organization which had never given prominence to individuals. *Rocket to the Moon* was a tender love story, thought by some critics to contain some of Odets's best dialogue, but its tone was wistful rather than tragic and for most people it remained a minor play. *The Gentle People* came closer to being a box office success, not only helped by the appearance of Tone and Sidney, but because there was something that tickled many fancies in the story of two nice old men whose happiness is threatened by a vicious racketeer and who are driven to murder and somehow get away with it. At a time when fascism in Europe was taking over one land after another, the play seemed to say that the meek would only inherit the earth if they were willing to fight for it, but it delivered this message in so good-humored a tone as to diminish its impact. Although business wasn't bad, things were not happy behind the scenes. Tone, recently separated from his wife, went night-clubbing after performances and often had to recover in Turkish baths; there were times when he was so hoarse that he could barely make himself heard from the stage. He felt, too, that the Group had miscast him in the role of a gangster and that they were capitalizing on his reputation. By the time the play ended he had become openly hostile, and he had lost money which he had invested in the show, which didn't help matters. There was some fretting, too, on the part of many of the actors about the choice of plays, which seemed to them weak and equivocal. It was true that every play had some connection with American life, but the link with serious political or social issues appeared increasingly tenuous. At about this time, in a radio speech delivered on Station WINS by a Group Theatre representative, much was made of the fact that the Group had always been, and was still, a social theatre, the work of which was "the expression of its social environment, the reflection of the drama in the daily life of the mass of society. Out of the need for this kind of drama," the speech continued, "grew hundreds of small workers' theatre groups, such as the Theatre of Action and the New Theatre League. . . . There was a need for a more highly developed group to invade the sacred grove of Broadway, and this is what we tried to be." To a good many of the actors, the Group seemed to be contradicting its avowed aims.

While *Rocket to the Moon* was running, Luther Adler suggested that *Awake and Sing* be revived and run alternately with it. Three actors from the original production were already in *Rocket,* and a fourth, J. Edward Bromberg, had returned from Hollywood to work with the Group again. Julia Adler took on the role her sister, Stella, had played, while the part of Ralph was taken by Alfred Ryder, one of the Group's students. The production, according to Clurman, was "distinctly inferior" to the original, but no fault could be found in it by the press. "[The] play and production were now accorded the reception of an honored classic," Clurman wrote. "Brooks Atkinson . . . asked me one day whether *Awake and Sing* had improved since he first saw it. 'No,' I answered, 'you have.' "[71] The venture proved profitable and drew large audiences during its limited run.

The Group now turned to a pair of fantasies, *Quiet City* by Irwin Shaw and William Saroyan's first play, *My Heart's in the Highlands.* In a brief article for the press, Clurman explained the Group's position on experimentation. "In the halcyon days before 1929," he said, "what used to be called an experimental play was often something noisy, disagreeable, pretentiously dolorous in thirty or forty half-lit scenes." However, for the Group, experiment in the theatre meant either "productions which are trying to extend the means and meaning of theatrical expression . . . or plays that are sincere attempts to put down states of being . . . that are special and limited in appeal, a sort of minority report of perhaps peculiar but nonetheless real emotions." *Quiet City*, directed by Kazan, fell somewhere between reality and fantasy and was judged "not at present complete enough to present as a successful solution of the theatrical problems the script had set for us." It was given two Sunday evening performances. The Saroyan play, so whimsical, deliberately naive, and vaguely mystical that some of the actors weren't sure what it was saying, was directed by Robert Lewis in a delectably stylized way which gave it more meaning than it actually had. It contained only one Group regular, Art Smith, but provided an opportunity for work for many young people who had been in the studio or in previous productions. The production had its impingement on the Group's past. An old friend of many of the members, Phil Loeb, was given the lead; he had been the Theatre Guild's general stage manager when Clurman worked for the *Garrick Gaieties* of 1925. The Group had had a hard time raising money for the production of *My Heart's in the Highlands*, and called in the Guild's board, hoping either to get backing from them or to have the play chosen as a subscription presentation. The Guild gave it five performances to begin with, and then decided to make it the fifth subscription play of the season of 1938–39. It was greatly liked by the critics, but it was not really popular with subscribers, a failure the Guild attributed, according to Clurman, to the fact that Loeb looked too Jewish to be a poet. In any case, Saroyan had attracted a good deal of attention and he brought his next play, *The Time of Your Life*, to the Group. Clurman made the mistake of rejecting it. Eddie Dowling bought it instead, and it became one of the hits of the year.

"I have often thought, in retrospect," Clurman wrote in his autobiography, "that the Group might have done well at the end of its 1938–9 season to announce its dissolution. In this way it might have called sharp attention to the fact that while its services had been acclaimed by practically all camps, it had achieved everything that could be achieved without the aid of any organized support."[72] Its next two plays were the struggles of a drowning concern.

They were at the bottom of their bank account. Unrest plagued the actors; there had been departures and there were to be more.

Jules Garfield, who had left *Having Wonderful Time* to appear in *Golden Boy*, had packed up abruptly midway through the run and gone to Hollywood, his place being taken by Will Lee. While his departure was viewed as treason, it could not but breed restlessness, especially among the newer members who wanted the Group to provide them with at least as nutritious an alternative. In July, 1939, the Group assembled at Smithtown, Long Island for the summer, but it was to be more than simply preparation for the next play. In their hearts, everyone knew that the whole future of the organization was at stake.

It was a large gathering which met for the first day of discussion, but there were few of the original Group members left. Many people were uneasy; some confessed that they were downright uncomfortable in the Group as it was then constituted and that, as Sanford Meisner put it, there was "a vast exciting field of the theatre out there" which he for one felt he'd like to explore. Frances Farmer said that she was certain by now she didn't want to work anywhere but in the Group, but that there were four women, herself, Ruth Nelson, Phoebe Brand, and Eleanor Lynn, and only limited parts for them. There had been some resentment in the past among the Group's women because they had often felt shut out of decisions. Clurman brought the discussion to a head by insisting that the company should allow him to be their leader in fact, not only in name. He ended the session by asking, "Are you willing to go on with the Group Theatre if the sole direction of its artistic life, without explanation to you, is in my hands, the hands of your director? Are you willing to . . . let me be the absolute dictator for one season?" He urged them to think things over and to give him their answer. The following day, at a particularly turbulent meeting, all but one or two said, in effect, that they loved him, trusted him, and wanted to work with him, but that the answer to the question was no.

For all their discontent, they did want to continue, and to continue as the Group Theatre. But in the days that followed, while issues, policies, and plays were debated, the links of fellowship that had bound them for so many years were ruptured. Much of what was said was inconclusive. Roman Bohnen asked nervously for a five week leave of absence to make a movie for Lewis Milestone, and half a dozen others said with asperity that they could have taken outside jobs but had stayed because they were needed. "A matter like this must be decided on by democratic discussion," cried Kazan. A vote was taken, and the decision was that Bohnen should decide for himself what to do. Some of the juniors—Will Lee, Norman Lloyd, Curt Conway, Martin Ritt, Alfred Ryder—were accused by Clurman of being part of an "insurrection." They denied it, and Lee demanded that the newcomers should be given more responsibility. "We haven't got the problems of the old timers," he said. Michael Gordon charged that people were thinking about big parts and little parts, not so much about acting for its own sake as how it would affect their status on Broadway or in Hollywood. Several people said, woundedly, that they loved everyone but that no one seemed to love them or understand them, and the stage manager, Bill Watts, remarked, "The Group Theatre isn't a theatre, it's a religion."

At one of the early meetings, Odets's *Silent Partner* was read to the company. It took four hours, and Clurman noted that everyone was impressed by its power, and its spiritual and physical dimensions. But a couple of weeks later, Odets announced that he did not want them to produce it. It was, he said, unsatisfactory to him, and rather than rewrite it, he'd bring them a new play. They determined, meanwhile to do something they had long had in mind, a revival of a classic, Chekhov's *Three Sisters*, which provided excellent parts for the women. While it was being rehearsed they would look for other scripts. A new play by Irwin Shaw was submitted but was vetoed. Work began on *Three Sisters* but bogged down in squabbles among the cast, capped by a kind of lassitude that prevented Clurman from concentrating properly on his direction. The summer waned to an end.

The play finally chosen for the beginning of the fall season was Robert Ardrey's *Thunder Rock*, with Kazan as director. A fable about a man who becomes a lighthouse keeper to escape the troubled world and who is taught by the ghosts of the past that he must return to take up the fight, it was also an allegory about liberals in modern times and the resemblance betweeen the lighthouse and the ivory tower could hardly be missed. However, to many it was too imprecise, and while Ardrey's ability was recognized—he was given an award by the Playwrights Company as the most promising young playwright of the year—it had to close in three weeks.

After it, Odets's promised new play, *Night Music*, was put into rehearsal. It was a rather slight comedy with little of his usual bite. Jane Wyatt was brought in for the feminine lead, and few of the Group members were in it although two of the original ones, Walter Coy and Tony Kraber, had small parts. The others began to take up offers which had been pressing from outside. *Night Music*, which opened in February 1940, was a fiasco. The actors were not happy with their own performances or those of their colleagues; Odets was dissatisfied with Clurman's direction and infuriated because a critic compared him to Saroyan; Clurman was wretched because everyone seemed to him to be engaged in re-crimination; and everybody was thoroughly put out at the press, which had joined in the shilly-shallying by applauding the Group and in the same breath running it down. The play could not even equal *Thunder Rock*'s brief run, and after it closed recovery was impossible.

There was, nevertheless, one more attempt. Irwin Shaw had written a play called *Retreat to Pleasure*, a lightweight effort which Clurman later gloomily confessed was "unredeemed, despite dexterity, by either a sure hand or a clear spirit." Nothing better offered itself, and Clurman saw it as a way of holding at least a fragment of the Group together. It was too late for that. At a final meeting at which tempers were lost and insults flew, the last bonds that had held them together were undone. Clurman went ahead with the play on his own, using a few of the old hands, Art Smith, Dorothy Patten, and Ruth Nelson. The production was an unqualified disaster.

This time there was to be no recovery for the Group. But Clurman had summed up its undying spirit when, during the long impassioned arguments of its final summer, he said, "The Group Theatre . . . is one of the few which said at the beginning of its work, plays have a meaning, theatres have a meaning, we fight for the meaning of these plays because they are good for our life, they are good for the lives of those who love us and those whom we love, theatre is one clear, strong, definite form of the expression for us of the meaning of our life and also the life of our families, of our cities, of our states, the United States, the world." Its epitaph, however, was spoken by Morris Carnovsky. Even as *Retreat to Pleasure* was foundering in December 1940, he appeared as Mr. Appopolous, the eccentric landlord of a Greenwich Village apartment in *My Sister Eileen.* A friend met him on the street and slapped him on the back. "Well, Morris," he said, "how does it feel to be in a success." Carnovsky shrugged. "I've been in a success for nearly ten years," he replied.

It seems obvious, at this remove, that the Group Theatre's defeat was the result of trying to keep a foot on several pedestals at once. Its strong collective structure, the very thing that made it a group, weakened its leadership. Its refusal to leave the Broadway arena meant that it had to fill theatres at competitive prices, but its insistence that "plays have a meaning" made it turn away from scripts which might have given it an easy popularity. By its very nature it could never cater to an orchestra-seat subscription list like the Guild's, nor survive on the pennies of those who supported the Theatre Union. Its members were, in a sense, the victims of their own talent; the closer they came to perfection as a unit, the more temptations were offered them to leave the unit. And for some, the Group's ideals were too hard to live up to and too hard to live without. Their problems were those of artists in a commercial world, and America has never been particularly kind to its artists. It has always been readier to equate financial success with artistic merit and to regard creative innovation with indifference, except in those cases where it finds something aberrant enough to be seized on as a fad. The Group was too serious to be taken either way. Unlike the Guild, from which it sprang, it rested on a whole company rather than upon a directorial board and in consequence it could not adapt, as the Guild could, to the tempests of the commercial theatre by taking refuge in any port that offered.

The Guild's directors had forged an organization, in fact, so flexible and so conformable to many layers of taste as to outlast the board itself. When the Theatre Union closed down, its remaining subscribers were offered preferential subscriptions to the Guild. When the Actors' Repertory Company showed what it could do with *Bury the Dead,* the Guild went into association with them to do a complicated piece of political looniness called *Washington Jitters,* by John Boruff and Walter Hart. Once the Group had given

William Saroyan his start and then failed to do his next, and better, play, *The Time of Your Life*, the Guild joined with Eddie Dowling to produce it. They never forgot that most theatre-goers pay to see stars, and so they devoted much of their attention to finding vehicles for Katherine Hepburn or the Lunts. They also kept in mind that there was money to be made from Hollywood, and quietly entered into an agreement with Paramount whereby some of their productions were underwritten with an eye to film adaptations.

They did not hesitate to take long chances when a project seemed worthwhile. Thus, when George Gershwin wrote an opera based on *Porgy*, although there was a lot of head-shaking over its expense, and even more over its unusual musical form—its songs were based on the rhythms of natural speech rather than on singable tunes—the Guild backed it. In the light of the importance of *Porgy and Bess* as the first native opera of any consequence, it is hard to believe that it was received with some demurral by critics; its run of 124 performances was good but by no means outstanding. The Guild also, in its own moderate way, continued to sponsor an occasional social-conscious play, although these tended to stick to safe ground. When, in 1937, they did Sidney Howard's *The Ghost of Yankee Doodle*, John Mason Brown observed, "What they [the play's arguments] say is what everyone knows."

Their relations with authors did not improve. During 1937–38, four playwrights, Robert Sherwood, Maxwell Anderson, Elmer Rice and Sidney Howard, formed their own producing association, the Playwrights Company, which was later joined by S. N. Behrman. This deprived the Guild of a source of scripts. They were also sometimes singularly blind; they turned down such important plays as T.S. Eliot's *Murder in the Cathedral* and Giraudoux's *Tiger at the Gates*. Yet they somehow managed, at the very moment when things looked blackest, to come up with winners which rescued them, as Philip Barry's *The Philadelphia Story* did in 1939.

Nor did the relations among members of the board mend, and the split between the "artists" and the "managers" widened. After the spring season of 1939, Alfred Lunt, who had been made a director four years before to keep him and Lynn Fontanne tied to the Guild, resigned. Policy-making fell more and more into the hands of Lawrence Langner and Theresa Helburn, while Philip Moeller, Lee Simonson, and Helen Westley were only called upon for consultation on the choice of plays. Finally, in 1940, the latter three gave in their resignations. But the structure that had been built was too strong to collapse with the dispersal of the board of directors. There were some 20,000 subscribers in New York and more than twice that number on the road. One of the first actions of the remaining pair of directors after the separation was the co-production, with the Playwrights Company, of a sturdily anti-fascist play, Robert Sherwood's *There Shall Be No Night*, which allowed the Guild to take advantage both of its waiting supporters and one of its major rivals. And, after some years of faltering, in March, 1943, it popped up with its greatest triumph of all time, *Oklahoma!* by Richard Rodgers and Oscar Hammerstein 2nd. This musical version of *Green Grow the Lilacs* had been driven ruthlessly to its opening by Theresa Helburn in the face of all obstacles—"Helburn's Folly" it was called in some circles—and it ran for over five years in New York alone, hatching a whole new breed of shows closer to opera than to old-fashioned musical comedy, so that the latter soon became as difficult to find as the passenger pigeon.

Looking back, it may seem that between the two great wars a new kind of American theatre, with its eye on social realities rather than on the refined taste of the carriage trade, rose, flourished, and then dismally failed. For after all, the main stream of the theatre seems to have continued as it always had, with its strength lying, as one historian has concluded, "in the spirit of fun, not in social significance."[73] That would be as illusory a conclusion as that the history of art in this century should be gauged by the popularity of Norman Rockwell.

It is axiomatic that creative innovation in the arts is regarded with suspicion and hostility. It is not how explorers themselves are received that counts, but how their explorations affect those who come after. *Lightnin'*, with its thousands of performances, may have been a success, but after it closed nothing remained to show that it had ever existed; the ripples begun by *Stevedore* are still spreading. Today, the fabric of the theatre, the films, and the ubiquitous television is so shot through with the threads of the socially-conscious theatre and the forms it established over twenty-five years that no one any longer sees the connection. Yet it exists. The experimentation of the expressionists, the insistence that theatre should have a meaning, the realism of the Group's acting, the irreverence of the workers' theatres, the acceptance of social and political comment, the breaking down of the proscenium, all worked to change the atmosphere and even the structures of the theatre so that today a title like *Jesus Christ Superstar,* which would surely once have been condemned as the work of atheistic Reds, lifts not a single eyebrow, and a set composed of bare platforms draws no special comment. The groundwork for *West Side Story* and *Fiddler on the Roof* was laid by *The Three-penny Opera* and *The Cradle Will Rock,* dramatic plays supported and illustrated by music which couldn't easily be hummed on the way out of the theatre. One can imagine the plays of Becket and Pinter in the repertory of the New Playwrights Theatre or the Provincetown Players, so advanced were those groups beyond the perceptions of their own times. In a fading echo of the 1930s, *Hair* was attacked as the glorification of "draft-card burning, desecration of religious and patriotic symbols . . . and youthful rebellion in general,"[74] but although two astronauts walked out of the show because they didn't like "what you're doing to the flag," most audiences everywhere remained and accepted its iconoclasm with equanimity and pleasure. Black plays of protest have become as commonplace as minstrel shows once were, and the appearance of black actors in a cast is as universally mandatory as it once was for the workers' theatres alone. The simple political parables of Archie Bunker, now viewed by millions, might well have been seized upon as one-acters by the New Theatre League—with a few obvious changes. Arthur Miller's first play, a forgotten comedy called *The Man Who Had All the Luck,* ran for a week in 1944; his next play, *All My Sons,* a forthright condemnation of war profiteering which would have been called propaganda if the Theatre Union had done it in the 1930s, received the Critics Circle Award when it appeared in 1947. It was produced by Harold Clurman, Elia Kazan, and Walter Fried (who had worked as a business manager for the Group), in association with Herbert Harris; it was staged by Kazan, and had sets and lighting by Mordecai Gorelik. The greater part of Miller's plays were pointedly social-conscious, and many had former Group Theatre people involved in them. Even the faces of film stars have been transformed from the clean-cut profiles of the past into a proletarian homeliness. Marlon Brando and Paul Newman would have been chosen at once by the Theatre of Action as working-class types.

Certainly, no one can put a finger on any one factor which changed the outlook of society during the decades since the Second World War. But the theatre in all its forms—even those masquerading under the fashionable neologism of "the media"—has helped to make a climate for that change, and the forms which were hammered out, chiefly by the rebellious avant-garde, have fallen ready-made into the hands of the moderns.

If the life of some of the early groups was short—and in the theatre few producers can point to a continuous working span of more than a few years—their influence was long. It would be unthinkable nowadays, for example, for an actor not to have some general working acquaintanceship with the Stanislavsky method. That they could not continue indefinitely is no mark of failure except in the most primitive commercial terms; we might as well say that Dylan Thomas and Brendan Behan failed because their output was small and they died relatively young and poor. The dissolution of the companies this book has dealt with did not come about because they were unsuccessful, but because their ends were inherent in their structures and in the nature and development of the theatrical scene, as their history shows. But by the time they finished they had already spread their influence in ever-widening circles around them, and in the very act of collapse they released a swarm of proselytizers who perpetuated, each in his own version, the original gospel. The groups of the Twenties and Thirties concerned with making the theatre reflect in positive ways the conflicts and ideals of its time did not fail. They accomplished precisely what they set out to do, which was to present before audiences the abstracts and brief chronicles of a real America which they helped to change.

STAGE LEFT 258

Fire ravages the tenement house, Howard Bay's basic setting for the Living Newspaper's *One-third of a Nation. New York Public Library Theatre Collection.*

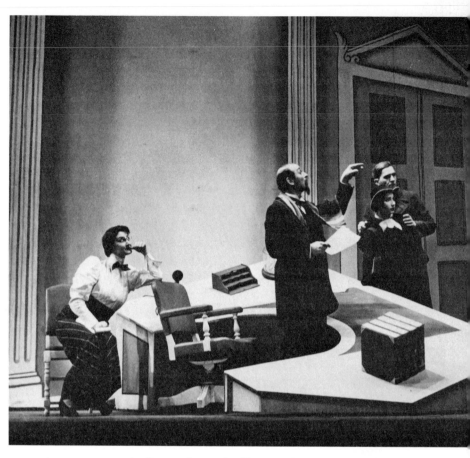

A tense moment in the psychiatrist's office, in JOHNNY JOHNSON. Left to right: Kate Allen, Morris Carnovsky, Phoebe Brand, Grover Burgess, and Russell Collins. *Photo by Alfedo Valente, courtesy Queens College Library Theatre Collection.*

Puppets by Nat Messik and Morey Bunin in a skit called "Schnozzle Durante Gets the News." *Photo by Messik.*

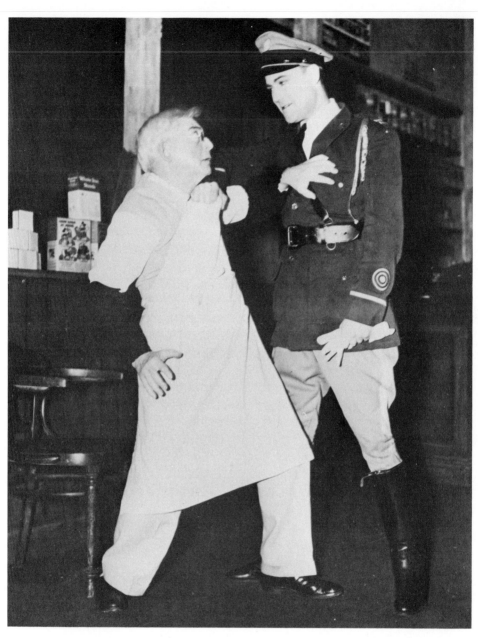

Corpo Commissioner Swan (Frederic Tozere) threatens a small town shopkeeper (George Henry Trader) for daring to protest Corpo actions, in IT CAN'T HAPPEN HERE. *New York Public Library Theatre Collection*

Footnotes

1. Quoted in *The American Theatre as Seen by its Critics* Montrose Moses & John Mason Brown, eds. (New York: W.W.Norton Co., 1934).
2. N. Bryllion Fagin, "American Drama Today," in *Present-Day American Literature*, 3, no. 3, Dec. 1929, New River State College, Montgomery, W. Va.
3. Quoted in Helen Deutsch and Stella Hanau, *The Provincetown* (New York: Farrar & Rinehart, 1931).
4. Ibid.
5. Provincetown Playhouse mailing, 1925
6. Walter Prichard Eaton, *The Theatre Guild* (New York: Brentano's, 1929).
7. Ibid.
8. Ibid.
9. Provincetown Playhouse, letter, 1925
10. N. Bryllion Fagin, "A Radical Theatre," in *Present-Day American Literature*, 3, no. 3, Dec. 1929.
11. Provincetown Playhouse mailing, 1925
12. John Dos Passos, "Did the New Playwrights Theatre Fail?" in *The New Masses*, 5, Aug. 1929.
13. *Workers Theatre*, Aug. 1931
14. *Workers Theatre*, April 1931
15. Ibid.
16. Ibid.
17. Ibid.
18. *Workers Theatre*, June 1931
19. Hallie Flanagan, "A Theatre is Born," in *Theatre Arts*

Monthly, 15, no. 11, Nov. 1931
20. *Workers Theatre,* Feb. 1932
21. *Workers Theatre,* April 1932
22. Ben Blake, *The Awakening of the American Theatre* (New York: Tomorrow Publishers, 1935).
23. *Workers Theatre,* Aug. 1931
24. *Workers Theatre,* May 1932
25. Harold Clurman, *The Fervent Years* (New York: Alfred A. Knopf, 1949).
26. Ibid.
27. Ibid.
28. Constantin Stanislavsky, *An Actor Prepares,* trans. Elizabeth R. Hapgood (New York: Theatre Arts Books, Robert M. MacGregor, 1955).
29. Quoted in *Cue Magazine,* 10 Jan. 1970
30. Harold Clurman, *The Fervent Years.*
31. Ibid.
32. Irving Werstein, *A Nation Fights Back* (New York: Julian Messner Inc., 1962).
33. Quoted in Eric Bentley, *Thirty Years of Treason,* (New York: Viking Press, 1971).
34. *Workers Theatre,* June-July 1932
35. *Workers Theatre,* Sept.-Oct. 1932
36. *Workers Theatre,* Feb. 1932
37. *Workers Theatre,* May-June 1933
38. Morgan Y. Himelstein, *Drama Was a Weapon* (New Brunswick: Rutgers University Press, 1963).
39. *Workers Theatre,* May-June 1933
40. *Workers Theatre,* April 1933
41. Al Saxe, *Newsboy,* in *New Theatre,* July-Aug. 1934.
42. Maxwell Anderson *Both Your Houses,*
43. Quoted in Roy S. Waldau, *Vintage Years of the Theatre Guild* (Cleveland: The Press of Case Western Reserve University, 1972).
44. Ibid.
45. Ibid.
46. *New Theatre,* Feb. 1934
47. Burns Mantle, ed., *The Best Plays of 1929–30.* (New York: Dodd, Mead & Co., 1930).

48. *Daily Worker,* N.Y., May 23, 1934
49. *New York Times,* 6 Jan. 1935
50. Elmer Rice, *We, the People.*
51. *Theatre Arts,* 1916
52. *Theatre Arts,* 1917
53. This and following quotes from *Theatre Arts Monthly,* Jan. 1934
54. This and following quotes from *New Theatre,* Jan. 1934
55. *New Theatre,* July 1934
56. *Daily Worker,* 14 June 1934
57. *New Theatre,* July 1934
58. *New Theatre,* Nov. 1934
59. Ibid.
60. Harold Clurman, *The Fervent Years.*
61. *New Theatre,* Feb. 1935
62. Ibid.
63. *Daily Worker,* New York, 28 Dec., 1935
64. *Vanity Fair,* Sept. 1934
65. Harold Clurman, *The Fervent Years.*
66. *The Flying Grouse,* 1, no. 2
67. Robert Lewis, *Method or Madness* (New York: Samuel French Inc., 1958).
68. *New Theatre,* June 1934
69. *New Theatre,* Nov. 1935
70. Hallie Flanagan, *Arena,* (New York: Benjamin Blau, Inc., 1965).
71. Harold Clurman, *Fervent Years.*
72. Ibid.
73. Morgan Y. Himelstein, *Drama Was a Weapon*
74. Warren Hall, in *Sunday News,* 5 Jan. 1969, New York

Index